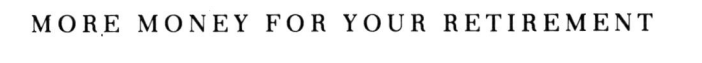

MORE MONEY FOR YOUR RETIREMENT

MORE MONEY FOR YOUR RETIREMENT

JOHN BARNES

1817

HARPER & ROW, PUBLISHERS

NEW YORK, HAGERSTOWN

SAN FRANCISCO

LONDON

FIRST EDITION

Designed by Sidney Feinberg

Library of Congress Cataloging in Publication Data

Barnes, John, date
    More money for your retirement.
    Includes index.
    1. Retirement Income—United States. 2. Finance,
Personal. 3. Saving and thrift. I. Title.
HQ1064.U5B27   332'.024   77–11530
ISBN 0–06–010228–4

78 79 80 81 82 10 9 8 7 6 5 4 3 2 1

Contents

The dominance of the present should never be a denial of what has been.

MORE MONEY FOR YOUR RETIREMENT

1

How to Increase Your Income

Most of the twenty million people who are now retired, and those who are ten years away from retirement, have been raised on the concept that when they stopped working they would carefully conserve their capital and spend only the income from it.

In these days of inflation and high taxes this principle, for the most part, can no longer be followed.

If you want to live better and enjoy yourself more when retired—and who doesn't?—you should abandon this lifetime concept. You should change your basic thinking and realize that, in your own best interests, you should spend a small percentage of your capital each year, for this is one sure way to increase your cash flow. Admittedly this is a jolt to the way you have always thought you would manage your finances. It raises the specter of running out of money some day, a truly frightening prospect.

But wait a minute. Let's take a second look (for you don't have to adopt the concept, you know) and see what would be so terrible about spending 3 percent of your capital every year, though retired. At the end of ten long years, you would have used up 30 percent of your assets. Your heirs will then receive only 70 percent instead of 100 percent of your estate. Is this such a bad thing after all?

We assume that you carefully accumulated your estate over the years so you could enjoy using some of it yourself. We hope that you haven't saved it to leave to your heirs or to be turned over to strangers through the imposition of death taxes or to be squandered through probate administration expenses by law offices.

You saved, we are sure, to be financially secure and to enjoy your leisure years to the fullest extent possible according to your past earning capacity. You were willing to deny yourself some of life's pleasures while working in order to enjoy them later.

So we come back to our basic proposition. Why not spend a small percentage of your capital each year when retired in order to live better?

There is an important advantage to this concept. You can stop at any time. If you spend some capital for a couple of years, to go to Europe or what have you, there is no reason to continue at the same rate, although you may find you're having too much fun to stop. You can always revert to spending income only in order to conserve all of your capital for an extreme old age that may never come or for that catastrophic illness that may never happen.

If you face facts squarely, it's the first ten years after you retire that you want to be on the go the most. After that it might be more fun to stay home and enjoy your friends and your grandchildren.

Let's say that you have $100,000 (in addition to your home) on which you are receiving an average return of 6 percent. This would produce an income of $6,000 a year, or $500 a month, which is not much these days but it's far better than nothing. Let's suppose that you change your thinking and decide to use 3 percent of the principal of your $100,000, and therefore have $9,000 instead of $6,000 to spend this year. Wouldn't you say that your horizons had suddenly expanded? Where would you spend that extra $3,000—*this year?* Think about it. Or let's assume that you have $40,000, where would you spend the extra 3 percent, or $1,200—*this year?*

We have in mind Mrs. Alice Adams, an extreme case, but sometimes an exception is one way to demonstrate the soundness of a concept.

Mrs. Adams was a widow, with a single sister who lived with her, not only for love and companionship but because her sister had no money. Both of them were in their late sixties, Mrs. Adams's husband having died several years earlier. Besides their Social Security checks, both ladies were trying to live on Mrs. Adams's income, which was $3,600 a year from dividends on some stocks that she owned. They were not doing very well; their living room had become so shabby that they had virtually stopped seeing their friends.

A widow acquaintance, sensing that something was wrong, suggested that Mrs. Adams see her investment representative. What he discovered flabbergasted him. Mrs. Adams had no knowledge of money and, like so many widows, knew no better than to retain her assets in exactly the same position in which her husband had left them. She had $20,000 in a checking account and $40,000 more in matured E bonds in a safe-deposit box. None of this $60,000 was giving her a current income. In addition, she had $90,000 in securities that were paying her an average dividend of 4 percent, or $3,600 a year. It was on these dividends, besides their Social Security checks, that Mrs. Adams and her sister were supporting themselves.

The investment representative had Mrs. Adams cash the E bonds and sell her stocks, and invest the proceeds in AAA utility bonds that paid 8 percent. By this method he increased her income from $3,600 to $10,400 a year. Three thousand dollars more from her checking account was used to refurbish her apartment, and another $4,000 booked the two ladies on a Mediterranean cruise.

The transformation in their way of life was nothing short of astounding.

Furthermore, the investment representative advised Mrs. Adams to spend $4,200 a year of principal, thereby increasing her cash flow to $14,600 a year, or to over $1,200 per month!

Such a change in a way of life is a rare exception, but it does demonstrate the soundness of a principle. It's possible to live better in retirement if you can change your fundamental thinking and every year spend a small percentage of your capital, rather than hang on to it for dear life for the benefit of your heirs.

Retired people should spend all of their income.

We have to admit that there are those who simply cannot bring themselves to spend a part of their capital. But retired people should, at the very least, spend all of their income. Many do not. Thousands, like Mrs. Adams, own government E bonds that don't pay a current income. The semiannual interest is automatically compounded, which simply increases the bonds' redemption value, with the income not being paid to anyone. The bondholder is still saving money, though retired.

Many people hold stocks and bonds in a street name with their stockbroker. By this method the interest and dividends are automatically added to their account, and when they accumulate to a sufficient sum, the owners buy more securities with them.

They should not do this. They should take all of their income, no matter how much they may be worth.

Mr. and Mrs. Archer were retired and worth a million dollars, give or take a few thousand. One day they made an additional investment of $50,000 in a balanced mutual fund, and the question arose with their stockbroker about what they should do with the dividends and realized capital gains.

"We don't need them, dear," suggested Mr. Archer, as they sat at the broker's desk. "Why don't we just reinvest them? There is no charge."

Their broker demurred. "I don't think so, though you can do as you like. Take the dividends even though you don't spend them. If they pile up in your bank account you will know for sure they are excess dollars; then you can give them away to your heirs. If you compound them in your mutual fund account, they won't be distributed to anyone. They will just increase your death taxes, which are already high enough."

So the Archers agreed, and took the income.

After hearing a speech to a retired group one noon, a member of the audience rushed up to the speaker at the end of the luncheon and pumped his hand.

"You're right!" he exclaimed. "I'm going to stop saving money. I'm going home and cash my E bonds."

And he did.

He didn't have to cash them, of course, in order to receive a current income. Government E bonds can be exchanged for current income H bonds, without having to pay an income tax on the accumulated interest. This way the bondholder still owns government bonds, but now he receives a check twice a year from Washington, D.C. The interest is the same as on the E bonds.[1] A word of caution, however: if the H bonds are cashed at any time in the future, the holder has to pay a tax on the accumulated E bond interest at that time. The tax obligation is stamped right on the face of the H bonds when they are purchased.

Another way to increase your income drastically is to buy a lifetime annuity from an insurance company.

Only a part of your assets can be used this way, for now you have exchanged this much of your capital for an income that is guaranteed for life. There is no longer a lump sum available

---

1. The interest is the same if H bonds are held to their maturity, which is ten years. They earn at the annual rate of 4.2 percent the first six months, 5.8 percent the subsequent 4½ years, 6.5 percent for the final five years.

from this money. For those who qualify, though, annuities can greatly increase spendable income. For a male, age 75, for instance, a life insurance company will guarantee to pay 13 percent no matter how long the annuitant may live. This will approximately double current income. Annuities must be understood, however, before any decision is made to buy them. Therefore a whole chapter in this book is devoted to them.

If you own permanent cash value life insurance and you are retired, you should stop paying the premiums.

This might seem like a drastic suggestion. It's not. It will increase your income, not only by the amount of the saved premium, but also by the interest that can be earned on the cash surrender value when the policy is surrendered.

This, too, should not be done unless permanent life insurance, with its nonforfeiture values, is completely understood. Again, an entire chapter is devoted to this important way of increasing income.

You should shift out of common stocks that are paying low dividends.

It doesn't make sense to retain an asset that is returning 2 percent when you can almost quadruple your income by buying bonds, or by receiving 7½ percent from a savings and loan time certificate.

It's true that a capital gains tax will have to be paid when low dividend paying stocks, or any other capital assets for that matter (such as real estate), are sold at a profit. But the capital gains tax should not be a deterrent to selling because, retired or not, it's not that big a problem. So let's take a look at this tax, since most people don't understand it.

The first confusion lies in the statement (which is true) that the maximum capital gains tax is 25 percent. Twenty-five percent of what? Of the whole profit. Let's assume that low dividend paying stocks that have a cost basis of $20,000 are sold for $40,000. The owner in that event has made a profit of $20,000, on which the maximum tax would be 25 percent, or $5,000. But most people don't have to pay this maximum rate, particularly when retired. Instead of paying 25 percent on the whole profit, most people divide the profit in one-half and then pay on this one-half according to their tax bracket. The other one-half is tax-free. This results in their paying less than 25 percent.[2]

For example, let's assume that you, married and filing a joint return, have a taxable income of $8,000 that requires you to pay an income tax of $1,370.

You decide to sell your $40,000 in low-paying stocks and take a $20,000 profit.

Dividing this profit in one-half adds $10,000 to your taxable income. The other one-half of the profit is yours tax-free. Your taxable income, because of the stock sale, has now gone up from $8,000 to $18,000. This causes you to pay an income tax of $3,820. The increase in your tax looks like this.

Taxable income before the sale	$ 8,000
Income tax	1,380
Taxable income after the sale	$18,000
Income tax	3,820
Difference	$ 2,440

Your capital gains tax is therefore $2,440, not the maximum of $5,000. This is at a tax rate of 12 percent on your $20,000 profit, not 25 percent.

It is true that you will have to deduct this increase in your taxes from the gross sale price, which enables you to invest only the difference. The increase in your income from the new investment in 8 percent bonds looks like this.

$40,000 at 2 percent	$ 800.00
$37,560 ($40,000–$2,440) at 8 percent	$3,004.80

Even though you had to pay a capital gains tax, you have increased your income on the $40,000 in stocks by $2,204.80 a year!

2. For a more detailed explanation the reader is referred to Chapter 12.

There is another way that people who own stocks can increase their income. This is by correctly computing the current dividend yield.

Too many persons make the mistake of basing the calculation of their dividend income upon the original cost of their stocks. They feel that they are receiving 4 percent from the above $40,000 in securities, not 2 percent, because their cost basis was only $20,000. This is not the way to compute the income from an investment. The dividend should be calculated on the *current market price,* for it is this amount of money that is available for investment elsewhere at higher interest rates, minus of course the capital gains tax (as demonstrated in the above example).

Investing at the bottom of a bear market can increase income.

This is not easy to do. It is difficult to be optimistic when everyone else is pessimistic. Also most retired people feel that they are not in a position to risk capital.

However, if you are a well-to-do, knowledgeable investor, it can be done with a minimum of risk.

Determining when a rising bull market has peaked out is very difficult, even for the experts. By comparison it is relatively easy to determine the bottom of a bear market.

Why? Because the percentage drop in a bear market is already an established fact.

As an example, let's take the bear market of 1973–74, which hit bottom in October of 1974 and again in December, three months later. In the previous bull market the Dow Jones Industrial Average had gone through 1,000. It dropped in the fall of 1974 to below 600. The DJIA had gone down over 40 percent. If it went back again to 1,000, the subsequent rise would be 66 ⅔ percent.

A drop of over 40 percent was a known fact; it was not guesswork upon the part of the investor. The only question at this point was whether or not stock prices would go any lower. Already stocks had gone down, however, to a level that was almost ridiculous. At this point, and this is the important consideration, the risk of securities going down further in price had been reduced to a minimum.

The next question becomes what stocks to buy at the bottom of a bear market?

The market is dominated today by the big institutional investors—mutual funds, pension funds, and insurance companies—who account for 70 percent of the buying and selling on the New York Stock Exchange. So stocks should be purchased only if they are owned by at least twenty institutions. This information can be found in Standard & Poor's Stock Guide which is published every month.

Another rule. Never buy a stock unless it is going up in price. *Never.* No matter what you think of it, or the prospects of the company.

So at the end of 1974 the knowledgeable investor stepped in and bought. In the first five months of 1975 the market went up almost 50 percent. It would take six years to earn that much by buying corporate bonds at 8 percent!

Surely this is one way to increase your income.

Keep most of your money in fixed dollars when interest rates are high.

When 7½ interest can be earned from certificates of deposit, and 9 percent interest can be obtained by investing in industrial and utility bonds, they should be bought to increase income. Since buying bonds is only for the sophisticated investor, the average person should confine his or her high-interest investing to certificates of deposit. Many people shy away from them, however, because of the "severe penalties" for early withdrawal that are imposed by federal law. These penalties, however, are not as severe as people are led to believe.

There are two penalties imposed: (1) There is a loss of interest for 90 days, and (2) the entire contract reverts back to passbook interest from the date of the investment to the date of withdrawal.

Example. You purchased a four-year time deposit for $10,000 at a return of 7½ percent, which was 2 percent above the passbook rate. Two years later you cashed in. Your penalty was computed as follows:

Ninety-day loss of interest (One-fourth of $750)	$187.50
Two-year loss of 2 percent on $10,000 (Assuming a passbook rate of 5½%)	400.00
Total	$587.50

Your actual loss was only the $187.50, because this was the only time you received zero interest on your money (during the ninety-day period). The other $400 was deducted from your account because you did not receive the *extra* interest that you originally planned on, but (and this is important) you did obtain the regular passbook rate. You simply did not receive the additional interest you thought you were going to obtain when you bought the investment certificate in the first place.

Retired people, or anybody else, should not view a time deposit as a frozen account because of the penalties. Sometimes this cash is needed, and a financial hardship should not be endured just because of a loss of interest. The money should be withdrawn and the penalty paid to increase cash flow.

Another income loss can occur from a time deposit because people are careless about their maturity date.

A bank or a savings and loan institution does not notify holders of investment certificates that their accounts are maturing, although they should be required by law to do so. If holders do not notify the financial institution in writing of their intention to withdraw their accounts within ten days after their time deposits have matured, they are automatically renewed for the full term. As a consequence, if depositors want their money, they had better be careful about the maturity date.

Mr. Altman had been retired for many years, and though physically spry enough and sharp mentally, he could hardly be expected to be as alert as a man thirty years his junior. He was mistaken about the maturity date of his two-year $10,000 certificate of deposit and thought it was June 1 when it was actually May 1. When he went to withdraw his money in June, the savings and loan association would not give it to him without the ninety-day interest penalty, because the account had been automatically renewed. It took the intervention of his investment adviser, and a talk with the branch manager, before the association would consent to pay him his full $10,000.

Sitting at the manager's desk, the adviser protested: "Mr. Manager, this shareholder is elderly. Before the next maturity date he will be 80 years of age. He wants his money now, and it should be paid to him without penalty."

It was only with extreme reluctance that the branch manager, after a telephone consultation with his head office, agreed to the request. Obviously a younger person would not have had a chance.

When short-term interest rates are high, it's possible to obtain even higher rates than those that are available from time deposits and bonds.

A well-to-do investor can do this by buying bankers acceptances through that individual's bank. Bankers acceptances are the method by which large corporations with the highest credit rating borrow from each other for short periods of time. During a period of high interest rates, it's possible to earn as much as 12 percent from their purchase.

Even the so-called little man is not shut out from participating in these unusually high rates, due to the proliferation in recent years of the money mutual funds. These funds invest in short-term fixed obligations for high income. Since it takes knowledge and a lot of money (at least $100,000 for bankers acceptances, for instance), the average investor cannot obtain these high rates except through the mutual fund concept. This way a person can invest a small amount of money (the usual minimum is $3,000), and by pooling it with thousands of others, obtain the advantage formerly reserved for the well-to-do. Hundreds of millions have been invested in these new money funds as a consequence.

Long-term high interest rates from bonds can be used
effectively to increase income.

We have already mentioned that this is a sophisticated market, but industrial and utility bonds should not be ignored when existing conditions of the money market make it possible to obtain 9 percent and more from them. This is an excellent way to increase income.

The usual minimum investment in bonds is $5,000 because the commission is low, and the average stockbroker simply can't be bothered with a lesser sum. Once again, when reaching out for a higher return, the investment must be understood.

A bond is an interest-bearing certificate of indebtedness issued by a corporation or a government. They are sold in $1,000 denominations. Three facts should be kept in mind.

1. A bond is an evidence of a debt.
2. The corporation or government issuing the bond is a borrower.
3. The investor purchasing the bond is a creditor.

A bond is the issuer's promise to repay the lender the face amount at a specified time known as the maturity date. The borrower also promises to pay interest on the principal of the loan at a specified rate. Failure to pay either the interest or the principal when due is a legal default, and court proceedings may be instituted.

When bonds are purchased they are registered, or not registered, on the books of the company that issues them. Therefore they are sold in three different forms.

A *coupon bond* is not registered and has a coupon attached to it for each interest payment. When the interest falls due, the bondholder simply presents the coupon to a bank teller for cashing. From this arose the old cliché: "He's retired now. All he does is clip coupons." Coupon bonds are known as bearer bonds because whoever is in possession of them (the bearer) may cash them. Great care has to be exercised when handling these bonds because they are not registered; title is passed upon delivery, and no endorsement is necessary.

The owner of a *fully registered bond* has his or her name and address registered on the books of the issuing corporation. Such a bond can be cashed only by endorsement and submission of the bond to the issuing company. Instead of clipping coupons, interest is mailed to the bondholder.

The owner of a *partly registered bond* also has his or her name registered on the books of the company, as well as on the face of the bond itself. Coupons are attached to it for the interest. From this it can be seen that just because the bonds bear coupons does not mean that they are automatically bearer bonds. They could be partly registered (as to who owns them, but not as to who is entitled to receive the interest) and as such require endorsement by the owner before they can be cashed.

The great majority of all corporate and utility bonds are coupon bonds. Investors prefer them because of the ease with which they can be transferred.

Bond prices vary inversely as to interest rates. When interest rates go up, bond prices go down; and when interest rates go down, bond prices go up.

Example. If you own a $1,000 bond that pays 6 percent, and interest rates go up to 7 percent, your bond will sell at a discount. Investors will not pay the full face amount for a $1,000 bond that earns 6 percent when they can obtain 7 percent elsewhere.

Since bond prices fluctuate, they can't be viewed as fixed dollars like a bank account. Also, since they will go down in price only if interest rates go up, they should be purchased only when interest rates are high. Subsequently, when interest rates go down, as they will sooner or later, the market price of bonds will hold steady or even increase in value.

2

How to Avoid Probate

Probate is a procedure whereby the assets of the deceased will be administered by a court of law, and a legal representative (either named in the will by the testator, or appointed by the court) will manage the estate during the period of administration.

Probate of an estate should be avoided whenever possible.

Distribution of property by will or a trust, or by state law because the property owner died intestate (without a will), involves unnecessary trouble and expense, and time-consuming legal entanglements. It should be shunned especially by couples with small estates, where it is intended that the survivor should inherit everything.

Once an estate is caught up in the web of probate court proceedings and bureaucratic regulations, there is nothing that can be done by the eventual heirs except to stand by in anger and frustration waiting for this slow process to grind to a halt, eventually terminating in a final order of distribution, a result that may not occur for a year or two, or even more.

On the other hand, if probate is avoided, distribution of a small estate can take place in a few weeks, and release of bank and savings and loan accounts can be obtained in many states within a matter of hours. Even an estate that is large enough to be subject to death taxes can be transferred to the heirs in three or four months. Certainly this is a preferable method of passing on property to one's heirs.

Probate costs are approximately 5 percent of an estate appraisal. When assets are worth $100,000, this amounts to $5,000, which is a sizable sum. On small estates the percentage is greater. On an appraisal of $40,000, it is almost 7 percent, at a cost of $2,660.

Minimum probate fees are charged according to the following schedule.

	Percent	Amount	Cumulative cost
First $1,000	7%	$ 70	$ 70
$2,000 to $10,000	4	360	430
$10,000 to $40,000	3	900	1,330
$40,000 to $100,000	2	1,200	2,530

The above schedule of fees is charged by both the probate attorney *and* the executor, therefore they have to be doubled. In addition there are always some nominal court costs and filing fees.

Most people don't know that probate of an estate is a matter of public record. Anybody can walk off the street into the county clerk's office and ask to see the probate file of a deceased person. No reason has to be given for anyone has the right to look at the records because probate falls into the area of the public domain.

After you die, any stranger, friend, or relative can find out exactly what you died possessed of down to the last penny, and in what bank you kept it. Your will, and the record of the step-by-step probate proceedings, including the names and addresses of your heirs, can be read by anyone. Many people are appalled when they learn of this and will take every possible step to avoid having this happen to their estates, and to protect those who are inheriting from them, particularly a surviving widow. In many cases privacy is of the utmost importance. There are three ways to avoid probate:

1. Joint tenancy with right of survivorship
2. Naming a beneficiary
3. Creating a living trust

The first two are accomplished by holding the assets of an estate in the correct ownership. The third entails the drawing of an involved legal document, a procedure that should not be followed except by those who are wealthy enough to have a serious death tax problem.

Joint tenancy

There are many advantages, and certain disadvantages, in using this form of ownership. It should not be entered into until its various ramifications are understood. The matter of joint tenancy is complex, and since the laws of the states vary widely, there is no alternative but to ascertain the law of the state wherein the property is located to determine the future status of assets following the death of the first tenant.

Some states provide for joint tenancy, others legislate against it. However, even in those states that do not favor its creation, as long as the correct wording is employed in the title to the property, it can be used effectively. The wording should be as follows: "John Jones and Mary Jones, as joint tenants with right of survivorship, and not as tenants in common." This eliminates all other heirs, and the property will be inherited by the surviving joint tenant.

There are several forms of plural ownership, which is the reason for using the exact wording above. The other forms will be discussed in detail in Chapter 6.

Joint tenancy is not confined to couples. It can be used by any two people, or by any number more than two. If several people own real estate, for instance, and one of them should die, the others still own the property in joint tenancy. If one remains it becomes single ownership, and if not changed, results in the probate of that asset upon the death of the last tenant.

In joint tenancy with right of survivorship, a tenant may dispose of his or her part of the ownership to another. If that individual does, and just two people are involved, the ownership now becomes tenants in common, meaning that each tenant may will his or her portion to anyone.

A joint tenant may also convey his or her interest to the other tenant. He or she may *convey* it, meaning that the interest can be released to the other joint tenant while that tenant is alive, but it can't be *devised or bequeathed.* To devise or bequeath property means, in legal lexicon, to leave it by will to another. This is not possible because the surviving tenant automatically inherits. This is one reason why lawyers hate joint tenancy; property that is held this way cannot pass by will or by trust. It cannot, and will not, be probated. The chief distinguishing feature of joint tenancy is the right of survivorship. By the death of the first joint tenant, the other tenant falls heir to the entire interest.

Joint tenancy therefore prevents lawyers from collecting a probate fee. Despite this, many attorneys honestly feel that an estate that has been probated (proven) has been subjected to a more legal change of ownership, for transfer to the heirs now has received the formal approval of a court of law. But where the property is left to the immediate family, such as a surviving spouse or children, this argument falls rather flat. It is quite obvious that the court would rule that they are the legal heirs and, therefore, probate is hardly necessary.

Dissolving a joint tenancy is a relatively easy matter for the surviving joint tenant. It simply means removing the deceased tenant's name from the various assets. Two basic forms are needed to accomplish this—a certified copy of the death certificate and an inheritance tax release from the state taxing authorities.

Mr. Mason's wife died. All of the assets in their joint estate, which amounted to $50,000, were held in joint tenancy with right of survivorship. After recovering from the shock of his wife's death, Mr. Mason made an appointment with the nearest office of the state inheritance tax division. He was told to bring with him a certified copy of the death certificate, their marriage license, a copy of the will (if any), the deed to their home, and proof of any other assets (which in his case amounted to two passbooks for a bank savings deposit and a savings and loan account).

Mr. Mason encountered one major difficulty, however. To his consternation, he couldn't find the deed to their home. At the inheritance tax office he was told that he would have to produce it before a waiver could be granted. Since he was eighty-two years old, and not sure of what to do, he elicited the help of a business acquaintance.

Seated in the living room of his home the following day, his friend asked him: "When did you buy your house, Mr. Mason?"

"In 1940, just before World War II," he replied.

"Are you sure? For example, did you buy it or build it?"

"Well, no. I didn't buy it. I had it built on a lot that I owned."

"When did you buy the lot?"

"The same year, I think," Mr. Mason replied. "I'm not sure."

"You see," explained his friend, "the deed would have been issued when you bought the lot, not when you built your home. Let's go down to the county recorder's office and see what we can find out."

Fortunately when Mr. Mason and his friend arrived at the recorder's office, they found it almost empty and a cooperative clerk on duty. Starting with 1941, the clerk went through the records clear back to 1929, without finding a copy of the deed to the property. But the friend still wasn't satisfied.

"Are you sure that you didn't buy that lot prior to 1929?" he asked.

At this point Mr. Mason was so confused he wasn't sure of anything.

"Let's go back to another department," the clerk suggested. "Deeds that were issued prior to 1929 have been put on microfilm. Maybe we'll find it there."

And sure enough, they did. When the microfilm was blown up on an enlarger, there was the deed to the lot as big as life, dated October 1, 1922! Mr. Mason could hardly believe it.

For a five-dollar fee he obtained a copy of the deed, and upon returning to the inheritance tax department, he secured his release.

Since Mr. Mason's estate amounted to only $50,000, he did not owe a federal estate tax, and by the laws of the state where he lived, he didn't owe an inheritance tax either. In some states, if a state tax had been due, the approximate amount of the tax would have been frozen, and the balance of the estate released.

Armed with the tax waiver, and certified copies of the death certificate, Mr. Mason went to the bank and the savings and loan office and had these two accounts transferred to his name, and upon returning to the recorder's office, experienced no difficulty in recording the house in his name alone.

Certainly, despite the problem in regard to the deed (which would have been encountered in court administration as well), this was far less trouble and expense than going through probate.

Quite often when a widow is the survivor, especially where she has had little experience in money matters, she prefers to have an attorney dissolve the joint tenancy for her. It will usually take longer, but his fee will be about one-third of the probate schedule.

Fortunately, all of Mr. Mason's assets were held in joint tenancy with right of survivorship; none of them were held in his name alone. If probate is to be completely avoided, the property owner can't be too careful in this regard. He should inspect each document to ensure that title to all of his property is held in joint tenancy. If any of the assets are not so held this much of the estate will have to be probated.

There are some valid arguments against using joint tenancy with right of survivorship. If any of them apply to you, perhaps this type of ownership should not be used.

Joint tenancy should never be used in large estates that have a death-tax problem. The escalation of federal estate and state inheritance taxes in the second estate is too severe. Upon the first death, one-half of the joint estate will be taxed, and then (because the survivor owns the entire estate) the first one-half will be taxed again upon the death of the second joint tenant. It's better in large estates to have a trust drawn by a competent attorney so that the first one-half of the joint estate will be taxed only once. A complete discussion of how this can be accomplished is found in Chapter 13.

Often property that is held in some other form of ownership is changed to joint tenancy. Now costs are involved. If real estate is the property, quite often the title will have to be searched to determine that no cloud exists, and always a new deed has to be prepared and recorded. Also a gift tax could be incurred if the property conveyed is large enough to exceed the gift-tax exemptions. Rather than go into the matter of gift taxes (without an adequate explanation of them), the reader is referred to Chapter 13, which deals with the gift-tax laws.

In these days of increasing longevity, hundreds of thousands of people are marrying a second time upon the death of their first spouse. Extreme care should be exercised about placing separate property of either spouse in a joint ownership. This could result in disinheriting the children of the tenant who is first to die.

Mr. McAfee, a widower with three children, married a second time to a widow with one child. He owned 1,000 shares of a corporation, which at the time of his second marriage didn't have much value. He placed this stock in joint tenancy with right of survivorship with his new wife. With the passage of years the corporation prospered, and the stock increased in value tremendously. Mr. McAfee in the meantime had forgotten how title to the stock was held. He died, and shortly thereafter his second wife died also. Now something happened, due to joint tenancy with right of survivorship, that neither of them had intended. Mrs. McAfee had inherited all of the valuable stock (which had become their principal asset), and in her will she left everything of which she died possessed to her only child. Mr. McAfee's own three children were disinherited!

Despite these few adverse features, if none of them apply to you, joint tenancy with right of survivorship is still the best way for couples with small estates to hold their assets. Probate is completely avoided, and the property will be inherited by the survivor with the least trouble and expense.

Naming a beneficiary is the second way to avoid probate.

Most people are acquainted with this form of ownership because of their life insurance.

A frequently used beneficiary form on a life insurance policy reads as follows: "To my wife, Mary, if living; if not, to my children equally, the survivors equally, or the survivor."

The wife of the insured is called the primary beneficiary, and the children are called contingent beneficiaries, meaning that their interest is dependent upon their surviving their mother. Contingent beneficiaries can be provided for only on life insurance policies. On other property only a primary beneficiary can be named.

A primary beneficiary can be named on bank and savings and loan accounts. Both of these institutions over the past few years have relaxed their restrictions on this type of ownership, and naming a beneficiary is now widely accepted. This form of ownership may also be used on government bonds. As a consequence all of this property will avoid probate. This is advantageous for persons with small estates consisting solely of one or all of these three assets. It is particularly useful for widows and widowers who want their children to inherit this kind of property with the least trouble and expense.

However, if other assets are owned this form of ownership can't be used. Transfer agents of securities will not accept a beneficiary designation, nor will the custodian banks of most mutual funds. It can't be used at all with real estate. As a consequence these assets have to be probated. The use of this form of ownership is therefore severely limited.

The third and final way to avoid probate is by the creation of a living trust.

This is the only way the well-to-do and the wealthy can avoid probate. They can't use the two previously discussed ownership forms because of death taxes.

Before creating a living trust, the grantor must understand the basic difference between a will and a trust. A will simply states who inherits the assets of the estate, and when probate is over, title to the property passes to the legal heirs. The new owners may then use these assets as they see fit.

When a trust is created, the property owner doesn't want his or her estate to be inherited immediately by his or her heirs. Title passes to a trustee, who then administers the property according to the terms of the trust for the benefit of someone else. Disposition of the capital and/or the income to the beneficiaries of the trust usually will take place over a period of many years

Normally a grantor creates a testamentary trust that, like a will, does not go into effect until the testator dies. Also like a will, it may be revoked at any time; and like a will, the property will be subject to probate administration.

A living trust on the other hand goes into effect while the grantor is alive, and can be made revocable or irrevocable. One of the main advantages of a living trust is the avoidance of probate. Title passes directly to a successor trustee upon the death of the grantor. Court administration of the estate is bypassed completely.

While this saves time and some legal entanglements, the

main objective is quite often complete privacy. Since there is no court record of any kind, no one can find out the size and nature of the estate, or to whom it was left. This protects the heirs from innumerable telephone calls and letters from friends and total strangers whose sole purpose is to participate in the estate by extracting part of the money from the legal owners by one means or another, many of them not very beneficial. It also frustrates those who are simply curious.

Mr. and Mrs. Yates had a $700,000 estate, which they had built as the result of owning a profitable business in a small town. They had no children, so they decided to leave their assets upon the death of both of them to their favorite charities. They had been exceptionally frugal in building an estate of this size. As Mr. Yates said to his lawyer: "I'm like a squirrel. I bury those nuts and forget about them." As a consequence, their friends and acquaintances had only an inkling of the size of their estate, and upon the death of the first spouse, the survivor didn't want anyone to know.

When Mr. Yates died, the complete lack of information as to the size of the estate so frustrated people that Mrs. Yates would be stopped on the street with a leading question, such as: "I assume that Jack left you pretty well off?" But she would just smile and walk on. If privacy in estate matters is desired, a living trust will guarantee it.

Sometimes the desire for privacy is caused by the inherent frugality of heirs who, while they inherited a relatively modest sum years before, now find themselves possessed of a sizable estate without having increased their standard of living. Knowledge of the amount of money that has been accumulated is completely unsuspected by their friends and relatives.

Two maiden sisters inherited the income from a trust that had been created by their surgeon father. All of the proceeds from the trust investments were paid to them by a university trustee, until the death of the sister who survived, at which time the college as the remainderman would inherit the principal.

The two sisters were frugal, so they spent very little of the income from the trust; in addition they shrewdly managed some real estate that had been left to them outright. After forty years, one of them was dying. The other sister became panic-stricken at the thought of the publicity that would result when it became known that she and her sister had accumulated $600,000. A living trust to prevent the public disclosure of their assets was the only solution.

Many lawyers don't know how to properly draw a living trust. It's a complicated document, and they would prefer a large estate to go though probate anyway. The proper choice of a lawyer therefore becomes a crucial decision. The wrong attorney will either draw a bad document, which may not stand up in court, or he or she will present so many objections to a living trust that a client will be talked out of it.

When drawing a living trust, you should be convinced that you truly want to avoid probate. This should be your major objective, for a living trust will still cause time and trouble for the trustee. Since the estate is large, it will have to be appraised, and both federal estate and state inheritance tax returns filed. To accomplish this, the trustee will have to work closely with an accountant and with the attorney who drew the agreement.

As with all trusts, a trustee has to be named. Since there is no court administration, someone has to be appointed to take over and capably manage sizable assets in the absence of the grantor.

Who should be named trustee?

Where a couple is involved, they should name themselves as cotrustees while they are both alive, and provide that the surviving spouse be the successor trustee. Most people don't know that they can be trustees of their own property, but they can. In a properly drawn document, they can continue to manage their assets just as they had before the trust was created. They will hardly realize the difference.

A bank trustee should not be named. Doing so introduces a third party unnecessarily into the management of the assets. Where avoiding probate is the primary objective in creating the trust, the advantage to be gained may not be worth the inconvenience.

3

Help for the Potential Widow

When a wife suddenly becomes a widow she faces financial problems that seem to her almost insurmountable, particularly if she has had little experience in money management.

Most times she is confronted with the probate of her husband's estate. Too many couples do not provide for ease of estate settlement. They distribute their assets by will, or worse yet, die intestate. In either event, the widow is faced with probate administration.

The first thing she must do is find and read her husband's will. If it is kept in a safe-deposit box, this presents an immediate problem because state law usually prohibits a bank from granting access to it once the death of the testator becomes known. Most states require a representative of the state inheritance tax department to be present when the box is opened, for taxing authorities are well aware that most valuable documents are kept there. When a box is opened under their supervision, its contents will give them an estimate of the size of the estate to determine if an inheritance tax is due.

Despite this, a bank official is authorized to grant access to a vault in advance of a supervised inventory so that two vital documents can be obtained—the will and the deed to the cemetery plot.

In the average small estate the widow is usually the sole heir, but sometimes in both small and large estates she is not the only beneficiary. In this event, she has the right to take her share under the will or to inherit according to state law. If the latter is more advantageous to her, she has the right to ignore the will and take that portion that she would have received if her husband had died intestate, or without a will. This can be extremely important under circumstances where the widow is left less than her legal share.

If the widow decides to use the will (the normal procedure), it must be filed promptly with the probate court, or with whatever court has jurisdiction in the state involved, such as the orphan's court or the surrogate court. The person who has custody of the will has the responsibility of filing it. Normally it should be lodged with the court within ten days. Willfully failing to comply with the law is a criminal offense.

After obtaining the will and the deed to the cemetery plot, the widow can now make the necessary funeral arrangements. This can be an immediate and sometimes serious mistake. Funerals can be costly, but they don't have to be. Good taste and common sense should govern here, but sometimes it's extremely difficult for a grief-stricken widow to think clearly and sensibly. Unfortunately some funeral directors may prevail upon her to spend more than she should.

The best way to solve this problem is to turn it over to a sensible friend, or one of her husband's business associates, who can make the arrangements on an unemotional basis.

Death creates financial obligations that did not exist before. As a consequence no estate is completely debt-free. Besides the funeral arrangements, there are the expenses of last illness and the costs of probate administration. If the estate is large enough, state inheritance taxes and federal estate taxes will have to be paid, and certainly income taxes for that part of the year for which no return has yet been filed. With a costly funeral, there may be insufficient liquid assets with which to meet these obligations.

Certified copies of the death certificate should be ordered immediately. These can be obtained from the county public health service for a dollar or two. Since the cost is nominal, at least six should be ordered initially; more can be ordered later if the size and number of assets in the estate should require it. Quite often the funeral home will obtain them as part of their service.

Copies of the death certificate should be used to release at once all bank or savings and loan accounts that are held in joint tenancy, and to collect the proceeds of life insurance policies in which the widow is named the beneficiary, even though the balance of the estate is in probate.

Rules of the various states vary widely in regard to savings and checking accounts held in joint tenancy. In most states, money can be made available to the surviving joint tenant, if not in full, then up to a certain maximum such as $5,000.

Life insurance proceeds are different. An insurance company will pay the death proceeds to a named beneficiary, regardless of the provisions of a will or the dictates of state law. A certified copy of the death certificate and a claim form are usually sufficient.

Scott Avery died, leaving his widow as the sole beneficiary of his estate, including a $25,000 life insurance policy. Their home, a small bank account, and some securities, all of which were in Mr. Avery's name alone, were all they had besides the insurance. Since the balance of the estate was in probate, Mrs. Avery desperately needed the insurance death benefit to be paid as quickly as possible.

Fortunately the company maintained an agency office in the metropolitan city where Mrs. Avery lived. She wasn't sure of what she should do, but being a forthright woman, she went to the company office armed with the policy (which Mr. Avery kept in a strong box at home) and with a certified copy of the death certificate.

The female clerk behind the counter, after extending her sympathy, was helpful and efficient.

"I knew your husband well, Mrs. Avery," she said. "A fine gentleman. We saw the notice of his death in the newspaper and have a copy of it in his file. Since you are the sole beneficiary, if you will answer a few questions, there shouldn't be any trouble."

"What is it you want to know?" asked Mrs. Avery.

"Just the information on our claim form," the clerk replied. "If you like, I can help you fill it out. The newspaper clipping, along with the death certificate, should satisfy our home office that the benefit should be paid."

After the form was completed, Mrs. Avery asked: "How soon will I receive a check?"

"Oh," replied the clerk, "I should say in about four or five days."

Mrs. Avery's case illustrates that a widow doesn't have to hire a lawyer to collect insurance proceeds for her. The procedure is too simple. It's a completely unnecessary legal fee, even though the balance of the estate is in probate. An insurance policy that names an individual beneficiary is what is known as a non-probate asset, as we shall see later in Chapter 6. Payment by the insurance company is immediate because they don't have to wait on an order of the probate court.

The probate attorney lodges the will by filing a petition with the court for a hearing to formally admit the will to probate. The attorney also asks the court to issue letters testamentary, which is a fancy name for a written order of the court appointing the widow as executrix, if her husband named her in his will. If he failed to name his wife (or anyone else), and the court appoints her, she is called an administratrix. Both terms mean the same thing. The individual who receives the letters testamentary is empowered to take over and manage the estate during probate administration.

Every executrix should fully understand that she is in charge of the estate, not the probate attorney. She also may choose any officer of the court to represent her and file the necessary petitions and documents; she doesn't have to hire the attorney who drew her husband's will. If she hasn't previously met him, there could be a conflict of personality or a lack of trust. If there is, she should hire someone else.

When a date has been set by the court for a hearing to admit the will to probate, all of the heirs have to be notified by registered mail. These people must include not only the heirs who will participate in the estate according to the will, but also those who are left only one dollar. The latter people are mentioned because they stand in line to inherit from the testator under state law, and consequently could contest the will if they were so inclined.

Once letters testamentary are issued, formally appointing the widow as executrix, she is empowered for the first time to take charge of the assets. Armed with this court order, she should now change the ownership of each savings and checking account to read: "Mary Jones, executrix of the estate of John Jones." Henceforth all checks drawn by her must be signed this way, and all moneys received must be deposited to these accounts.

The next order of business is to make an inventory of the assets that comprise the estate. This is not a formal appraisal. An appraiser will be appointed later by the court for this purpose, but this preliminary list forms a basis for his or her estimate. If the inventory filed with the court by the executrix is accurate and complete much time can be saved.

It is sometimes difficult to obtain an accurate inventory, particularly when the widow has not participated in managing the couple's finances. A list of all property, kept with the will and maintained up-to-date by the testator, is invaluable in this regard. Here is a sample copy of a Confidential Inventory of Assets.

A Confidential Inventory of Assets

Name _____ Date of birth _____

Wife's name _____ Date of birth _____

Address _____ telephone _____

City _____ state _____ zip code _____

Social Security numbers: husband _____ wife _____

Total value of the estate _____

1. Names of children (include name of spouse if child
   is married) birth dates—residence

   _____

   _____

   _____

2. Names of grandchildren—birth dates—residence
   (if not living with parents)

   _____

   _____

3. Last will and testament—date—where kept

   _____

4. Advisers: name—address—telephone

   Lawyer _____

   Banker _____

   Life underwriter _____

   Accountant _____

   Investment representative _____

   Signature _____ Date _____

Assets

	Present value	Ownership
1. Checking accounts	$ _____	_____
2. Bank savings	_____	_____
3. Savings and loan associations	_____	_____
4. Credit unions	_____	_____
5. Securities (see page 4)	_____	_____
6. Mortgages and trust deeds	_____	_____
7. Notes receivable	_____	_____
8. Home	_____	_____
9. Other real estate	_____	_____
10. Life insurance death benefit	_____	_____
11. Business equity	_____	_____
Total assets	$ _____	_____

Liabilities

	Amount
1. Mortgage or trust deeds	$ _____
(a) Home	_____
(b) Other	_____
2. Notes payable	_____
3. Other liabilities	_____
Total liabilities	$ _____

Total assets	_____
Total liabilities	_____
Net value of the estate	_____

2

Current Income

Salary or business income $ _____

_____

Bank accounts

_____

Savings and loan

_____

Credit unions

_____

Securities

_____

Mortgages and trust deeds

_____

Real-estate income

_____

Notes

_____

Annuities

_____

Company pensions

_____

Other pensions

_____

Social Security
Railroad Retirement

_____

Other

_____

Total monthly income $ _____

Securities

Common stocks

No. shares	Company	Cost basis	Current value	Ownership
_____	_____	_____	$ _____	_____
_____	_____	_____	_____	_____
_____	_____	_____	_____	_____
_____	_____	_____	_____	_____
_____	_____	_____	_____	_____
		Total value	$ _____	

Preferred stocks

No. shares	Company	Cost basis	Current value	Ownership
_____	_____	_____	$ _____	_____
_____	_____	_____	_____	_____
		Total value	$ _____	

Industrial and municipal bonds

Face amount	Description	Interest	Current value	Ownership
_____	_____	_____	$ _____	_____
_____	_____	_____	_____	_____
		Total value	$ _____	

Government bonds

Face amount	Description	Interest	Current value	Ownership
_____	_____	_____	$ _____	_____
_____	_____	_____	_____	_____
		Total value	$ _____	

Total value in securities $ _____

4

Comments by the Property Owner

_____

_____

_____

_____

_____

_____

_____

_____

_____

_____

_____

_____

_____

Date   Signature

In the absence of such an inventory, there is no alternative but to use every possible source of information to ensure that nothing has been overlooked. These sources include a safe-deposit box (or a strong box at home), bank statements and canceled checks, passbooks, income-tax records for the previous three years, brokerage statements and confirmations, and all documents and papers, including memoranda.

It's amazing how people keep records for years that have absolutely no value. One nephew had to go through a whole trunk full of papers kept in the corner of his aunt's bedroom to find assets that in the final analysis amounted to only $3,000. Receipts had been kept for bills that had been paid for twenty years. A paid promissory note was found for a loan that had been made to a brother in 1924! Besides an up-to-date inventory, every testator should periodically go over his or her papers and documents and throw away all those that are no longer of any value. It is of tremendous help to the legal representative later on.

A notice has to be published in a legal newspaper notifying everyone concerned, mainly creditors of the estate, that the will has been lodged with the court and that an executor or executrix has been appointed. The number of times this has to appear, and for how long, varies from state to state. The minimum time given to creditors to file their claims is usually from four to six months, and many states grant them a year. This is one of the major reasons why probate takes so long.

The probate attorney must file an affidavit with the court that public notice has been given that the estate is in probate. Failure to do so can seriously delay the probate proceedings, because the length of time that must elapse for the benefit of creditors is not from the date of publication, but from the date the affidavit is filed.

Robert Ashford died leaving his estate to his widow, except for some minor cash bequests. All of the property required probate administration.

Mrs. Ashford, as executrix, knew nothing of her duties. She was fortunate to have a brother-in-law as an investment representative who had specialized for years in estate planning. As a consequence, she turned to him for all of her advice, with the result that he, in effect, became the executor, although she had to sign all the papers, including the checks.

He helped her choose the attorney, and thereafter handled every step of the probate process, including filing the state inheritance-tax return and making the final accounting to the court. He left one thing, unfortunately, to the lawyer. Since he didn't live in the city where the probate court was located, he left it up to the legal representative to publish the notice to creditors in the local newspaper and file the affadavit with the court that this had been done. From the very outset he had made it clear to the attorney that he wanted the estate out of probate in the minimum time permitted by law, which in the state of domicile was four months. He made one mistake. He didn't ask the lawyer to mail him a copy of the newspaper notice and proof that the affadavit had been filed.

The estate was due for final distribution on February 9 as far as the brother-in-law was concerned. He frequently checked with the lawyer to be sure that this date was firm and that everything was in order. On January 25 he again contacted the lawyer by telephone.

"Are we still all set for February ninth?" he asked.

"February ninth? No. You mean April twenty-sixth, don't you?"

"April twenty-sixth!" the brother-in-law exploded over the phone. "What are you talking about anyway?"

"You've known all along," the attorney replied, "that the minimum time for filing claims in this state is four months. The affadavit wasn't filed with the court until December twenty-sixth."

"Why haven't you told me this before now?" the brother-in-law demanded. "You knew I was counting on February ninth."

"Well, it's the first time that it's happened to me," replied the attorney. "I usually leave it up to the newspaper to see that the affadavit is filed. They failed to remind me."

"They failed to remind you!" replied the brother-in-law sarcastically, for he was really incensed. "You know that an executrix in this state can't invest in securities. The market is forty percent off. My sister-in-law wants her share of the cash invested as soon as possible. Now she can't invest for another two-and-one-half months. Your mistake is liable to cost her a lot of money."

And it did. The market went up drastically from February 9 to April 26, and it cost her $10,000 in lost profits, simply because the attorney failed to file an affadavit on time.

When the bills from the creditors come in, the widow-executrix should not pay them at once but file them into classes that are fixed by state law. First preferred would be funeral expenses, expenses of last illness, and court allowances (if any) to the widow and minor children. Second preferred would be taxes, wages for labor performed, and bills for necessities. Third preferred would be the remainder. After waiting for a few weeks to be sure that she had received all of the claims, or most of them, she should pay them in this order.

All casualty insurance policies should be examined as to their due dates to be sure they are kept in force. Automobile insurance and fire insurance on real estate are particularly important. Property taxes should be paid promptly to avoid interest charges and penalties.

Social Security and Railroad Retirement benefits are often a major source of family income. As we shall see later in Chapter 9, the widow's check if she is 65 increases from 50 percent of her husband's monthly benefit (which she received as his wife) to 100 percent, which she is entitled to as his widow. Application should be made immediately and in person at the nearest Social Security office for it takes two to three months for a claim to be processed. Even though the benefit will be retroactive to the date of death, it is still better to receive the monthly check as soon as possible.

Social Security also pays a death benefit of $255 to help defray funeral expenses. This should be applied for immediately. If the widow prefers, in order to reduce her cash outlay, she may direct that the $255 check be paid directly to the funeral home. If she does, the funeral parlor should be notified so she can subtract this amount from their bill.

Often a pension was received by the testator from his former employer. The widow may or may not be entitled to a reduced portion of this monthly check. Query should be made promptly, and a claim filed if one is in order. Sometimes this takes months.

Mr. George died leaving his widow in rather meager circumstances. Unfortunately he also died without a will, which placed his small estate in probate. He had been a teacher for forty years and had frequently reminded his wife that upon his death the City of New York would pay her 50 percent of his $600 a month pension, having purposely chosen this option at age 65.

Mrs. George had a terrible time finding the necessary documents to substantiate this. Her husband had not been a tidy man, and he had been a meticulous saver of every scrap of paper. It was only after weeks of frantic searching that she found a copy of the original pension award and the document that he had indeed elected to include her in his pension.

After mailing these papers to the proper New York City office, as indicated on the forms, she heard nothing for two months. So she wrote again. Finally after three months had elapsed, she received an answer requesting a certified copy of the death certificate, which she mailed, and again she heard nothing. Upon once more querying the office she was sent still another document, which required her signature to be notarized. Obtaining a notary was difficult because she was confined to a wheelchair. To solve this problem, a friend persuaded a notary to come to her apartment. Finally at the end of seven months she received her first monthly check.

Money is often due an estate. The executrix should be diligent in collecting what is owed. Debtors often feel that they can ignore a widow because probably she has had no business experience, and she may not even be aware of the obligation. In one instance, a husband had loaned $50,000 to a builder, receiving for it a first mortgage on an apartment house. Upon his death the contractor-owner promptly stopped making payments. It was only after many months, and after the widow hired a lawyer who threatened foreclosure, that the monthly payments were resumed.

In another instance, the only remaining payment due the estate was from a pension plan, and then for only a part of one month. The husband had died on May 12, and the pension died with him. However, by reading the fine print in the pension agreement, the executrix determined that the pension was due up to the date of death. The amount due for the twelve days was $154.20, not much money, but still something. It took several months of correspondence, and two long-distance telephone calls, before the money was finally paid.

When an estate is appraised, a copy of the inventory and its evaluation is sent to the state inheritance tax department and the Internal Revenue Service by the court clerk. If these agencies determine that death taxes are owed, it is the duty of the legal representative to prepare and file a state inheritance tax return, and a federal estate tax return for the IRS. The probate attorney usually prepares these returns and advises the executrix of the amount owed. This is one of the most time-consuming processes of the entire probate administration. The attorney often procrastinates at this point, for these forms are complicated. Constant prodding by the executrix is sometimes the only solution.

If the estate is large, or consists of real estate or closed corporation stock, the evaluation can be difficult and often results in an argument as to what is a fair appraisal. This can be an honest difference of opinion, but nevertheless this by itself can delay the closing of an estate for many months and sometimes years.

The executor or executrix also has the option under the law of evaluating the estate at the time of death or six months later. In a declining stock market, or deteriorating economic conditions, the alternate six months date can result in considerably reducing death taxes.

Often inheritance and estate taxes can't be paid within the required time of nine months after death. An extension can be obtained in this event, but the government charges interest on any unpaid balance after the due date. Therefore every effort should be made by the executrix to pay these taxes on time.

It is also the duty of the legal representative to file an income-tax return for the decedent up to the date of death.

For example, the testator died on August 15. Obviously no income tax return had been filed by the property owner for the period from January 1 to the date of his death. A return has to be filed the following April (or before) and the taxes paid just as though the property owner were still alive.

During the period of administration, income is collected by the executrix and deposited to the estate bank accounts. If taxable income amounts to more than $600, an income tax return has to be filed for the estate as well as for the decedent.

State law varies widely in regard to what the executrix can and cannot do about investments during probate administration. Sometimes this is controlled by the testator himself by instructions he has left in the will. If state law permits it, complete power can be granted by the testator to his legal representative to invest or not invest as he or she sees fit. Then there is no problem.

On the other hand some states don't allow an executor or executrix to invest at all. In still others, all investments must be converted into cash, unless the testator specifies otherwise. This can result in severe losses in a bear stock market, or when real-estate prices are depressed.

The widow-executrix has no alternative but to make sure of the law in her particular state. Rather than trust the advice of her attorney (who may not be too knowledgeable in this regard), she should discuss her investment powers at the county offices with the probate clerk. She may, if she likes, even ask to see the records of several probate proceedings to obtain more information. This is important when other heirs or legatees are involved because she is personally responsible for any losses that may occur because she acted outside the law. In some states she may not even settle a claim for less than the full amount, for if she does, she is liable for the difference.

Whom should the widow trust, if like Mrs. Ashford she isn't fortunate enough to have a knowledgeable brother-in-law?

The answer lies in the Confidential Inventory of Assets that has been previously discussed. In the example given, there is a place at the bottom of page one for the testator to list the names, addresses, and telephone numbers of his advisers. If this procedure is followed, the widow-executrix will be in good hands.

But what if this hasn't been done?

The survivor has but one recourse—not to trust strangers, no matter how well recommended, nor should she follow the advice of well-meaning friends and relatives. It's sad but true that, even with all the protection provided by the law today, the average widow is broke in just four years.

She should listen only to proven experts who have spent years in the financial world.

Mrs. Casey was a widow and went to see a banker, but she refused to follow his advice without first consulting her cousin. Admittedly the banker was not an expert on investments, but he had years of experience that had given him a lot of common sense.

"You evidently have a great deal of faith in your cousin," said the banker, as she sat at his desk.

"Well, he keeps all my books for me, and I don't know how to do that."

"What books does he keep for you, Mrs. Casey?"

"Well, he pays my property taxes and car insurance and makes out my income tax return."

"And what does your cousin do?"

"He's retired."

"And before he was retired?"

"He drove a truck for an oil company."

The banker threw up his hands. "And you are going to follow his advice?"

"Yes. If I don't, maybe he won't keep my books anymore."

The result was that Mrs. Casey was broke in less than the average four years. The well-meaning cousin was going to make her rich by buying stocks on margin. The next down market took care of that.

During the entire period of administration, a careful record has to be maintained of all collections and disbursements and of all changes in the nature of the assets. Then a final accounting has to be made to the court that clearly demonstrates that the income and the property have been properly managed, according to the dictates of state law and the will of the testator. The bookkeeping obviously must be in balance. In large estates an accountant should be hired to maintain records and render the final account.

Here is a copy of an accounting to the court on a small estate.

Summary of Account

Assets of Estate, per Inventory and Appraisement		$41,014.53
Receipts, per Exhibit A		1,122.12
Total Estate		$42,136.65
Disbursements, per Exhibit B	$5,206.84	
Distribution, per Exhibit D	500.00	$5,706.84
NET ESTATE ON HAND, PER EXHIBIT C		$36,429.81

Exhibit A—Receipts

Date	Received from Purpose	Amount
12-2-74	Crocker Bank—Interest on savings account	$ 151.23
12-2-74	Guaranty Savings & Loan—Interest	92.35
12-2-74	Guaranty Savings & Loan—Interest	17.53
	Plaza Art Galleries, Sale of personal effects:	
8-8-74	By check	193.79
8-19-74	By check	30.60
8-29-74	By check	167.20
9-4-74	By check	46.49
9-11-74	By check	129.20
12-17-74	Beverly Manor Inc.—refund of money	99.00
12-28-74	Beverly Manor Inc.—refund of money	18.75
12-29-74	Final pension check to date of death from the Acme Corporation	79.12
12-29-74	Gibraltar Savings & Loan, accrued interest	96.86
	Total receipts	$1,122.12

Exhibit B—Disbursements

Date	Paid to Purpose	Amount
10-11-74	John Baldwin, reimbursement for funeral expenses, Catholic Cemeteries	$ 260.00
10-11-74	Dickerson, Higbee & Lightfoot, funeral expenses, balance owing on account	184.00
10-15-74	Abbey Rents, for rent of wheelchair	18.55
10-21-74	Alfred Morino, M.D., medical expenses	32.00
10-27-74	Pacific Telephone, closing bill	7.25
11-09-74	Bradford Hull, inheritance tax referee	5.68
11-09-74	County Treasurer—state inheritance tax	2,267.76
12-12-74	Martha Kennedy, executrix, part payment of commission	1,200.00
12-21-74	Medical Science Laboratory, expenses of last illness	40.50
12-21-74	Martin Douglas, attorney, repayment of costs of administration	117.10
12-21-74	Plaza Movers, Baltimore, moving personal effects to auction house	74.00
12-21-74	Redemptorist Mission House, bequest in will	1,000.00
	Total disbursements	$5,206.84

Exhibit C—Property on Hand

(1)	400 shares Tandy Corporation common stock at appraised value, date of death	$ 5,175.00
(2)	100 shares Tandy Corporation common stock, value at date of purchase March 10, 1975	2,930.75
(3)	200 shares Intel Corporation common stock value at date of purchase March 10, 1975	9,648.41
(4)	100 shares Digital Equipment common stock value at date of purchase March 10, 1975	7,980.73
(5)	Bank of America, Commercial Account 095–9–01422	157.95
(6)	Bank of America, Passbook Account 5–80502	10,000.00
(7)	Merrill Lynch, Pierce, Fenner & Smith, Inc. Cash balance on hand in Account 286–32105	536.97
	Total estate on hand	$36,429.81

Exhibit D—Personal Property Distributed

10–10–74	Distribution to Robert Revoir, personal effects and household furniture by terms of will	$400.00
10–10–74	Distribution to Marth Kennedy, personal effects and household furniture by terms of will	100.00
	Total distribution at appraised value	$500.00

The court can now issue a final decree of distribution authorizing the executrix to distribute the balance in the estate according to the will.

At this point, if legatees have been named in the will who are to receive a specific amount, checks for these sums should be drawn and a receipt obtained from each legatee so it can be filed with the court as proof that the instructions of the testator have been complied with in this regard.

Probate is then finally over.

One more thing, however, is essential for the protection of the widow-executrix. She should instruct her attorney to obtain from the court a written order that she has fully and faithfully performed her duties, and that therefore she is discharged as executrix.

If securities are in the estate, the ownership of them has yet to be changed. This is because transfer agents for stocks and bonds can't transfer title until the final decree of distribution has been issued by the court, which involves another delay. Mrs. Ashforth inherited several securities. After probate was over, it took another four months before they were issued in her name. Despite a knowledgeable brother-in-law, and a state law that allowed distribution within four months, due to an error on the part of her attorney and because stocks were a part of the estate, it was one year before she finally had all of the assets in her name.

In view of all of the above, there is a serious question about the advisability of making a widow the executrix. And certainly poor Aunt Mathilda shouldn't be named just so she can earn the executrix's fee. Far better that Aunt Mathilda be left a cash bequest.

No, in many estates it is better to name a bank as executor and not the widow at all. The trust department of a bank has a probate division that handles estate administration every day as a matter of routine business. They won't do the work any faster than an individual executor or executrix, maybe even a little slower for that matter, but at least it will be done right and according to the strict letter of the law. And the charge will be the same.

Admittedly the widow is now completely at the mercy, not only of the probate attorney, but of the corporate executor as well. She will have lost control of the estate during the long period of probate and, like any other heir, will not be able to do anything about it but stand by in frustration until the final decree of distribution is issued by the court.

4

Proper Ownership of Your Assets and Community Property

Proper ownership of assets cannot be discussed intelligently unless property is clearly defined first, especially since an attorney is often involved, as when drawing a will. The possession of property is the right to use, enjoy, and dispose of land, and other things of value, and to bar others from the ownership of it.

Property is either real or personal.

Real property is a general name for land and the things that are attached to it. Real estate is basically land, even though there are buildings on it. This is why title to one's home is by legal description of the land only, for automatically it includes the house. Real property also includes things that are attached to the land by roots (trees and shrubs), imbedded in it (posts), and things permanently attached to buildings.

Personal property includes movable objects that one may possess, use, enjoy, and dispose of. It is further classified as being either tangible or intangible.

Tangible personal property includes the furniture and fixtures in one's home, jewelry and art works, and one's clothing. It also includes the furniture and equipment in an office or store, business inventories, equipment on a farm, automobiles, airplanes, and livestock.

Intangible personal property consists of rights one has to the possession, use, enjoyment, and disposal of stocks and bonds, bank and savings and loan accounts, stockbrokerage accounts, mortgages and notes, rights in contracts, leases, options, copyrights, and patents.

A lawyer frequently refers to personal property as chattels. Holding the correct title to all of these assets is of the utmost importance. It will determine which of them will be subject to probate administration and which will not. It will determine who will be in immediate possession of part of your estate, and who of your heirs will have to wait for months, and maybe years, to inherit what you left them. Carelessness in how you hold your assets can completely disrupt your estate plan. It can seriously escalate death taxes, and it can result in disinheriting your wife of two-thirds of your estate, even though it is your intention that she should inherit the whole of it. It could result in such bad management of your assets that your widow will be broke in just four years. Improper ownership can allow relatives, friends, and even absolute strangers to participate in the fruits of your labor, although this is the last thing in the world that you want to have happen.

Correct title can avoid probate. But even when you want to avoid court administration of your estate, your attorney will often raise so many objections to the types of ownership that permit this that you may throw up your hands and tell him to arrange your affairs as he thinks best.

Nevertheless, probate of an estate is advisable in many situations. Single persons, those who have heirs who are minors (or mentally or physically incompetent), and those people with large and complicated estates, usually find that probate is their best solution. These testators must understand, however, that they can't hold their assets in joint tenancy or in beneficiary form, for such assets cannot be willed, and therefore will pass to the named beneficiaries or to the surviving joint tenant, regardless of what kind of testamentary document is drawn by the testator (whether it be a will or a trust).

If assets in an estate are held in the name of an individual alone, and the property owner leaves no will, the estate will pass to his heirs by operation of law. The distribution will depend upon the law of the state where the deceased was domiciled. This varies widely from state to state. It would be wise for everyone to determine the law of succession where they reside. The result of dying intestate, with all of the assets in the name of the deceased, may be so shocking as to prompt some people who have no will to go to a competent attorney and have one drawn at once. In some states, where there are no children and a widow and his parents are the surviving relatives, the widow receives one-third and his parents two-thirds of her husband's estate. If he doesn't get along with his in-laws and his wife would need all of the assets, this result could be disastrous.

In the state of Ohio if a person dies intestate (without a will), and all of the assets are held in the deceased's name alone, his or her assets will be divided among first, second, and third cousins, if these people are the only relatives.

Mildred Long died in Columbus, Ohio, without a will. She was a retired maiden schoolteacher, age 80, who held her assets in her individual name. She was an only child, with one aunt and uncle, both deceased. However she did have two widowed cousins of whom she was fond, who lived nearby. She always felt that she would leave what little she had to them, if they outlived her. But it didn't happen that way, for she never got around to changing her individual ownership or to making a will.

When Mildred Long died the probate division of the Court of Common Pleas appointed an attorney as the administrator. She left a very simple estate, consisting of $24,000 in two savings and loan accounts. The attorney was faced not only with probate administration, but with locating all of the heirs which by Ohio state law (as we have said) consist of first, second, and third cousins if they are the only relatives, which was the case with Mildred Long.

Almost four years after she died, one of her first cousins who lived in Florida received an unexpected long distance telephone call one day from Columbus, Ohio.

"Is this Mr. Robert Long?" the voice asked at the other end of the line.

"Yes, it is."

"I'm John Hull, attorney-at-law in Columbus, Ohio. Do you happen to know a Mildred Long of Columbus?"

"Yes, I do. I'm her first cousin."

"I hoped you'd say that. I've been looking for you. She died several years ago and you are one of the heirs."

"Mildred Long," mused the cousin. "That's a name out of the past. I haven't seen her for forty years. Why would she leave me anything?"

"Well, she didn't, really. She died without a will, and I'm the administrator of her estate. Her heirs by state law are her cousins. Unfortunately, there seem to be quite a few of you. I have spent the last several years tracing the family tree."

"What is the estate worth? Do you know?"

"Oh yes. Twenty-four thousand dollars, all in cash."

"How many cousins are there?"

"Sixteen, including you."

"That doesn't leave much to divvy up, does it?"

"No, it doesn't."

"What do you want me to do?" asked the cousin.

"Nothing actually, now that I've located you," replied the attorney. "You're the last one I had to find. I'll mail you a court summons for a Hearing on Complaint to Determine Heirship. But you don't have to appear. The court should declare the sixteen of you as heirs. But not in identical shares, however. As a first cousin, you inherit one-tenth. Since there are five first cousins, the five of you will inherit one-half of the estate, the other eleven will divide the other half."

"Well, thanks anyway for calling."

"Don't mention it."

What was the result? Mildred Long's estate was distributed

four years after she died among sixteen people, fourteen of whom she had never seen, or hadn't laid eyes on for thirty or forty years! Her two first cousins, living right in Columbus and whom she wanted to inherit her estate, actually received one-tenth each, after attorney's fees and probate costs.

Because of the lengthy search for the cousins, John Hull was paid attorney's fees of $3,528.20, an administrator's fee of $250.78, a reimbursement for long-distance telephone calls of $340.16, and for cash advanced, $416.30. This was a total cost of $4,875.60, of which the lawyer received for his services $3,778.98, as both the attorney and the administrator for the estate. He therefore became the largest single heir of Mildred Long. The two first cousins who lived in Columbus each inherited $1,912.44 (after deduction for their one-tenth of the costs). With a simple will they would each have inherited over $10,000, and within one year, not after four long years of waiting.[1]

Furthermore, if Mildred Long had understood proper owner-ship, she could have made it easy for her two cousins to inherit from her. She could have named them as beneficiaries on her two savings and loan accounts. This way there would have been no delay, no probate, and no expense, except for the Ohio estate tax.

In many estates title is left to chance. Assets acquired over a period of a lifetime are bought without regard to correct title. In others, where ownership was chosen with care, conditions changed, which resulted in the titles becoming obsolete for various reasons, usually because of death, births, marriages, or a divorce. Titles that were correct, or that seemed to be correct at the time that the assets were acquired, no longer applied. And yet mainly through inertia, they weren't changed.

1. For sake of simplicity, the interest earned on the savings and loan accounts has been ignored. Likewise the Ohio estate tax, which is 2 percent on the first $40,000 (after exemptions) hasn't been taken into account.

Tom Wilson died after a relatively short marriage of ten years. There was no issue, so his will left everything to his beloved wife, or so he thought. One asset was left out, however, his life insurance. He had bought a $50,000 policy before he was married, and had named his brother as beneficiary. Through neglect he didn't change the beneficiary designation when he married, and later he completely forgot that he hadn't taken care of this very important matter. When he died the insurance company had no alternative but to pay the $50,000 to his brother. His widow was very upset, for this was their major asset; but the brother wasn't—for he kept the money.

From the two examples of Mildred Long and Tom Wilson the importance of proper ownership is obvious; it is of overriding importance in many estates. Therefore the various types of ownership, and their uses, must be clearly understood. There are a number of different kinds. They comprise both probate and non-probate assets. Since non-probate assets are the most widely held, these will be considered first.

Non-Probate Assets

Joint tenancy with right of survivorship, and not as tenants in common

This is the principal title that is used to avoid probate, which is why it was discussed in Chapter 2. It applies ideally to a couple with a small estate and no death tax problem. The objectives of these couples, where they want the survivor to inherit everything, is to avoid probate administration and cause the least trouble and expense for the survivor. Joint tenancy will do this.

However, to accomplish this, all assets must be jointly owned. If something is left out, that item will have to be probated. By all assets, we mean securities and real estate, bank and savings and loan accounts, government bonds, mortgages, notes. The only assets that can be excluded are household furnishings and furniture.

Many people have the mistaken notion that joint tenancy with right of survivorship avoids the payment of death taxes. It does not. If an estate is of sufficient size to entail the payment of federal or state taxes, they have to be paid. The fact that the assets escape probate administration has no bearing whatsoever.

Sometimes assets are held in another state besides the one where the deceased was domiciled. Ancillary probate proceedings are then required in that other state. This can be avoided by placing out-of-state property, particularly real estate, in joint tenancy with right of survivorship. Since the survivor automatically inherits, ancillary probate proceedings will be avoided. Where intangible personal property is the asset, such as bank accounts or securities, they should be physically transferred into the state of domicile as the simplest way of handling the problem.

Sometimes property is placed in joint tenancy with children. This shouldn't be done when the child is a minor. If the other tenant wants to sell, the child's consent is required; and if the other tenant should die, the child now becomes the sole owner, which may not be desirable for several reasons.

Many property owners don't realize that there are potential gift taxes when assets are placed in joint tenancy. Generally, a gift occurs when an individual uses his or her separate funds for the purchase of property and places the ownership in joint names. This most frequently happens when a couple wants to obtain the advantages of joint tenancy, so the husband changes the title from his individual ownership, or the wife does. If the asset has a value of $6,000 or less, this still doesn't involve a gift tax because a donation of $3,000 or less comes under the annual exclusion (the donor tenant still owns the other one-half).

When property is worth more than this, there is a possible gift tax obligation. It then becomes important to know at what point a gift actually occurs when an asset is placed in joint tenancy. When securities are put in joint names, a transfer occurs the minute the ownership is changed. In real estate a gift doesn't occur until it is sold, for the other tenant can't use any portion of the property until it is disposed of. If the donor tenant chooses to treat the transfer as a gift at the time, he or she may do so by filing a federal gift tax return and paying the tax, if any.

With bank accounts, there is no gift tax obligation at the time a joint tenancy account is opened. The sole contributing tenant can at any time close out the account and return the proceeds to his name alone, in which event no gift took place. However, if the noncontributing tenant withdraws any part of the account, this amount (up to one-half) becomes a gift. The same thing holds true with savings and loan accounts and government bonds.

This merging of separate property into joint tenancy with right of survivorship often occurs when second marriages are involved, or when one of the spouses receives a gift or an inheritance.

Just as care must be exercised when placing property in joint tenancy, so must caution be exercised when unraveling it. When property has been titled in joint names, and the joint owners decide that this ownership is a mistake, it is possible to undo what has been done. If no gift was made at the time the joint tenancy was created, a return to individual ownership presents no problem.

Naming a beneficiary

This was also discussed in Chapter 2. We have seen in the case of Mildred Long the importance of understanding when this type of ownership should be used, and how it can so easily avoid probate, delay, and costs, as well as preventing total strangers from participating in the estate.

A *living trust*

This was also discussed in Chapter 2 as the third way to avoid probate. Title to the property passes immediately to the successor trustee; it does not go through the executor's hands and probate administration.

Co-ownership

This title is used less and less frequently. It is still used extensively, however, on United States government savings bonds. The title reads simply: John or Mary Jones. The signatures of both owners is required when the bonds are purchased initially, but either owner may cash them. Because of this, the survivor inherits them without probate. The ownership, however, can't be changed during life; the coowners have to cash the bonds and purchase new ones if they want a different title.

Naming a beneficiary on pension and profit-sharing plans

These proceeds also pass directly to the named individual regardless of any testamentary disposition, like the death benefit of life insurance. This is a beneficiary form of ownership, but it's mentioned here separately because correct title to these plans is frequently overlooked, yet they are increasingly becoming a sizable portion of many estates.

When a pension or profit-sharing plan is sizable, care should be exercised when naming a beneficiary. The same considerations apply here as with the death benefit from life insurance. Is the beneficiary financially responsible and knowledgeable? If not, payment to the estate might be better, with distribution arranged by a will, or possibly a trust should be created.

Tenants by the entirety

This ownership is created by a conveyance to a husband and wife, whereupon each becomes possessed of the entire estate, and after the death of one, the survivor takes the whole. This ownership is available *only* between spouses, and *only* with real estate. In this relationship a husband and a wife are considered to be one person. The ownership is basically a joint tenancy with right of survivorship, but with a difference.

The chief characteristic that distinguishes it from a joint tenancy is that it can be terminated only by joint action of the husband and wife during their lives. Many people believe this to be true of a joint tenancy, but this is not so. In joint tenancy, either tenant may convey his interest to another. In this event, the new co-owners no longer hold the property in joint tenancy, but as tenants in common, with the property subject to probate administration.

Another important characteristic of tenants by the entirety is the possession by each tenant of the whole property. Because of this the real estate can't be attached by a creditor of either the husband or the wife alone. A judgment can be obtained only if they are *both* legally liable for the debt.

Tenants by the entirety is therefore used by couples for two different reasons.

First, because either the husband or the wife wants protection from the irresponsible financial acts (real or imaginary) of the other, which when resources are meager can be a worry. It gives protection to the other tenant because the creditor of the financially irresponsible spouse can't execute a judgment against property that is held as tenants by the entirety.

Second, couples use this form of ownership when there is a lack of trust between spouses. Real property held as tenants by the entirety can't be sold without the written consent of both parties. It prevents the possibility of the ownership being dissolved by one tenant without the consent of the other, thereby destroying the very important provision of survivorship.

Some states prohibit this type of ownership; therefore local law must be determined in regard to it.

Declaration of a homestead

The homestead laws of the various states are statutory provisions for exempting a home from execution of a judgment by the homeowner's creditors for the payment of general debts. This ownership is created by a declaration of homestead, acknowledged like a grant deed to real property, and recorded in the office of the county recorder.

The amount of the equity in a domicile that is exempted from the owner's creditors is limited by state statute. The exempt amount or value (and sometimes the number of acres, particularly if it's rural property) varies from a low figure of $1,000 to a high of $25,000. At least three states—Pennsylvania, Maryland, and New Jersey—have no homestead law at all.

In practically all states that have a homestead law, the property can be subjected to a forced sale if the value exceeds the allowable exemption (a common occurrence in these days of inflation). In the event of a sale, the exempt portion is set aside for the homeowner, and the overage is paid to the owner's creditors.

The purpose in executing a declaration of homestead and filing it with the county recorder is an obvious one. The owner has debts and wants to protect his or her home from general creditors. It doesn't shelter him or her from the payment of property taxes, nor from the claims of a mortgagor. Nor will it protect an equity that is greater than the amount of the homestead exemption according to the law of the particular state involved. But where an owner's debts are less than the exemption, and creditors insistent, it will give the property owner relief from execution of a judgment against the home.

When a residence is declared a homestead, the wife normally must join in its execution. In some states, however (as in California and New Mexico), she may make a declaration of homestead by herself if her husband does not. If a couple later wants to change the homestead status (because they have become free of debt, for instance), they may do so by making a declaration of abandonment, and filing it with the county recorder.

The amount of the exemption is so small in some states that it isn't worth the time and trouble to make a declaration; in others it is.

Generally speaking it is not worth it in the eastern part of the United States. We have already mentioned three eastern states that don't have a homestead law. In North and South Carolina, and Ohio, the homestead exemption is only $1,000, and in New York and Virginia only $2,000.

In the Midwest and Far West it is generally worthwhile to make a declaration of homestead if the owner's creditors are closing in. In California the exemption is high, $20,000, and in Wisconsin even higher, $25,000. In Minnesota no declaration is required. A person creates a homestead simply by residing in a house that is owned and occupied by the debtor as a dwelling place. It includes the land on which it is situated, and there is no limitation as to the value that is exempted. In Arizona and Louisiana the exemption is $15,000, and in the states of Idaho, Illinois, New Mexico, Nevada, Texas, and Washington it is $10,000. In Kansas there is no limitation, except when it is farm land; then the maximum exemption is 160 acres.

From the above it can be seen that the property owner who is considering a homestead declaration has no alternative but to ascertain the homestead law, if any, in the state where he resides.

Here is a copy of a homestead declaration. This form can be obtained from any large stationery store that maintains a supply of blank legal forms. It can be filled out and filed by the home-owner; the services of an attorney are not necessary, unless this is desired.

This form of ownership is a joint tenancy with right of survivorship. It is therefore a non-probate asset.

RECORDING REQUESTED BY

AND WHEN RECORDED MAIL TO

Name

Street
Address

City &
State

———— SPACE ABOVE THIS LINE FOR RECORDER'S USE ————

Know all Men by these Presents:

I, ... , do hereby declare:

That I am unmarried and am not the head of a family.

That I do now, at the time of making this declaration, actually reside on the land and premises hereinafter described;

That the premises on which I so reside are th...... certain lot...................................., piece....... or parcel...... of land situate, lying, and being in the .... County of ...., State of California, and bounded and described as follows, to wit:

Together with the dwelling-house...... and the outbuildings thereon;

That I do, by these presents, claim the premises above described, together with the dwelling-house......, and the outbuildings thereon, as a homestead; that all of said property is necessary to the use and enjoyment of said homestead;

* That following is a statement of the character of said property sought to be homesteaded showing the improvement or improvements which have been affixed thereto:

* That .... former declaration of homestead has been made ....

....

and this is .... an augmentation of value of a former claim.

That the actual cash value of said premises I estimate to be ....

.... dollars.

In Witness Whereof   I have hereunto set my hand this ....

day of.................................... one thousand nine hundred and ....

....

* Use of this paragraph is optional. Delete if it is not filled in. If it is filled in, affidavit must be attached. See C. C. Sec. 1263(4).

Cowdery's Form No. 434—DECLARATION OF HOMESTEAD—Single Person Not Head of Family   •   Printed 8/1/72

State of California, } ss.
County of ....

On this .... day of ....
in the year one thousand nine hundred and ...., before me,
.... a Notary Public,
State of California, duly commissioned and sworn, personally appeared ....
....
known to me to be the person described in and whose name is subscribed to the within instrument,
and acknowledged to me that .... executed the same.

IN WITNESS WHEREOF I have hereunto set my hand and affixed my official seal in the
.... County of ....
the day and year in this certificate first above written.

....
Notary Public, State of California
My commission expires ....

Declaration of Homestead

BY

Claimant

Dated. ...., 19......

State of California, } ss.
County of ....

.... being duly sworn, deposes and says:
That ...... is the declarant named in and who makes the within and annexed declaration of
homestead, that ...... has read the same and knows the contents thereof, and that the matters therein
stated are true of ...... own knowledge.   ....

Subscribed and sworn to before me this
.... day of ...., 19 ....

....
Notary Public, State of California

Gifts made during life by the property owner

This property, whether real or personal, is not subject to probate for a very simple reason. Title has already been changed into the names of the donee or donees. It completely bypasses a court administration as a consequence, except for one thing. The donated property is subject to death taxes in the donor's estate.

Probate Assets

Tenants in common

This is an ownership in joint names, without benefit of survivorship. Each tenant may will his or her share to whomever he or she pleases. This is because a tenant in common differs from a joint tenant with right of survivorship in that each tenant has a distinct estate in the property, with the same rights as though he or she were an individual owner.

In tenants in common there must be a unity of possession only, with each tenant having the right to occupy the undivided whole of the property in common with other cotenants. In joint tenancy with right of survivorship four different unities must exist at the same time. In addition to unity of possession, there must be a unity of interest, a unity of title, and a unity of time. This means that no one of the joint tenants can have a greater interest in the property than each of the others, that they must hold their property by one and the same conveyance (while tenants in common may acquire their interest by different titles), and the ownership of all of the tenants must be vested at one and the same time.

Tenancy in common is used when the tenants want the property to be probated because each tenant desires to make a testamentary disposition of his or her individual interest. It is a convenient ownership when the estate is large and death taxes are a problem. Each tenant can will to whom he or she pleases, thereby preventing the escalation of death taxes in the estate of the survivor.

In most of the United States the presumption is that all tenants holding jointly hold as tenants in common, unless a clear intention to the contrary is shown. This is why when a joint tenancy is desired the tenants should be explicit and have the title read: "Joint tenants with right of survivorship, and not as tenants in common." This way there can be no misunderstanding as to the intention of the parties.

A tenant in severalty

This is an individual ownership, despite its confusing name.

A tenant in severalty holds land and tenements in his or her right only, without any other person being joined or connected with that individual in point of interest. It is a title wherein only the individual's name appears.

Mildred Long held her two savings and loan accounts in her name only, or as *a tenant in severalty.* This required probate administration. And because she had no will, the accounts were subject to the law of succession in the state of Ohio.

Holding property as a conservator

A conservator is defined in the law as one who is a protector, a preserver.

When any person who owns property is found to be incapable of managing his or her affairs because of a defect of age, understanding, or self-control, the court appoints some person to be conservator. It is the conservator's duty, upon giving a probate bond, to take charge of the person and the estate of such an individual.

Obviously one who has been placed in charge of a conservator is incapable of making a will. The estate is therefore subject to probate.

Holding property as a guardian

This is different from a conservator in that a guardian legally has the care and management of the person, or the estate, or both, *of a child during his or her minority*. Incompetence in property management is due solely because the person is too young. Also, while a conservator is in charge of *both* the person and the estate of the individual involved, this is not necessarily true of a guardian.

A parent is the *natural* guardian of his or her own child, first the father and, upon death, the mother. But as a natural guardian a parent is in charge of the person of the child only. If a parent is to be a guardian of the minor's estate as well, he or she has to be named as such in the testator's will, or be appointed by a probate court.

In large estates it is not uncommon for the court to name some member of the family as guardian of the person of the child, so that the child will have the loving care and attention that might not otherwise be afforded, and to place someone else (such as a trust company, for instance) in charge of the minor's property. Notwithstanding this, if a guardian is appointed in a father's will, that person is a *testamentary guardian* of the minor, and as such will supersede the claims of all other guardians and have control of the person *and* the estate of the child until he or she reaches his or her majority.

If the child should die during his or her minority, the property would have to be probated.

Holding property as custodian for a minor

This is a different type of ownership than when acting as a guardian of the estate of a minor. This title is created when a gift is made to a minor child during the owner's lifetime of a specific property under the Uniform Gifts to Minors Act. For a donor to be able to use this ownership, the state where the donor resides must have adopted this uniform law. California, for example, has enacted it, so a resident of that state when making such a gift would have the title read: John Doe, as Custodian, Under The California Gifts To Minors Act.

When a gift is made under this uniform act, the property may be sold or cashed by the custodian for the benefit of the minor without having to obtain approval from the probate court. The most common use of this form of ownership is to set up a college educational fund, although any useful purpose may be served. A word of caution. This is an outright gift to the minor, and belongs to the child when the minor reaches his or her majority. For this reason the value of the gift is not included in the estate of the donor for death tax purposes, with one exception. If the donor is named as custodian, there is a possibility that it will return to the donor if the minor child should die. Because of this, the gift will be taxed in the donor's estate. If this is not desired, and a grandfather is making the gift to the minor, for instance, he should name one of the child's natural parents as custodian, not himself; this way the gift will not be taxed in his estate.

Anyone who is an adult may act as custodian; it doesn't have to be the minor's parent or grandparent. Also, all types of property can constitute the gift—cash in a bank or savings and loan account, government bonds, securities, a life insurance policy, an annuity, or real estate. In the 1966 amendments to the Revised Uniform Gifts To Minors Act, subsection (3) of section 4 was amended to read as follows:

> The custodian, notwithstanding statutes restricting investments by fiduciaries, shall invest and reinvest the custodial property as would a prudent man of discretion and intelligence, who is seeking a reasonable income and the preservation of his capital, except that he may, in his discretion and without liability to the minor or his estate, retain a security given to the minor in a manner prescribed in this act, or hold money so given in an account in the financial institution to which it was paid or delivered by the donor.

A gift, when it is made in the manner prescribed in the act, is irrevocable and conveys to the minor an indefeasible vested legal title to the security, life insurance policy, annuity contract, or money given.

A custodian, who is not the donor, may resign and designate his or her successor by:

1. Executing an instrument of resignation designating the successor custodian; and
2. Causing any registered custodial property to be registered in the name of the successor custodian.

The primary purpose in using this uniform act is to circumvent the jurisdiction of the probate court and to vest the power to act in respect to the gift property in the custodian.

William and Mary Talcott were wealthy grandparents who wanted to make a gift to each of their three grandchildren to help pay for their college education (which any parent who has a child in college will testify is a substantial financial burden).

Upon the advice of their attorney, and their tax consultant, they set up three separate $6,000 gifts for their grandchildren under the Uniform Gifts To Minors Act, naming their son as custodian. By making these gifts, they accomplished several objectives.

1. By joining in the gifts, each grandparent gave $3,000 to each grandchild under the annual exclusion. The total amount of the gifts was therefore $6,000 × 3, or $18,000, completely gift-tax and death-tax-free, provided they survived the gifts by three years.
2. By bypassing their son, the gifts would not be included in his estate if he should die, as they would have been if the gifts had been made to him outright.
3. The children's father (their son) as custodian could spend the money for their college education without having to resort to approval from the probate court.
4. If the children's parents did not need to use the gifts for which

they were designed (a college education) each child upon reaching his or her majority would have legal title to the property and could use it for some other useful purpose, such as a graduate degree, buying a home, or setting up a business.

5. They had the satisfaction of making a substantial gift to each grandchild during their lifetime.

6. Family income taxes were reduced, for each gift would have to earn in excess of $750 (the personal exemption allowed each taxpayer) before any taxes would have to be paid. If income from the gift eventually exceeded this amount, taxes would start at the lowest tax bracket.

A donation under the Uniform Gifts To Minors Act is a probate asset if the minor should die before reaching his or her majority. It would be distributed according to the child's will (if permitted in the state of domicile) or pass under the law of succession in that state.

Holding title as a trustee

A trustee is one who holds legal title to property for the benefit of another.

A trust may be created by the grantor either as a separate document or as a part of a will. It may be created for any purpose that is not illegal, and that is not against public policy.

Normally a testamentary trust is used (instead of a will) when it is the intention of the settlor that his or her property shall not be immediately inherited by heirs upon the conclusion of probate. Instead the property will be handed over to a trustee who will control and manage the property, and pay out the income and principal to the beneficiaries, according to the trust's provisions. A trust usually lasts for a period of years.

Community property

Property is owned this way by husband and wife only in the eight community property states. These states are Arizona, California, Idaho, Louisiana, Nevada, New Mexico, Texas, and

Washington. Forty million people are affected, four million of
them age 65 and older. For this reason a large segment of the
total population of the United States has to have a clear understanding of the community property system. Unfortunately,
however, the law in regard to community property is complex
and even varies from one community property state to another.

In these eight states, property that is acquired *after marriage*
is community property, while property that is owned by either
spouse before their marriage, or that which is acquired after
their marriage by gift, bequest, devise, or descent, is separate
property. Each spouse owns one-half of the community property while they are both alive, and each may will his or her
one-half of the community property to whomever he or she
pleases.

Because of the careful distinction that is made in these states
between what is community property and what is separate
property, a more complete definition follows.

Property that is acquired by a husband and wife, or either,
during marriage (when not acquired as the separate property
of either) is common or community property. This community
belongs one-half to the husband and one-half to the wife. This
kind of marital partnership, or community, consists of the
profits of all the effects of which the husband has the administration and enjoyment, and which is the produce of the reciprocal
industry and labor of both husband and wife, and of the estates
which they may acquire during their marriage, either by dona-
tions *made jointly to both of them,* or by purchase, or in any
other similar way. This is so even though the purchase is made
only in the name of one of the two, and not both, *because in this
case the period of time when the purchase is made is alone
attended to,* and not the person who made the purchase.

Separate property

All property, whether real or personal, which is owned by
either spouse *before marriage,* or thereafter acquired by gift,

bequeath, devise, or descent, and any increase thereof because of rents, issues, and profits, is the separate property of each spouse. Each spouse has sole management, control, and disposition of the rights in his or her separate property. The separate property of a spouse is not liable for separate debts or obligations of the other consort, and it may be conveyed without the other spouse joining in the conveyance. In other words, it is the property of a married person which that individual owns in her or his own right, and which she or he can encumber and dispose of at will. Separate property continues to be such as long as it can clearly be traced and identified as belonging to that spouse.

Since separate property of a spouse consists not only of what he or she owned *before* marriage, but also that which he or she acquired *after* marriage, by gift, bequeath, devise, or descent, these words must be understood.

In a will a testator bequeaths only personal property, and devises only real property, while property that is acquired by descent means that the decedent died intestate (without a will) and therefore the property is inherited by the laws of succession of the state wherein the deceased was domiciled.

A gift that is made to either spouse alone is also separate property of that consort; it doesn't have to be inherited.

It will be noted by the reader that the community property states lie only in the southwestern and western parts of the United States. This is because Louisiana and the southwestern parts of the country belonged at one time either to Spain or to Mexico. Mexico, in return for the payment of $15 million, ceded to the United States the huge territory from California to Texas at the conclusion of the Mexican War in 1848. The common law in these states therefore goes back to Spain because, as every schoolchild knows, Mexico was conquered by the Spaniards before that nation became independent. And Spain has always recognized the community property system, whereby one-half of the community belongs to the husband and one-half to the wife, during life, and in death. In the rest of the United States the law goes back to the common law of England, where the husband owns everything during life, and dies possessed of it all. The only two exceptions in the eight community property states (as to the origin of the law) are Idaho and Washington, which are community property states, not because of their original conquest by Spain, but because the legislatures of these states adopted the community property system by statute.

The community property system is very effective in protecting the rights of the wife in property that was acquired by the industry of both after the marriage. It also causes complications. The problems arise because of the very protection community ownership affords, not only the wife, but each spouse. The control, management, and disposition of the community property now becomes a problem, as does the matter of who may enter into contracts in regard to it. Also who, upon the death of either spouse, inherits the community property of the deceased if the deceased consort failed to exercise his or her right of testamentary disposition over his or her one-half of the community, and as a consequence died intestate.

Let's examine each of these problems, giving first the broad concept of the community property law, and then looking at to what extent, if any, each of the eight community property states has changed it by state statute.

Management, control, and disposition of community property during life

Property must be continuously managed if the maximum benefits are to be derived from it, and once in a while it should be sold.

The general concept in this regard is that each spouse separately may acquire, manage, control, or dispose of *community personal property*. However, a spouse cannot *give away* personal property, or sell or encumber furniture, furnishings, or wearing apparel of the other spouse, or that of minor children, without the written consent of the other spouse.

Either consort also has the management and control of *community real property;* but when selling or mortgaging it, the signatures of both spouses are required. This concept makes it easy to buy and sell securities, deal with bank and savings and loan accounts, and to manage real property. There are, however, adherence to and variations from it among the eight community property states as follows.

Arizona and *Washington* follow the above concept.

In California an exception is made for real estate. If either spouse holds the record title to real property that is actually community, he or she may execute a sole lease, contract, mortgage, or deed to a leasee, purchaser, or mortgagor in good faith, without knowledge of a marriage relationship, and it shall be presumed to be valid. The other spouse is given one year in which to take action to void such an instrument; after that it is binding. The practical effect of this law is to protect that person who enters into such a contract in good faith, not realizing that the person who holds record title is married.

In Idaho the husband has the management and control of the community personal and real property, but he cannot convey or mortgage real estate without his wife's signature.

In Louisiana the husband is head and master of the partnership or community during the marriage. He manages and controls it, and he may morgage it or sell it without his wife's consent. He may sell, lease, or mortgage real property even though title is in both names. If the wife wants to protect herself from this situation, she must record a declaration that her authority and consent to alienation of the property is required. Wives in Louisiana are hereby forewarned!

In Nevada the husband has control of the community property with absolute power of disposition, except that any real property can't be mortgaged or sold except by an instrument that is both executed and acknowledged by both husband and wife.

In New Mexico it is presumed that the husband has control and management of commercial community personal property, the proceeds of which support the family in whole or in part, unless the wife has assumed her rights of management by filing a written statement with the clerk of the county in which she resides.

Mr. and Mrs. Timothy Randall resided in New Mexico, and by the laws of that state all of their property was community, for neither one of them owned any property when they were married, nor had either one individually been given or inherited anything after their marriage.

Most of their property was in a sizable portfolio of stocks, all of it listed in Mr. Randall's name alone. Late in life Mrs. Randall became unhappy with the way her husband was buying and selling their securities, losing quite a bit of money in the process. To stop this trading without her consent, she filed a written statement with the county recorder. Thereafter, Mr. Randall had to obtain his wife's signature before he could buy or sell.

Mrs. Randall could have avoided making such a declaration if she had insisted in the first place that all of the securities be purchased in the names of both of them, for New Mexico law further states that both spouses must sign the instrument in any transaction where both their names appear, and they are joined by the word "and."

In Texas any property that stands in the spouse's name alone is presumed to be under his or her sole management and control. Joint conveyance, however, is required of a homestead, whether it is the community property, or the separate property, of either spouse.

Contracts

Community property is liable for contracts made by either spouse entered into after the marriage.

There are no variations to this rule in the eight community property states, except to a degree in Arizona and Texas.

In Arizona if a debt can't be satisfied from the community property, then it can be collected from the separate property, if any, of the spouse who contracted the debt.

In Texas a husband and wife, *without prejudice to preexisting creditors*, may by written instrument, as if the wife were single, partition between themselves all or any part of their existing community property. If they do so partition, such property becomes the separate property of the spouses.

If the Randalls had lived in Texas, and not New Mexico, Mrs. Randall could have solved the problem of her husband's stock market losses by this method.

Upon the death of either husband or wife

Under the general community property system, upon the death of either husband or wife, one-half of the community property belongs to the surviving spouse, and the other one-half is subject to the testamentary disposition of the decedent. In the absence of such a disposition it goes to the surviving spouse.

Warning! This is true only in four of the eight community property states—California, Nevada, New Mexico, and Washington. In the other four states, namely Arizona, Idaho, Louisiana, and Texas, when a spouse dies without a will his or her one-half of the community property does *not* automatically go to the surviving consort.

In Arizona, when a spouse dies intestate, one-half of the community property and one-half of the separate property goes to the deceased's descendants. Only if there are none does it go to the surviving spouse.

In Idaho the children inherit the community property of the deceased spouse who dies intestate. They also inherit two-thirds of the separate property (if any), and if there is only one child he or she inherits one-half. If there is no issue from the marriage, but a parent of the deceased spouse survives, the surviving consort inherits all of the community property, plus the first $50,000 of separate property, plus one-half of the balance. The parent receives the remainder.

In Louisiana the deceased's one-half of the community goes to his or her descendants. Only when there are no children, and no parents living, does the survivor inherit all of the community.

In Texas the deceased's share of the community, when he or she dies intestate, goes to the children, or to their descendants by right of representation. This means that grandchildren could inherit the community of the deceased consort if the immediate issue of the marriage are all dead. If there are children left alive, and separate property is involved, one-third of the real property goes to the widow for life, and one-third of the personal property is inherited by her absolutely. The balance of the separate property goes to the children.

In these four states, therefore, any assumption by either spouse that a will isn't necessary, *because they live in a community property state,* can be disastrous to the surviving spouse.

Mr. and Mrs. Ronald Hall were both born and raised in California and from their parents had become acquainted with the community property laws of that state.

Shortly after their marriage they moved to Idaho, also a community property state, where they had one child born to them. They assumed that the community property system was the same in both states; therefore they did not bother to make a will, even though Mr. Hall inherited a goodly amount of separate property upon the death of his mother, and also had made a lot of money early in life after moving to Idaho.

When Mr. Hall unexpectedly died, his widow was shocked to discover that the intestate law in Idaho gave all of his community property, and one-half of his separate property, to their only child. This could have been completely avoided if Mr. Hall had made a will leaving everything of which he died possessed, whether real or personal, community or separate, to his beloved wife.

Conclusion

It should be realized that non-probate assets, while avoiding court administration, are quite often assets without a plan. The testator should review all property titles by actual inspection of the documents, and view them not as individual assets, but as a part of an economic whole so that they will accomplish his or her overall objectives. In larger estates, it may well be that part of the property can be held as non-probate assets (the home and a bank account, for instance) but the majority of the estate left deliberately to testamentary disposition, particularly where death taxes are a major consideration.

At no time should title to property be left to memory or chance. And it should be realized that even though ownership of an estate is entirely in non-probate assets, or the property owners live in one of the eight community property states, it is still advisable to have a will. With a will, even though it never becomes necessary to prove it in probate court, there can be no question about the decedent's intentions in regard to his or her estate. When a testator has non-probate assets he or she should:

1. Recognize them as such.
2. Determine the tax consequences.
3. Provide for the payment of the death taxes on these assets.
4. Coordinate their disposition with the assets that will pass under his or her will.

5

Stop Paying Those Life Insurance Premiums When Retired

Retired people should not pay premiums on individual permanent life insurance policies. These premiums cut into retirement income, and the cash surrender value can be put to better use.

We realize that this is a drastic suggestion; therefore it must be substantiated.

It should be understood also that this suggestion does not apply to term insurance, nor to group term policies issued to members by such retirement organizations as the American Association of Retired Persons. It pertains only to those individual permanent policies taken out years ago by the insured, which have high cash surrender values. Unless this money is put to use by the policyholder, he or she will never benefit from it.

What should be done with this cash value? There are three choices.

1. The insured can take the cash.
2. The insured can use the cash surrender value to buy a reduced paid-up policy.
3. The insured can use the cash surrender value to buy an extended term policy for the full face value of the contract.

By any one of these methods, not only does the policyholder make use of the cash surrender value, but what is equally important, he or she stops paying premiums.

A retired policyholder, who is still making payments on these policies, is doing so because he or she justifiably doesn't understand permanent life insurance. Very few people do, retired or not. Therefore it's necessary to review some of the fundamental concepts behind whole life insurance, and how the general public has been brainwashed by the insurance industry into paying premiums for this type of insurance until they are dead. Basically there are only two types of life insurance—whole life or term.

Term insurance provides protection during the term of years specified in the policy, has no cash surrender value, and then ceases to exist. It is cheaper than whole life because the insured is paying for straight protection only; there is no cash value.[1]

Whole life insurance on the other hand lasts for the whole of life, and builds up a sizable cash surrender value for the insured. It has been the most widely sold policy in the United States over the last one hundred years.

Why?

The reasons are fairly obvious. When a man is young the chances of his dying are slim, therefore an appeal to take out life insurance based solely upon the likelihood of his premature death falls rather flat. The only ones who will benefit from the insurance will be his family, and then only if he dies prematurely. But if the insured can be offered a so-called savings program in conjunction with his life insurance, which gives the policyholder a sizable cash surrender value if he should live, then the proposition becomes much more attractive.

It was from this concept that the level premium theory for whole life insurance was developed. In the early years of the contract the insured pays more for his policy than the actual

---

1. Except in some term policies, and then only for a very small amount.

cost of pure insurance protection. Because of this deliberate overpayment, a cash surrender value can be generated. Also by this level premium concept the cost of the insurance remains constant during the term of the contract, no matter how long the policyholder may live.

However, the payment of this level premium does *not* mean that whenever the insured dies that his beneficiary will receive *both* the face value of the contract, and the cash surrender value. On the contrary, the beneficiary never receives as a death benefit any more than the face amount of the policy. This is because whole life insurance (also called straight life or ordinary life) is so designed that the amount of the insurance protection *and* the cash surrender value of the policy are at all times exactly equal to the death benefit.

Charts 1 and 2 illustrate this concept.

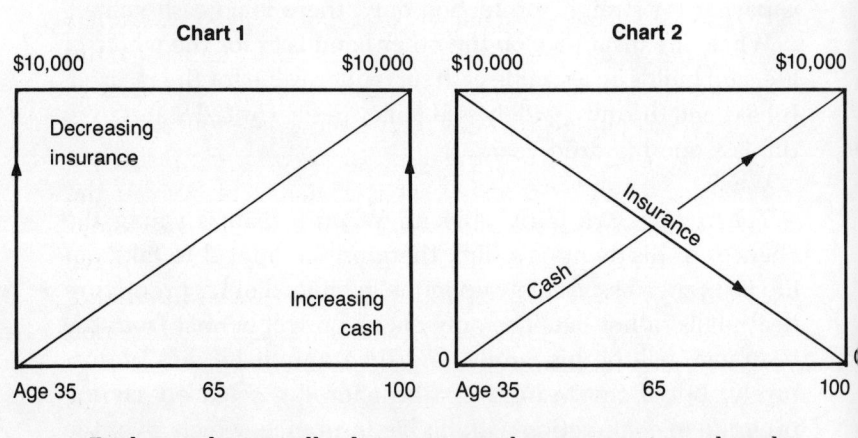

Chart 1

$10,000 $10,000

Decreasing insurance

Increasing cash

Age 35   65   100

Chart 2

$10,000 $10,000

Insurance

Cash

0

Age 35   65   100

Both graphs actually demonstrate the same point—that the policy is all insurance and no cash value if the insured should die immediately after taking out the policy at the average initial insurance age of 35. It is one-half cash surrender value and one-half protection at age 65. And at age 100, it is all cash and no protection; therefore if the policyholder should live to this advanced age, the insurance company will pay the insured himself the face amount, for a very simple reason. The number of people per million who are left alive at that age are so few in number that the insurance company mathematically ignores them.

The fact that the cash surrender value of permanent insurance is never paid to anyone upon the insured's death does not cheat the policyholder or his beneficiary, as many critics of whole life insurance contend. The amount of the level premium is computed on the basis that the combination of the cash surrender value *and* the amount of life insurance protection remaining in the contract shall be at all times exactly equal to the face amount. If this were not so, the level premium would have to be considerably higher in order to pay the beneficiary both.

Nevertheless, the cash surrender value build-up during the period that a permanent policy is kept in force *is not a savings program that belongs to the insured.* This money belongs to the insurance company, and must be retained by them in order to pay the death benefit to all of their policyholders. It is a *cash surrender value* only, and it means exactly what the insurance company calls it. It's money that is available in cash to the insured *only if he surrenders his policy.* To call it a savings program is duping the public because the insured can't have *her* or *his* so-called money unless the policy is surrendered, thereby canceling the insurance (which was the major reason the policy was taken out in the first place).

So now we return to our original suggestion at the start of this chapter—that a retired person should stop paying premiums on his permanent life insurance policies which he took out years ago, and which now have high cash surrender values.

In these policies, the insurance companies list the benefits available to the policyholder from the cash value in a table which they call Non-Forfeiture Values. This is a ridiculous title; it should be renamed. It should be called: What You, the Policyholder, Can Do with the Cash. Then every insured would examine the table very carefully and find out exactly what he or she could do with this "savings program."

As we have said, the policyholder has three options.

1. Surrender the contract and take the cash.
2. Convert to a paid-up policy.
3. Take out an extended term contract for the face amount.

None of these options, however, are explained in the policy in a manner that the insured can comprehend. Most policyholders don't understand the expressions "reduced paid-up" and "extended term," and when they should, or should not, exercise the privilege granted.

Option 1: surrendering the contract and taking the cash

Option 1, nevertheless, is fairly obvious. The amount of the cash surrender value per thousand that is available to the insured at his attained age is clearly stated in the table. On most policies (that were taken out at the average insured age of 35), this amount is approximately 50 percent of the face value of the policy at age 65. This means that if the contract calls for a payment of $10,000 in the event of the insured's death, $5,000 is obtainable.

However, if the insured elects to take the cash, the policy has now been *surrendered*. The insurance has been canceled; therefore, if the insured should die, his beneficiary would have only $5,000, not the face amount of the policy of $10,000. The beneficiary has been done out of $5,000 in this event, something that in many cases is not advisable. It must be emphasized that this so-called savings program is exactly what it is called— a cash surrender value, not cash.

It's also why retired people continue to pay premiums on their permanent life insurance until they die. But in doing so, they are forgetting an important precept. We do not live to save —we save to live.

Mr. and Mrs. Casey Chrisman were in their middle seventies and retired. They had no children and had been living comfortably until inflation caught up with them. Now they definitely could use more than their $500 per month retirement income.

One day a life underwriter called on them at their home. They had not seen an insurance salesman of the company from which Mr. Chrisman had bought his whole life policies for over twenty years. The agent was young, enthusiastic, and competent.

After they had become acquainted and were comfortably seated around the coffee table in the Chrismans' living room, the agent suggested that he review with them their three small whole life policies.

"Why?" asked Mr. Chrisman.

"Well," replied the life underwriter, with a smile, "you haven't seen a representative of the company for many years. I'd like to give you some service. Maybe I could make a suggestion or two."

"Why not, dear?" asked Mrs. Chrisman. "He seems like an honest young man."

"O.K.," her husband replied, getting out of his chair. "They're right here in the desk, although I don't intend to do anything about them. I'm still paying the premiums and I have to keep on paying them until I'm dead."

After carefully examining the policies, the agent went over the non-forfeiture value tables in the three contracts, ignoring the other two options, concentrating solely on the cash surrender values that were available at Mr. Chrisman's age of 75.

After writing the figures down on a pad of paper, the agent showed them to Mr. and Mrs. Chrisman and said:

"As you can see, the face value of the three policies is $20,000, while the total cash surrender value is $17,000. Now I'm going to suggest something that may surprise you. Why don't you surrender these policies and take the money?"

"Why should we?" asked Mr. Chrisman, who the agent by this time had discovered was very direct in his reactions.

"Let me answer that by asking you a question. If you surrendered the three policies and put the money in the bank, and then you suddenly died, how much money would you leave your wife?"

Mr. Chrisman was slightly puzzled. "Why $17,000, wouldn't I?"

"That's right," replied the agent. "And if you didn't surrender them, and died, how much would the insurance company pay your widow?"

Mrs. Chrisman was quicker than her husband. "Why," she exclaimed, "just $20,000. I would be only $3,000 better off."

"Exactly," replied the agent. "Which is the point I'm trying to make. You have only $3,000 of insurance protection left in all three contracts; the balance of the $20,000 is the cash surrender value. And for this $3,000 of insurance protection you are paying a total premium on all three policies of $460 per year."

"And besides that," exclaimed Mrs. Chrisman, "we don't have an income from the $17,000!"

"Exactly," replied the salesman. "So let's take a look at the loss of income as well." He then proceeded to show them the following computation.

Life insurance in force	$20,000
Cash surrender value	17,000
Insurance protection remaining in the three contracts	$3,000
Loss to Mrs. Chrisman as a widow if the policies were surrendered	$3,000
Increased income if the policies were surrendered:	
Annual saved premiums	$ 460
Income from $17,000 @ 6 percent	1,020
Total	$1,480

"Young man," exclaimed Mr. Chrisman, "that's a lot of extra income. How much is that a month?"

"Just a minute," replied the agent, figuring. "That would be an extra $123.33 per month."

"Mother," said Mr. Chrisman, "we're going to take that money. And young fellow, we want to thank you for coming around!"

So they took the cash surrender value, and started enjoying the extra income that this decision gave them.

Then something happened which neither the Chrismans nor the life underwriter thought would take place, although the agent had carefully pointed out this possibility to them. Despite his apparent good health, Mr. Chrisman died of a heart attack in just six months.

But Mrs. Chrisman didn't complain. She had fully understood their decision. They wanted to enjoy together the income from the $17,000 *while they were both alive* (and the money from the saved premiums), not for her to enjoy the income from the $20,000 face value, all by herself.

Another way to use the cash option, of course, is to spend the money. If the capital is going to be spent, the couple could take a trip to Europe together now, even though the cash surrender value is only 50 percent of the face value of the policy, rather than have the widow take *several* trips later alone, because she would have twice the money to spend and the expenses for only one.

A retired couple should remember an old maxim about life insurance. The death benefit of a life insurance policy is never paid to a man's wife. It's paid only to his widow.

Option 2: taking out reduced paid-up insurance

The second way to use the cash is not to surrender the policy at all. Instead, the money is used to purchase a reduced paid-up contract. A $10,000 whole life policy, with a $5,000 cash value, would provide approximately $7,500 of paid-up insurance. It's called a *reduced* paid-up option because obviously the cash surrender value of $5,000, used as a single premium payment, will not buy a policy for the full face amount of the original contract. Once again, however, and this is very important, the insured stops making premium payments for the rest of his life. When should this option be taken?

Only if the insured's health is good because, if he should die, his beneficiary would lose the difference between the original amount of the insurance and the value of the paid-up contract. But with good health, he has the probability of enjoying the saved premium money for many years; therefore, by a combination of these saved premiums and the reduced benefit, he and his beneficiary would not lose at all. And if he outlived his life expectancy, they would even be financially ahead.

When taking the paid-up option, the new policy is purchased at what the insurance industry calls net premium rates, which means without having to pay an agent's commission and, because no physical examination is required, without a doctor's fee. At these net premium rates, more insurance can be put in force with the cash surrender value than would otherwise be possible.

A reduced paid-up contract is chosen because a man and his wife want to stop paying premiums, thereby increasing their income for *both* of them to enjoy. Because his health is good, they are willing to risk a possible loss to his widow.

Mr. and Mrs. Sam Bartlett were retired and were considering how they could increase their income. When reviewing their assets, the question arose about the advisability of continuing to pay the premium on his $40,000 whole life policy, which Mr. Bartlett had taken out when he was thirty years of age. The premium was high, about $800 a year, and had become increasingly a burden as the years went by. One day they stopped into the regional office of the insurance company to see what could be done.

A female clerk, who had been with the company for many years, took them back to a small office where they could discuss their problem privately.

"Now what can I do for you?" she asked, when they were seated.

"Well," replied Mr. Bartlett, "I have this policy—here it is, I brought it with me—and we want to know what we can do, if anything, besides continuing to pay the premium. It's becoming a problem, but I don't want to cancel the insurance either. Quite frankly, if something happens to me Mrs. Bartlett will need the money."

The clerk asked to see the policy, and turning to the table of non-forfeiture values, computed the amount of the cash surrender value. She then asked Mr. Bartlett what he thought was an irrelevant question.

"You look well, sir. How is your health?"

"Why," he said, turning to his wife, "I would say excellent, wouldn't you, dear?"

She nodded her head. "Yes," she said, smiling. "There's nothing wrong with you, thank goodness." And turning to the clerk, she said: "He'll probably outlive me by at least ten years."

"Well, let's hope you'll both live to be a hundred," replied the clerk. "Since your health is good, Mr. Bartlett, let's take a look at the reduced paid-up option in the non-forfeiture table in your policy, and see what can be done with the cash surrender value."

She then explained to them that at Mr. Bartlett's attained age of 69 the cash available would buy a reduced paid-up policy for $32,000.

"This way," she explained, "you won't have to make any further premium payments. You can increase your income by the amount of the saved premium, or $800 a year. And whenever you die, Mrs. Bartlett will still receive $32,000. That's less than $40,000, it's true," she pointed out, with a slight smile, "but the new policy will be paid-up for life."

"Do I have to take a physical?" asked Mr. Bartlett.

"No," replied the clerk. "All you have to do is sign a change of policy form, and we'll convert the contract."

So that's what they did. Mr. Bartlett didn't meet his wife's expectations as far as his health was concerned because he didn't outlive her, but he did survive to the ripe old age of 86. In the meantime, for a long period of seventeen years they enjoyed the extra $800 a year income that the saved premium gave them. And when the reduced amount of $32,000 was finally paid to Mrs. Bartlett, the difference of $8,000 from the amount of the original contract was no longer of any importance.

Option 2 must be carefully understood. There is a loss in the amount of insurance remaining in force; therefore this nonforfeiture value should never be used if the beneficiary would desperately need the original face amount. But where the insured has reasonable expectancy of surviving for many years, it's a way for those retired people who have permanent life insurance with high cash surrender values to increase their income.

Option 3: using the cash surrender value to buy an extended term policy

This is probably the least understood of the three non-forfeiture options.

This alternative should be chosen *only* when the insured's health is poor, and he and his doctor both agree that the chances of his surviving another ten years are practically nil. When this choice is made, the existing permanent policy is exchanged for a *term contract for the same face value as the original policy,* again at net premium rates.

Calling this option *extended term* is confusing. It's true that it is a term policy, with the insurance terminating completely at the end of the number of years stated. It's called extended term, because the original amount of the insurance is extended, and put in force for a period of years, *without any further premium payment.* Whenever the insured dies while the policy is in force, the beneficiary receives exactly the same death benefit as in the original policy.

Mr. and Mrs. William Kelso were making some important

decisions, for he was about to retire. It was a question of how they were going to make ends meet on a much reduced income. As a man at work, Mr. Kelso was about to become unproductive; therefore property at work had to take his place to provide the necessary income.

They had two problems, actually, because his health was bad due to a serious heart condition. His doctor had warned both of them that they had better plan their finances around the fact that Mr. Kelso would not live too long. This meant maximum protection for Mrs. Kelso, whose health was excellent.

Their assets were meager, except for one thing, a $100,000 whole life policy on Mr. Kelso's life on which, during good times and bad, he had been sure to meet the premium payment. He was glad now that he had, considering the state of his health and his finances. But in talking it over with his wife, he didn't see how they could continue to pay an insurance premium of over $2,000 a year now that he was going to retire.

"Frankly, it bothers me," he said to his wife. "You need the insurance protection; besides it won't be too long before it's paid."

"Nonsense," she replied. "You're going to live for years, and besides, I'll manage somehow."

"No, that's not right," Mr. Kelso replied. "I've paid through the nose on that policy for too many years. There must be something that can be done."

"Well, let's call John Dahl then, dear. He sold you the policy, and it seems to me he did say something about the cash value years ago."

So they went to see their agent.

"Sure," he said. "There's no problem. I told you if there ever came a time when you couldn't pay the premium, to just let me know."

"What do you mean there's no problem," objected a worried Mr. Kelso. "If I don't pay, the insurance is canceled. You've told me that often enough over the years."

"That's true," smiled the agent, "because I didn't want you to drop the policy. Now things are different."

"Why different?"

"Because you've built up a high cash value, that's why. Fifty thousand dollars to be exact, which isn't hay. That alone would be a nice sum for Mrs. Kelso. But fortunately there's an option in the contract that will allow you to stop paying that big premium, and the company will still pay your wife the $100,000."

"You must be kidding."

"No, the option is buried in the table of non-forfeiture values. It's called extended term insurance. This means that we can use the cash surrender value to keep the full face value of the policy in force, in your case, for 13 years and 14 days without any further premium payment."

"And if I should die after that?" asked Mr. Kelso.

"Your wife wouldn't get a dime," said the agent cheerfully. "It's a term contract. If you outlive the term, the insurance would be caput. But we've talked several times about your health, Mr. Kelso. It's not good, is it?"

"No," said Mr. Keslo, "it's not. As a matter of fact it's lousy."

"Do you think you'll live thirteen years?"

"Not a chance."

"Then what's the problem? Let's convert to extended term."

So they did. And what was the result? Mr. Kelso lived five more years. But the full $100,000 was paid to his widow. In the meantime they had kept a very expensive policy in force without having to pay a cent in further premium payments. It would have been impossible for Mr. Kelso to have kept the policy without the extended term option.

There is an added benefit that is important when either option 2 or 3 is chosen. The cash surrender value hasn't been used up, or spent, by the insured. It's not gone forever, as some policyholders might assume. The insurance commissioners of the various states have concluded that immediate and complete dissipation of the cash value under these options would not be in the public interest. If a retired person should subsequently change his or her mind, and want the cash surrender value instead of the converted policy, it is therefore available. Of course, if the policy has been in force for a time, the insured has benefited from this, and as a consequence the premium that was necessary to keep the new policy in force for the length of time involved would be deducted from the original cash surrender value. Nevertheless, the amount left in the contract will be paid to the insured if he requests it. This means that the decision to take either option 2 or 3 is not an irrevocable one. The policyholder can change his mind later and take the remaining cash surrender value instead.

In addition to whole life, there are three variations to an ordinary life policy that must be understood. These are permanent policies also, each of them generating a higher cash surrender value per thousand than the straight whole life contract. Because of this, any decision on the part of the insured to surrender them is even more important.

The endowment contract

This policy is the answer to a prospective insured's desire to have his cake and eat it, too. In the endowment contract the face amount of the policy will be paid to the beneficiary as a death benefit if the insured should die, just as in a whole life policy, but if the insured should live to the end of the endowment period the policyholder himself will receive the face amount. In other words, at maturity (usually at age 65) an endowment contract for $10,000 (or for any other sum) will endow or pay the insured himself the amount of the insurance. The premium of course is considerably higher than for an ordinary life policy because the cash surrender value must equal the face amount of the contract *at age 65*, and not at age 100 as with whole life.

When the contract matures the insured has a decision to

make, for he may either accept the face amount of the policy in a lump sum, or take a monthly annuity for life under the various settlement options provided in the policy. If a monthly payment is decided upon, the insured has purchased a lump sum retirement annuity. The reader is therefore referred to Chapter 8 on annuities. The policyholder must understand, as with all annuity contracts, if he elects to buy a lifetime income with the endowment proceeds, he has irrevocably spent the cash. Thereafter he must be content with his decision, for he has exchanged this amount of his principal for a monthly payment which is guaranteed for life.

The twenty-pay life policy

This contract calls for the payment of the premium for just twenty years, at which time it becomes paid-up for life.

Many policyholders don't like the idea of paying premiums for the whole of life, nor do they want to pay them when retired —twenty years to their mind is enough. To meet the demands of these people, the life insurance industry devised the limited payment contract.

Once again the policy costs more than whole life. The premium is greater because the cash surrender value has to be sufficient at the end of twenty years so the interest earned on the money will be enough to pay the premium. Some people think of their policy as free insurance at this point. It's true that they are no longer paying premiums at the end of the payment period, but because of this, to call a policy "free insurance" is hardly the truth of the matter. The cost of the contract to the insured is the loss of interest on the high cash surrender value.

As with the endowment contract, the policyholder should make a decision at the end of his premium-paying period. Should he keep the policy and have "free insurance" for the balance of his life, or should he take the high cash surrender value and put it to work to increase his income? The latter course should be decided upon only if his health is good, and if he fully realizes that he is canceling out part of the insurance death benefit that would otherwise be paid to his beneficiary. The cash surrender value of a limited pay contract is always for a lesser sum than the face amount of the policy.

The retirement income policy

Of the three permanent contracts that are a variation of the whole life concept, this one is probably the least understood.

In this concept, the cash surrender value is greater at age 65 than the face amount of the policy, quite a bit greater as a matter of fact. A $10,000 retirement income policy taken out at age 35 will have a cash surrender value in excess of $16,000 at age 65. Why?

This is because the insured when he takes out the contract wants to have a policy that will pay him $100 per month for life. But no other permanent insurance can do this, not even the $10,000 endowment contract. There must be $16,000 available to pay this much monthly income. The retirement income policy therefore carries the highest premium of all the permanent type contracts.

As with the endowment contract, the insured at maturity has a decision to make because the conversion to a $100 per month life annuity is not the only option. The policyholder can take the cash instead.

Conclusion

A careful decision should be made by retired persons on their individually purchased permanent life insurance policies.

To repeat, on a whole life policy they have three choices.

1. To take the cash
2. To convert to a paid-up policy
3. To convert to an extended term contract

The correct decision in the vast majority of cases seems to be clear. One of the three options under the Table for Nonforfeiture Values should be taken rather than let the cash surrender value go "down the drain" as far as the insured himself is concerned.

With a couple, it is usually better for them to enjoy the income together or to spend the cash, rather than for the widow to enjoy more money alone.

Care must be exercised if an option is chosen, and when a widow will need every dollar of insurance protection that the policy provides, the contract should be kept in force and the premium paid for the entire life of the insured.

6

Why Everyone Should Have a Will

A will is often the most important document a person ever signs. It disposes of a lifetime accumulation of property, and determines who inherits it and in what amounts. Even if a person has a small estate, he or she should dispose of it properly through a will drawn by a competent attorney. The alternative, as we have mentioned before, is to die intestate (without a will), in which event distribution will be according to state law.

The effect of dying intestate can be disastrous, particularly for a widow, when it is the couple's intention that the survivor should inherit everything. State law varies widely in determining who gets the assets when a husband or a wife dies without a will. For exact information, the property owner has no alternative but to ascertain the law of the state in which he or she resides. As we have seen in Chapter 4, Mildred Long died intestate in the state of Ohio, and her estate was divided among sixteen different cousins, some of whom she had never seen.

In general, the various states provide for distribution according to the following set of circumstances.

1. When the spouse is the sole survivor
The estate goes to her or him.

2. *When the spouse and children survive*

The spouse receives one-third and the children two-thirds. This can result in real hardship for the widow, particularly in small estates where she desperately needs the entire property. It is worse when the children are minors, for in many states a guardian must be appointed and a bond posted. In some states the children's portion must be kept intact for them, not to be expended even for their support. This results in the widow's portion being dissipated, with the result that she has nothing when the children are grown.

3. *When a widow (or a widower) survives, with no living children, but the deceased leaves other relatives*

If the estate totals less than $25,000, the spouse takes all outright. If it is more than $25,000, the surviving spouse takes $25,000, and one-half of everything over that. The relatives get the remainder.

Example. An estate is worth $125,000, and the spouse dies intestate. The widow or widower receives $75,000 and the relatives get $50,000. In many states this is true no matter how distant the relatives may be.

4. *When no spouse, children, or other relatives survive*

All of the property now escheats (reverts) to the state where the deceased was domiciled. It would be far better for the property owner to leave the estate to his or her favorite charity.

Mr. Robinson was a widower with no children. He and his wife never bothered with a will because they lived in a community property state where the surviving spouse automatically inherited everything by state law. When his wife died, he still didn't make a will, feeling no compelling necessity to do so since he had no children, and as far as he knew no living relatives. When he died intestate, his sizable estate escheated to the state.

It was enough to make Mr. Robinson turn over in his grave. He lived in what he considered was a notorious welfare state, so bad in fact that during life he had become rabid on the subject of politicians who squandered the public's taxes on welfare projects, serene in their conviction that they could legislate poverty out of existence.

"The state will go broke," he warned ominously on many an occasion.

Even when New York City was threatened with default on its obligations, to the extent that it poised a threat to the solvency of New York State itself, he still didn't make a will.

Many people rightfully would fault Mr. Robinson for his procrastination, for he had incentive enough considering the way he felt.

Mr. Robinson's case also demonstrates the fallacious thinking of couples who feel they don't need a will because they have everything in joint tenancy with right of survivorship.

It's true that the will of the first spouse to die will not be used, for regardless of the existence of a will by the deceased spouse, the survivor automatically inherits everything that is held in joint tenancy. But what happens when the second spouse dies? This is when a will becomes of the utmost importance.

If Mr. and Mrs. Robinson had drawn wills before her death, each leaving his or her property to the survivor, and then to charity, their estate would not have escheated to the state because of Mr. Robinson's procrastination.

Anyone who is legally of age, of sound mind and body, and not acting under duress, may dispose of his or her property largely as he or she sees fit, except for taxes. Despite this, a man can't completely disinherit his wife. By law he may leave her everything, but on the other hand he can't leave her nothing. The law of most states protects her from being deprived of her just share. If a husband disinherits his wife, she can ignore the will and take her portion according to state law. This should be of considerable comfort to many wives who live in the forty-two non-community property states, who may be concerned as to the ultimate disposition of their combined estate, especially when everything is held in the name of the husband alone.

In general, a man may will everything away from his relatives (except his wife), including his children. But if he excludes his children, he must name them and purposely leave them one dollar.

It doesn't seem right somehow that, no matter how harshly he may treat his relatives, the testator's wishes in a properly drawn document will be upheld by the courts.

Mr. and Mrs. Gerald Bascom had accumulated an estate of approximately $200,000. They had no children and held everything in joint tenancy. They had an understanding that the survivor would not leave their combined estate solely to his or her side of the family, but in all fairness would divide the property in the survivor's will so that each side of the family would receive one-half of their estate, thereby enjoying the fruits of their labor and their frugality.

Since Mr. Bascom's health was poor, his wife was not too much concerned about this eventual distribution. She knew that she would do the right thing when the time came. But it didn't happen that way. Mrs. Bascom died suddenly in the matter of three days as the result of an accident, while Mr. Bascom lived for another ten years. When he died, his will left everything to his sister, who really didn't need it, and whom Mrs. Bascom had so thoroughly disliked that she had for years consistently refused her admittance to their home.

Distribution of their combined estate was not what Mrs. Bascom wanted, and her husband knew it. She wanted her one-half to go to her godchild, a favorite niece. It didn't because her husband had full ownership of the estate giving him the right to dispose of it as he saw fit.

What Mrs. Bascom could easily have arranged was to leave her one-half of the estate in trust for her niece, with all of the income to go to her husband. This way he wouldn't have been harmed financially in any way, but when he died he couldn't by his will disinherit her godchild. Her niece would have inherited Mrs. Bascom's one-half upon her husband's subsequent death. There was nothing that anyone could do about Mr. Bascom's will. The niece knew it was wrong, and so did the sister for that matter, for she was fully aware of how Mrs. Bascom felt. But that didn't make any difference. The will was legal, and the court was bound to uphold it. The niece could do nothing but stand by in frustration and see $100,000 that she knew her aunt wanted her to inherit go to a sister-in-law whom Mrs. Bascom despised.

With this in mind, there should be a free and open discussion between the two generations in a family, and between parents and their children, in regard to the ultimate disposition of property. Parents generally love their children and usually feel they should treat them equally in their wills—share and share alike is the expression often used. But in many instances this is not the way an estate should be divided.

If one child has done well in his business or profession, and the other has not, it would be a good idea to discuss this fact, particularly with the financially successful one. It could be suggested that perhaps the entire estate be left to the unfortunate one, not outright, but in trust with a corporate trustee empowered to hand over the income and principal to the beneficiary at the trustee's discretion. In such a frank discussion, the well-to-do child might readily agree that he didn't need any of his parents' estate, and that certainly he wouldn't feel that he had been cheated, or loved less, because of the lopsidedness of the will.

Without such a family understanding, outright distribution of such an estate would be made share and share alike to the two children. This simply would compound the death tax problem of the wealthy child, and could result in the dissipation of the indigent child's one-half because of bad management upon his part, since he had already demonstrated lack of business acumen.

There are standard phrases that lawyers use in wills which, if understood, will make an existing will more comprehensible and allow the testator to sign a new will with greater peace of mind.

There are eight of these standard phrases.

I hereby revoke all wills and codicils previously made by me.

This ensures that only the testator's latest will can be proved in probate court. No matter how many documents he may have drawn previously during his lifetime, none of them are in effect. They have been revoked by this statement in his latest will.

Sometimes a testator doesn't like his existing will, and so he destroys it with every intention of drawing a new one. But if he subsequently dies before signing a new will, he now dies intestate. This shouldn't be allowed to happen. An existing will should not be discarded until a new one is actually signed. It is better to die with a will that the property owner doesn't particularly like than with none, for it's probably better than the distribution provided by state law.

I hereby give, devise, and bequeath all of my property, whether real, personal, or mixed, and wherever situated.

This is a relatively simple statement, but it's certainly comprehensive!

You may *give* your property to someone, that is fairly obvious. But you may *devise* only real property, and you may *bequeath* only personal property; therefore you have now used the three ways available to you to dispose of your assets.

The expression *real, personal, or mixed* certainly takes care of all the property of which you die possessed, and in addition you state *wherever situated*.

By this statement in your will there isn't any question that you are disposing of your entire estate.

I direct first that my executor shall pay all inheritance, estate, or other death taxes, all expenses of administration of my estate, and all legal claims against my estate.

This means that distribution of the *residue* of your estate takes place only after all taxes, claims, and administration expenses are paid. This way all of the heirs have been subjected to their share of the death taxes and expenses.

But supposing you don't want this to happen. Instead you want specific dollar bequests to friends or relatives to be distributed to them first, so you know that they will receive these small sums undiluted by expenses and taxes. In this event you should have your lawyer state that these taxes and expenses should be paid by your executor from the *residue* of your estate, which means *after* payment of the various bequests.

The executor of my will shall be John Jones, and I request that he be permitted to serve without bond and that, without application to or order of the court, he have full power and authority to sell, transfer, grant, convey, exchange, lease, mortgage, pledge, or otherwise encumber or dispose of any and all of the real and personal property of my estate.

"Well," you might say, "that certainly gives my personal representative the right to do with my property as he pleases!"

And indeed it does.

But far more harm is done by granting only limited powers to your executor than in granting the broad powers quoted above. It's better to grant a power that isn't needed than to withhold from him or her the right to act, when this is the very power he or she might badly need to exercise.

This statement also gives your executor the right to act without appealing to the probate judge every time he wants to make a move in regard to the estate. He may do so *without application to or order of the court.* You have also given him the authority to act without bond. If you don't trust your personal representative to act honestly, you shouldn't have named him in the first place. If you demand that a bond be posted, some states require the signature of the bonding firm's representative on every check drawn by the executor. This is time consuming, expensive, and a terrible nuisance to your personal representative.

> *I further authorize my executor in his discretion to retain in*
> *my estate, and to distribute to the beneficiaries,*
> *divisees, and legatees hereunder, any property of any*
> *character of which I die the owner, or which comes*
> *into my estate during administration, without liability*
> *for any loss which my estate may sustain by reasons*
> *of such retention.*

In some states if retention is not authorized, the executor must sell all of the property in the estate at once, often at a great sacrifice, either because of a down market in securities or real estate, or because of adverse economic conditions.

And if you don't hold your personal representative harmless from such actions, he could under some jurisdictions be personally responsible for any and all losses that he may incur, even though no prudent man could have forseen them.

> *I give X number of dollars to John Jones if living at the time*
> *of my death. If deceased, this gift shall lapse.*

It's the second sentence that is important. You know how much you want to give John Jones, but what if he dies before you do, and you fail to state that your bequest to him lapses in that event. Did you intend for the gift to stand, and for it to go to his heirs per stirpes (as your lawyer is fond of saying), which means by right of representation, or not?

Example. You leave a bequest of $2,000 to John Jones, and he dies before you do, but you said nothing in your will about the gift lapsing in this event. John Jones has two sons. Did you intend that each of his sons should receive $1,000? It could be a nagging question.

I have the following children

and then you carefully name them.

You should not allow your attorney to be careless in this regard. He shouldn't be permitted to simply insert how many children you have, and that they shall share and share alike in your estate in the event of your demise. This is not good enough. Who are your children, exactly? In most cases it is obvious, but sometimes it isn't.

Walter Girard died, stating in his will that he had five children who were to share equally in his estate, but he did not name them. A woman, of whom none of the children had ever heard, claimed through her attorney that she was one of the five children named in the will because she was an illegitimate child, and that one of the legitimate children was not a legal heir. This child had been adopted as a baby when Walter Girard's first wife died. The baby was too young, he felt, for him to care for her properly. Twenty five years later (when the couple who had adopted his daughter died) he made himself known to her, and thereafter treated her as his own. This unknown woman's claim that she was entitled to inherit one-fifth of the estate was spurious, and a definite attempt upon the part of an absolute stranger to participate in a sizable estate. Her contention tied up the estate in probate court for five years; finally to get rid of her the executor compromised and paid her $10,000. How simple it would have been if Walter Girard had named his children, instead of just stating that he had five.

*If my wife should predecease me, then my estate shall be
distributed as follows.*

It's a simple statement, but exactly what does it mean?

It means that your wife has died, for you specifically state that
she has predeceased you, and if your will is being read, officially,
you are dead also.

This phrase means, if you inherited from your wife, that you
are disposing of the entire combined estate. A testator should
fully understand this.

Two apparently minor, but nonetheless important, items in
regard to the disposition of an estate seem to puzzle many
people.

First, how should they divide their assets?

The simplest method is to think of the total estate in terms
of 100 percent, and then divide it accordingly. This is particularly important when making bequests, with the remainder
(usually the bulk of the estate) being distributed to the other
heirs.

Example. As a widower you have an estate of $250,000.
It's a mistake for you to leave $12,500 to Uncle Charlie, and
$12,500 to your favorite charity, with the residue to be divided
equally among your four children. You might undergo financial
adversity before you die, and what was a minor 10 percent
share of your estate ($250,000/$25,000) is now a much larger
portion. This way you deprive your children, which wasn't your
intention.

If your estate should diminish from $250,000 to $75,000, and
you didn't change your will, you would now leave one-third of
your estate to Uncle Charlie and to charity, not just 10 percent.
This is the wrong way to do it. You should have left 10 percent
of your estate in the form of the two bequests. This way your
two legatees would receive $7,500 (not $25,000), which was the
share that you intended in the first place.

A better solution, even though you used the safeguard of dividing your estate into percentages, is to make a new will if your once sizable estate has shrunk to this extent, eliminating your bequests entirely because now you really can't afford them.

The second problem involves the disposition of tangible personal property.

This normally consists of furniture and furnishings in your home. Share and share alike among the children is again the method usually employed. But your chattels, as your lawyer calls them, shouldn't be divided this way, for too often the first child on the scene takes what he wants, and the other children get the remainder, causing in many instances a lifetime of bitterness.

As you go from room to room in your home and mentally inventory the contents, you will probably discover that there are only a few items that are valuable, either from a monetary or sentimental point of view. If you will put the name of the child who is to receive it on the under side of each of these items, or attach a simple list to your will, it will probably solve the problem. This method of distribution isn't legal; therefore your attorney will frown upon it, but legal or not, your children will usually abide by your wishes. The other method, which is legal, is to state in your will that an impartial executor shall have the right to determine the disposition of your personal property if there is a dispute among your heirs.

If personal property partly consists of business equipment, it's far better to bequeath it to those who can use it, such as your business partner, or another professional man, rather than leave it to your heirs. If it is farm equipment, and one of your sons operates the farm, then let him have it, for he is the one who can use it.

As we have mentioned before, ancillary probate proceedings of an estate should be avoided whenever possible. This occurs when there is property of the testator in another state than the one of domicile. This necessitates a second, or ancillary, probate in that other state. We also stated that the simplest solution involving real property is to place it in joint tenancy with right of survivorship. This is fine, but in your case it may not be the best solution. There are other ways to solve the problem if placing real estate in joint tenancy is not advisable.

1. By making an outright gift of the property

    For example, you are a widow with an only son. You should give him your out-of-state mountain cabin, which you visit only occasionally in any event.

2. By retaining a life interest in the property, including the right to sell

    You may not be financially in a position to irrevocably give the property away. By this method you have made a gift, but you cannot be dislodged from the property, or denied access to it, and in many states you may sell it.

3. By placing the real estate in a revocable living trust

    Any assets that are in a living trust are not subject to probate, even though they are in another state.

    Mrs. Berger, a widow living in California, owned a valuable piece of property in New York City, worth about $300,000, with a prime tenant who had leased it for a period of years. She did not want to go through probate proceedings in the state of New York. Her lawyer suggested that she create a revocable living trust in which the only asset would be this particular piece of property. The balance of her estate in California would be disposed of by her will.

    When Mrs. Berger died she effectively avoided ancillary probate proceedings in the state of New York. As a matter of fact, the New York property was turned over to her heirs years before the balance of her estate in California was released from the jurisdiction of the probate court.

4. By incorporating the property

    Mrs. Berger could have chosen this route, in which event the shares of the corporation (whose sole asset would have been the New York real estate) would have been distributed according to her California will.

Every year great numbers of people die without a will for a wide variety of reasons—fear of dying, procrastination (I'm not going to die), distrust of lawyers (a widespread feeling), unwillingness to pay the cost. It would be better if these people had a will, any will, rather than die intestate.

Because of this there are many people who should know how to draw their own will, for it can be done. We don't recommend it, but it's far better than dying intestate, and if it's drawn right, it can be legal. We repeat, we don't believe in do-it-yourself legal documents of any kind, but a handwritten will does solve the problem for those who would otherwise die intestate. It is also useful as a stop-gap measure until the testator has time to see a lawyer, particularly when the property owner is taken unexpectedly and seriously ill.

A will drawn by the testator himself is called a holographic will. The rules for drawing it vary from state to state, but if the following is adhered to, it will probably stand up in court, for no state demands greater requirements, and some demand less.

The will should be drawn in your own handwriting on a completely plain piece of paper. There can't be printing on it of any kind, not even the name of the firm who manufactured it. It must be dated and signed by you, with your signature witnessed by three persons. It doesn't have to be notarized.

Your witnesses should be adults who know you well by sight and who are considerably younger than you. They should be persons of good standing in the community, and none of them can be the testator's spouse, or a beneficiary named in the will, or the spouse of any such beneficiary. In other words, a person who is going to benefit from the will, or might benefit, can't witness your signature. The witnesses should be younger than you because one of the three should be alive to testify in court when your will is probated. All of them should be of good reputation so that when any one of them states in court under oath that the will was signed in his presence, that the signature on the will as far as he is concerned is the signature of the testator, and that he knew it was the deceased who signed the document because he knew him well by sight, these statements will be accepted as the truth.

The will must be signed and witnessed in a certain prescribed manner. The testator should sign first, after stating to those assembled that he is signing his last will and testament (though they don't have to read it) and that he is going to ask them not only to witness his signature, but the signatures of the other witnesses as well. The testator then signs the document. He must be the first one to sign, and he must also date the will at the same time.

Each of the witnesses should then sign in turn in the space provided, and put down his or her address while the testator and the other two witnesses look on. No person is allowed to move the will at any time out of the line of vision of those who are signing it. The witnesses should also be able to testify that the testator was of sound mind and body as far as they knew at the time he signed the will, and that he wasn't acting under duress of any kind.

If the above rules and procedures are followed, it should satisfy the requirements of the state in which you are domiciled. In some states a holographic will may be typewritten, in others only two witnesses are required, and so forth, but if your will is written in your own handwriting on a plain piece of paper, and is signed and witnessed in the prescribed manner, you won't have to ascertain the law of your particular state to have it legal.

There is a definite reason for all of this stilted formality. When the testator dies, nothing remains to speak for him except this piece of paper. It's an important document, for it distributes all of his worldly possessions, acquired for the most part over a lifetime.

A holographic will drawn in such a manner will be accepted by the court of jurisdiction provided one of the witnesses can appear in court and testify to the above formality. A few states will allow the will to be lodged with the court without this requirement, particularly when no witness to the signing of the will can be found.

If an attorney draws your will, and we repeat this is by far the better method, he or she should be given all the information about your family. You should also provide the attorney with a complete list of your assets, which you may not want to do for fear that a larger fee will be charged if your net worth is known. This is a mistake. Only by knowing the size of your estate can an attorney determine if you have a death-tax problem. If you do, he can provide for the payment of these taxes, giving particular attention to the problem of liquidity for they are due within nine months.

Mr. and Mrs. Eric Rasmussen were born in the old country and had emigrated to America early in life without even the benefit of a grade-school education. They were shrewd enough to buy farmland shortly after the turn of the century, worked hard at clearing the mortgage, and when in their eighties finally decided to make a will in favor of their three children. They did not tell the lawyer how much they were worth, and he assumed that this rather plain couple, speaking broken English, had a minor estate. On the contrary, their land was worth $700,000! When Mr. and Mrs. Rasmussen died some years later in their nineties, the lawyer who drew their wills was appalled. If he had known the size of their estate, he could have drawn a testamentary trust to save death taxes and could have advised them to sell part of their land to provide the necessary liquidity.

When they died, the real estate market was depressed, so rather than sell under these conditions, the three children mortgaged the property and spent the next ten years paying off the loan.

People should not procrastinate for so long a time before having a will drawn that extreme age causes them to make the wrong decisions. We don't mean that by waiting that they become senile; many people are in full possession of their faculties well into their eighties and nineties, particularly in this age of greater longevity. It is just that this late in life they may not exercise good judgment as far as their family is concerned. They are of sound mind and body and are not acting under duress; therefore their wills are upheld in court, but that doesn't mean that the disposition of their assets was wise.

Mrs. Wilson outlived her husband and two of her three children. The last child, a daughter, was married to a lawyer (and Mrs. Wilson basically disliked all lawyers). She was then 82 years of age. She decided without consulting her daughter that she was well provided for by her husband's will; besides her only child was "poorly" as she described it, and would probably die soon anyway. So she changed her will and left $1 million to charity, cutting off her only daughter with a bequest of $100,000.

When her will was read her daughter was furious. Her lawyer husband had just died without an estate of any kind. But the court upheld the will.

Mrs. Wilson probably would not have virtually disinherited her only daughter if she had made her will at a younger age, particularly if she had discussed the matter with her husband while he was still alive.

Conclusion

Don't procrastinate until you are so old that you may make bad decisions in regard to the disposition of your property.

7

What to Do About Real Estate

The ownership of real estate presents many perplexing problems. For example:

1. How is the income tax computed if a home or other property is sold?
2. If it is a home that is sold, what is the special tax break for those who are 65 and older?
3. Is income property a good investment?
4. How should real estate be divided in a will when there is more than one heir?
5. Should you retain a home as the surviving spouse or sell it?
6. Is it more economical to own a home or to rent? How are the comparative costs computed?
7. Should real-estate investment trusts (REITs) be considered?

These are real problems, but there are solutions to them, so let's consider each one in turn.

Computation of the Income Tax

Real estate that has been held for a period of years is usually sold for a profit. When it is sold for more than you paid for it, you have made money, and the Internal Revenue Service wants part of it in the form of a capital gains tax.[1]

This problem is encountered most often when, as a retired person, you sell your home. The income tax on the profit is computed by dividing the gain in one-half, and then reporting this one-half as increased income in the year that you sold it.

But how much was your profit? This is where it becomes a sticky problem for many retired people.

Your cost basis for determining your profit is what you paid for your home originally. For a home that was bought thirty or forty years ago this can present a real problem. The best solution, as with all tax problems, is adequate records. If you have the original deed proving when you bought it, a copy of the note and mortgage agreement, and a canceled check showing your down payment, you're in good shape. If not, you are probably faced with an argument from the IRS.

The original cost, however, is not the only basis used in calculating the amount of your profit. You can considerably reduce your gain, and therefore your tax, by increasing your original cost basis by the amount of any permanent improvements you made to your home over the years. Expenses such as repainting a bedroom don't count. But the addition of a swimming pool, or an extra room, or the erection of a fence to enclose the property are permanent improvements which increase its value. When these are added to your original purchase price, this becomes your cost basis that, when subtracted from your sales price, determines the amount of your profit. Once again you should have kept the proof of these improvements in order to add them. Sometimes this means retaining the records for years, for without them your claim of an increased cost basis will often be disallowed. Your profit will then be computed on the difference between how much you paid for your home originally, and how much you sold it for, no matter how unfair this may seem to you.

1. The capital gains tax was discussed in Chapter 1 in relation to selling stocks. The same rules apply when real estate is sold.

There is no time limit as to how long you should keep records of home improvements, for whenever you sell, you have to satisfy the IRS that your increased cost basis is justified.

The Special Tax Break for Those Who Are 65

Instead of paying the full capital gains tax according to the above rules, if you are 65 or older, you obtain a tax break. You may exclude all or a part of your capital gain under the following conditions:

1. You must be 65 on the date of the sale. It isn't sufficient that you would become 65 sometime during the year. If you are 65 on June 10 and sold on June 1, you would not qualify.
2. You must have owned and used your home as your principal residence for five of the preceding eight years.
3. You or your spouse cannot have used the exclusion at any time in the past. The election to exclude gain may be made only once in a taxpayer's lifetime.

You can exclude the entire gain if you sold your home for $35,000 or less. If you sell for more than $35,000, you can exclude that portion of the gain that is in the same ratio to the entire amount of the gain as $35,000 is to the sales price. This seems like a complicated statement by the IRS, but actually it is simple enough.

Mr. and Mrs. Marshall Coleman sold their home and moved into an apartment when he was 69 years of age. Their sale price was $70,000 and their profit was $20,000. The portion of the $20,000 long-term gain that was exempt is determined as follows:

$$\frac{\text{Tax exemption}}{\text{Sale price}} \times \text{Profit} = \text{Profit exemption}$$

$$\frac{\$35,000}{\$70,000} \times \$20,000 = \$10,000$$

The home in which you live, including condominiums and cooperative apartments, is classified as your permanent residence.

Qualification of a home as a residence is very carefully defined. You must have "owned and used" your home as your principal residence for five of the preceding eight years.

Example. Mr. Sidney Fiedler, age 66, lived with his son and daughter-in-law in a house owned by the son from 1955 through 1969. On January 1, 1970, he bought the house from his son and continued to live there until December 31, 1973, when he sold it. Although Mr. Fiedler "used" the property as his principal residence for more than the required five years, he could not exclude any of his gain from the sale because he did not "own" the property for the required length of time.

Short, temporary absences for vacations or other seasonal periods (even though the property is rented during that time) can be counted as periods of use, but not more permanent lengths of time that you are away.

Example. Jeff Fergusen was 65, single, and a teacher. On January 1, 1968 he bought a home and used it continuously as his principal residence until February 1, 1972, when he went abroad for a one-year sabbatical leave. He left it unoccupied and on March 1, 1973 he sold it. Since his leave was not a short, temporary absence, the period of time that he was out of the country couldn't be counted. He was not entitled to exclude any of his gain since he did not "use" the house as his principal residence for the required period of time.

When property is owned jointly by a husband and a wife and they file a joint return, the age requirement will be met as long as one of the spouses is 65 or over; it is not required that both of them be 65.

If the property of a deceased spouse is sold by the survivor and the surviving spouse has not remarried, the sale will qualify for the exclusion as long as the deceased spouse could have met the conditions.

Example. Paul and Lucille Williams were married on February 1, 1970. Both were 70 years of age. After their marriage they lived in a house that Mr. Williams had owned and used continuously as his principal residence since February 1, 1964. Mr. Williams died on January 1, 1973. Mrs. Williams did not remarry and continued to live in the home until she sold it on December 10, 1973. Since Mr. Williams satisfied the other requirements, and Mrs. Williams was over 65, she could exclude from her gross income all or a part of the gain from the sale.

But supposing you don't move into an apartment when you sell your home, but you buy or build another one instead? Now it is ruled by the IRS that you don't have to pay a capital gains tax at all. The amount of the tax is deferred (unless you should sell the second house).[2]

The rules for deferring the tax on your profit if you buy or build another home are as follows:

1. If you *buy* another home within an eighteen-month period, either before or after the sale, the capital gains tax is deferred and you pay nothing on your profit.
2. If you *build* another home, the time limit is extended to two years.

These two rules apply regardless of age. You don't have to be 65 or older to qualify.

Sometimes retired people don't sell their homes but give them to their children. This is one way for them to completely escape the capital gains tax. A word of warning—if you give a home that has appreciated in value to your daughter, for instance, you have simply shifted the capital gain to her. If she subsequently sells the property she has to go back to *your cost basis* in determining the amount of her capital gains tax. Therefore if you make a gift to her of your home, you had better include with it your cost basis records.

2. If you should sell your second house, you have to go back to the cost basis of your first home in order to determine your tax.

Depreciation cannot be taken on a home. It can be taken only on income property. However, when this type of real estate is sold, the depreciation *decreases* the cost basis for income tax purposes, which *increases* your profit and therefore your tax.

Is Income Property a Good Investment?

Yes and no, which is a bad answer, but we'll qualify it.

It is a good investment in the hands of knowledgeable retired people, who live on the property and have a small number of good tenants, particularly if the husband is good at do-it-yourself work, and therefore expensive hourly workers such as plumbers and painters don't have to be called when something needs to be done.

It is a bad investment for a widow who has none of these qualifications.

Owning income property when you are past 65, having to deal with the never-ending problems of tenants, is not true retirement. If your particular ownership prevents you from enjoying your later years, you should sell your income property and invest the money elsewhere.

Mr. and Mrs. Ralph Grant were in their late sixties and found themselves in this position. They lived in San Francisco where it was cold and foggy much of the year, and Mr. Grant was bothered by arthritis. One day his doctor told him that he would definitely feel better if he would move to a warmer climate.

"I can't do that, Doc," Mr. Grant protested. "I own a twelve-unit apartment house and I manage it myself."

So he kept on living in the building and working for his tenants.

One day an investment representative called on them at the suggestion of a friend.

He said: "I see from your list of investments that you own a mutual fund worth $20,000, and that you are reinvesting the dividends. At your age, why don't you take the income instead? It would give you an extra $100 a month."

"There's no sense to that," objected Mr. Grant. "We couldn't spend it."

The representative was surprised. "Why not?"

"Because we are tied down to this apartment house seven days a week. We'd like to go to Reno. Can't do it. Right now if I don't get down to apartment 14 and repair the lock on the hall door before dark, that spinster lady who has been a tenant for ten years is going to move out!"

"You know something," the account executive replied, "you ought to sell the property."

"How can we do that?"

"Simple. Put it on the market. What's it worth?"

"One hundred and eighty thousand dollars," Mr. Grant promptly replied. "I wouldn't take a penny less. And it's free and clear."

"Let me ask you a question," said the representative. "If you had a $140,000 first mortgage on this property at 8 percent, would you consider it a safe investment?"

"The best. Why?"

"Then sell the building for $40,000 down and take back a first mortgage for the difference. One hundred and eighty thousand dollars invested at 8 percent will give you an income of $14,400 a year. With Social Security, this would give you almost $20,000, without any work."

After thinking it over, the Grants took his advice and sold. Soon afterwards they moved to Palm Springs in southern California, where Mr. Grant's arthritis greatly improved, as his doctor had forecast, and they started enjoying their retirement years.

How Should Real Estate Be Divided
in Your Will?

This is a difficult decision when you have several heirs. Share and share alike would seem to be the best solution, especially when equal division among children is desired. If your home is the only real estate involved, this is probably the best way to dispose of it. After probate is over, the children can sell the home and divide the proceeds.

However, if several parcels of income property are involved, some other method is often chosen. Sometimes an undivided interest in all of the properties is left to the heirs. But it must be borne in mind that management of income property presents a problem. Which one of the heirs is capable enough, and willing on top of that, to accept the burden? And if one of them does assume the management, how long will it be before there is dissension among the heirs about the fair division of the net rents? Certainly anyone who is managing the property will demand a reasonable compensation for his or her work, and therefore be unwilling to divide the profits equally with the other heirs.

One of the devisees also may need money and therefore force a sale. Any heir has the right to do this, and if the others can't buy out this individual the property will be sold, often at a sacrifice. Smart real estate buyers are constantly searching for estate sales of real estate because they know they can buy the property at a bargain.

Sometimes if there are three different pieces of property and three heirs, each one is left his or her own individual parcel. But even though the properties are apparently of equal value when the will is drawn, it would be unusual for this to remain true over the years. As the values differentiate more and more there is bound to be dissatisfaction on the part of that heir who feels he or she was left the poorest of the lot.

So maybe it would be better to hand the problem over to your executor, giving him the power to dispose of the property at a fair market value within a reasonable length of time, and then divide the proceeds according to the terms of your will. Any attempt to arbitrarily retain the property in the estate by putting it in the hands of a corporate trustee is usually a mistake. Too much of the income is dissipated in maintenance and decorating charges because of the high cost of material and labor. After all, the corporate trustee doesn't live on the property and doesn't do the work. Professional firms are employed to make the repairs and do the painting which drastically reduces the net rent.

As the Surviving Spouse, Should You Retain a Home or Sell It?

The survivor should not sell a home immediately. A rash and sudden decision, made when emotionally upset, can lead to years of regret. The surviving spouse should wait a year or two. If a home is sold after that length of time it should be a sound decision. Quite often a widow feels she can't stay in familiar surroundings, where there are too many memories; or she thinks the house is too big and lonely; therefore she sells immediately.

Emily Bonner was a grief-stricken widow who felt that way, so she sold her home just after her husband's death. Three years later she regretted it and tried to buy it back. She could have, because it was up for sale, but she couldn't for a very good reason. It had gone up in value 30 percent, and she couldn't afford the higher price.

No, it's better to wait. The home can always be sold later, but too frequently it can't be repurchased, if this is desired.

Is It More Economical to Own a Home or to Rent?

Unfortunately each case must be considered separately. Once the arithmetic is understood, however, the respective costs can be accurately computed. But there are a few general ground rules to remember first.

1. Emotions aren't being considered. Comparative costs only are being determined.
2. The major expense of owning a home outright as a retired person is the loss of interest on the money invested.
3. The next major expense is property taxes.
4. As a renter, who will pay for the utilities, the landlord or the tenant?

Example. You own a home that is worth $40,000 on today's market, and you are wondering if it wouldn't be cheaper for you to rent an apartment.

Your property taxes are $700 a year, your bill for utilities is $360, and your annual premium for a comprehensive home insurance policy is $100. You do your own yardwork, but you feel that in the light of past experience that you have to set aside an average of $300 a year for maintenance and repairs. You add up these figures and conclude that it costs you $1,460 a year to live in your home, and decide you couldn't possibly rent for that.

But wait a minute. You forgot rule number 2. If you sell your home, you would have $40,000 to invest. You could easily obtain 7 percent on this money, which would give you an additional income of $2,800 a year. This is just as much an expense of living in your home as the outlay for property taxes and insurance. This brings the total to $4,260 ($1,460 + $2,800). This is $355 per month.

If you could rent an apartment (one you feel you would be happy in) for $300 per month, utilities included, you would be $55 per month better off. If you would have to pay $400 per month to find what you want, it would cost you $45 per month more than to stay where you are. It's just that simple. The main thing homeowners overlook in comparative costs of home ownership as against renting is the loss of interest on the money that they have buried under the house—in other words, its current market value on which they are receiving no interest.

In many communities and cities across the country property taxes have escalated so much in recent years that it is becoming increasingly difficult for retired people to retain their homes, even though this is what they really would like to do. There is something very satisfying about owning your own home, particularly one that you have lived in for years, and on which you have spent most of a lifetime paying off the mortgage.

If costs have become prohibitive, however, there is no alternative but to sell and rent instead, in order to reduce costs. Unfortunately there is little one can do as an individual where property taxes are concerned. Only mass protest against increase rates make any impression, and too often even this produces no results.

Should Real Estate Investment Trusts (REITs) Be Considered?

In the light of the recent events of the last few years—NO.

Real estate investment trusts, especially those that invested in mortgages, have had a sorry performance. They were supposed to be safe investments, even for retired people, because like mutual funds they provide diversification and professional management instead of the individual investing in mortgages or real-estate equities on his or her own. In addition they have millions at their disposal which gives them, or so the theory goes, the opportunity for greater profit because only large properties, which are beyond the reach of the small investor, are in the portfolio. It didn't work out that way. Even some of the largest commercial banks in the country were caught napping.

The cause of the debacle in real estate investment trusts was inflation and excessively high interest rates. Nobody in the business expected such high prices for land, outrageous construction costs, and the high cost for borrowed money. In too many mortgage REITs over half of the loans in which they had invested were not only receiving no payment on the principal, but no interest as well.

To use an expression of one trust promoter: "We got into trouble with real-estate developers who we thought were sound, but whose arrangements somehow fell through. The trust began to record a lot of non-earning assets." Which is just a fancy way of saying that the trust had too many bad loans on the books on which no interest was being paid.

Mr. and Mrs. John Kelley, a retired couple, invested in the debentures of a mortgage REIT, which was promoted and managed by a firm that had been in the mortgage business exclusively for over fifty years and was one of the biggest in the country.

Two years later, although still receiving their interest, they were disturbed by the trust's annual report, so they wrote for an explanation. The reply wasn't very encouraging—the trust was without question in financial trouble—so they sent their certificate in for redemption. The firm replied that they might be able to receive their money in about two years; in the meantime they would continue, for the time being at least, to receive their quarterly interest check.

This was decidedly bad news for Mr. and Mrs. Kelley. But they had understood what they had bought, so there was nothing they could do but wait it out and hope that the real-estate market would improve. Fortunately they had other invest-ments that were sound so they wouldn't be hurt too badly if they lost the $20,000 they had invested. But nobody likes the prospect of losing that much money, especially a retired person who has no possibility of saving it again.

In view of the record in recent years, real estate investment trusts should not be considered by those who are 65 and retired.

8

Annuities—A High Cash Flow If You're Old Enough

Annuities are ignored by most retired people. They shouldn't be, for they are the best means of obtaining a large assured income. Moreover, they are to a large extent exempt from income taxes.

Annuities are not life insurance. A lump sum immediate annuity, which provides a fixed sum per month, is simply a return to the annuitant (in a series of payments) of his or her own money plus interest. Then why should retired people buy them? Because the monthly payment is larger than from any other fixed dollar investment, and it is *guaranteed for life*. It is because of this latter feature that only life insurance companies can sell them.

The principle behind annuities is a simple one. All annuitants agree in advance that the money which is not returned to them, because they die too soon, may be retained by the insurance company to pay those other annuitants who live beyond their life expectancy. This way insurance companies can guarantee to every annuitant a monthly payment for life, no matter how long he or she may live.

How much assured life income can a person who is 65 or over receive?

A male annuitant who purchases a non-refund annuity at age

65 can obtain approximately 10 percent; at age 70, approximately 11 percent; and at age 75 approximately 14 percent. Female annuitants, because they live longer, receive about 1 percent less.

Admittedly this isn't straight income. Most of the money the annuitant receives is a return of capital, which is why the majority of the monthly payment is nontaxable. But it makes no difference if the payment is largely from principal, for no place else can a retired person obtain this high a check per month and still be assured that he or she will not run out of capital some day.

As we suggested in Chapter 1, retired people should deliberately spend a part of their principal in order to live better. However, there is one thing wrong with this concept. Unless some method of monthly payment is chosen that automatically uses capital, property owners don't do it, even though they may agree with the principle.

Several years ago mutual funds started offering their shareholders a solution for a higher cash flow, which they call a systematic withdrawal plan. Shareholders can choose any percentage return that they want on their investment, and the custodian bank will send them monthly checks. The percentage chosen usually varies between 6 and 8 percent a year. It's not so popular anymore because the dissipation of the shares has been so great for many investors (especially for those who bought their shares at a historically high price), that they have had to reduce the amount of their monthly withdrawal.

With an annuity this never becomes necessary because the monthly payments are guaranteed for life; therefore annuitants know that they can't run out of the capital that they invested in the contract. It's one of the best ways for persons to spend part of their principal in order to enjoy themselves more when retired.

We repeat, the average retiree will not spend some of his or her money simply by withdrawing it each month from a savings account. It goes against his or her basic save-the-capital philosophy. But if a check arrives every month that is part principal, he or she will treat the entire payment as income and enjoy the extra money.

The annuity does exactly this. And because the larger portion of the payment is a return of capital, there is a decided tax advantage. The monthly payment comes under the cost recovery rule of the Internal Revenue Service, meaning that you are allowed to recover your cost each month before you have to pay taxes on the balance. The tax-free part is a percentage of each monthly payment, derived by dividing the cost of the annuity by the number of years that you are expected to receive them.

Example. You are a female, age 75, with an IRS calculated payment-expectancy of twelve years.[1] You buy a non-refund annuity for $10,000 that pays you $100.62 per month, which is 12 percent a year. You can deduct $69.44 from each monthly payment as the tax-exempt portion because this amount is a return of your own capital.

The computation looks like this:

Expected return from the contract	
(144 months × $100.62)	$14,489.28
Cost of the contract	10,000.00
Interest portion	$ 4,489.28
Monthly payment	$ 100.62
Interest portion each month	
($4,489.28/144 months)	31.18
Return of cost, or principal	
($10,000/144 months)	$ 69.44

And what is important, as far as taxes are concerned, you may continue to exempt $69.44 of your monthly check from your tax return, no matter how many years you may live.

Annuities must be fully comprehended before they are purchased, including the following essential features.

1. According to the expected return multiples issued by the Internal Revenue Service, page 31 of Publication 76.

1. Annuitants must understand that they have spent the money that they paid for the contract. The capital is gone the minute they sign the agreement. There is no cash value, and they can't change their minds. They have exchanged this much of their principal for an income that is guaranteed for life.
2. There is no protection from the inroads of inflation. If the cost of living rises, the income remains the same.
3. Even though annuitants buy refund annuities (explained later), nothing is paid to their beneficiaries if they outlive their life expectancy. There is a refund only if the annuitants should die in the early years of the contract.

An annuity should be purchased, therefore, only under the following conditions.

Only a part of a retired person's capital should be invested this way. Since there is no cash value, the annuitant must keep a sufficient reserve in liquid assets. How much should be retained depends upon individual circumstances.

One should be 65 or older before considering an annuity. Many people retire before reaching this age. Cash that would otherwise be available for an annuity should be invested elsewhere until the retiree reaches 65. This is because the payment is too low for those who are younger than this; also the early retiree may want to try for inflationary protection through fluctuating investments because of a longer life expectancy.

There should be no desire on the part of the annuitant to leave this money in his or her estate. This would particularly be true of people who have no children.

In view of the above, what is important, and what is not important when considering the purchase of an annuity?

What is important is obtaining the largest possible spendable income during the rest of one's life.

What is not important is leaving a large capital fund after death.

Once this is agreed upon, annuities can be considered in more detail.

Immediate annuities are of two types—the refund annuity and the non-refund annuity. Both of them are sold to retired persons, who give the insurance company a lump sum of money to obtain a monthly payment that is guaranteed for life.

The refund annuity

In this type of annuity a refund is paid to the beneficiary if the annuitant dies in the early years of the contract. As with all immediate annuities, the annuitant is paid a guaranteed life income, but if that individual should die before the total monthly payments received equal or exceed the amount of the single premium that was paid, the insurance company will make a refund to the annuitant's beneficiary. The amount refunded will be the sum by which the premium exceeds the total monthly payments the annuitant has received up to the time of his or her death.

This refund, if any, can be arranged in either one of two ways: A lump sum will be paid by the insurance company to the beneficiary, or the monthly payments will continue until the cash is exhausted. Which option goes into effect depends upon the one chosen by the annuitant at the time the contract was purchased.

The refund annuity should be bought by people who have children. Sometimes, however, a parent doesn't do this.

The non-refund annuity

Mrs. Manchester was an example of a person who bought the wrong contract. She was a widow, age 70, who had one married son. She purchased a non-refund annuity for $20,000, which would start paying her $200 per month at age 72. It was still considered by the insurance company to be an immediate annuity even though the payments did not start for two years. By leaving the money on deposit and withdrawing nothing for two years, the contract cost her less than if she had asked for the payments to commence at once. She also received more per month by not having to pay for a refund feature.

Shortly after she made the investment she went to live with her married son. When he discovered that she had purchased an annuity, he became upset and arranged a consultation with the life insurance agent who had sold Mrs. Manchester the policy.

At this meeting he demanded that a refund be made to his mother of the entire $20,000, especially in lieu of the fact that not a single payment had been made under the contract.

"I'm sorry," said the agent, as they all sat around the dinette table in the son's home. "We can't do that."

"Why not?"

"Because," explained the agent patiently, "your mother bought a non-refund annuity."

"What does that mean?"

"It means there's no cash available, even though she hasn't received a payment."

"You mean to tell me," demanded the son, "that if my mother dies tomorrow the entire $20,000 is gone?"

"That's right, sir."

"There ought to be a law," the son almost shouted, he was so upset. "It's highway robbery, that's what it is!"

But Mrs. Manchester wasn't upset. She knew what she had bought, which was the maximum monthly payment guaranteed for life, so she would be financially independent of her son.

Nevertheless, she was wrong.

She should not have bought a non-refund annuity, thereby risking the loss to her son of a substantial sum of money. She should have purchased a refund annuity, and taken less per month, for there wasn't that much difference. Her payment would have been $180, instead of $200, per month. If she didn't like this, her son would have been glad to pay her the additional $20 each month rather than possibly lose $20,000.

Mrs. Manchester's case demonstrates the care that should be taken in the type of annuity that is purchased. When immediate family heirs are involved, particularly children, a refund should be arranged rather than risk a severe loss of capital to the estate.

It's all right to purchase this type of annuity, however, where there are no heirs, and the maximum monthly payment is desired.

For example, all that Mark Schmidt had in the world was $30,000 and his Social Security check of $110 per month. He desperately needed more income, for even with a 5 percent return on his savings account, his total monthly income was only $235. He was 76 years of age, his wife had died, and they had no children. He had no one to whom he cared to leave his money.

He therefore asked his life underwriter to obtain for him a non-refund annuity proposal on $25,000. The insurance company replied, guaranteeing him $289.45 per month.

When his life underwriter pointed out to Mr. Schmidt that this monthly payment was equivalent to a 13.89 percent return on his $25,000, he bought the annuity. With his Social Security check this gave him an income of approximately $400 per month. He couldn't possibly have obtained this much cash per month from any other source, and have it guaranteed for life. The $5,000 he still had in the bank, after buying the annuity, gave him the necessary cash reserve.

Mark Schmidt (in contrast to Mrs. Manchester) bought the right contract—the non-refund annuity. There was no reason for his taking less per month in order to leave an estate if he should die too soon. He did not care that the money would be gone when he died.

The joint and survivor annuity

This type of annuity is purchased when a couple wants the same payment made to the survivor that is paid to both of them. When two lives have to be taken into account instead of one, obviously the monthly payment is less, because the life expectancy of two people is involved. The table for a non-refund joint and survivor annuity is shown here.

Example. You are a couple, male age 79 and female age 75.

FIXED DOLLAR ANNUITY BASIC RATES TABLE
SINGLE PURCHASE PAYMENT COMBINATION IMMEDIATE ANNUITY
JOINT AND FULL TO SURVIVOR
NON-REFUND

Monthly Income Purchased by $1,000 Net Purchase Payment
Applied to Provide a Fixed Annuity*

MALE AGE AT ISSUE	FEMALE AGE AT ISSUE														
	56	57	58	59	60	61	62	63	64	65	66	67	68	69	70
55	5.96	6.00	6.04	6.08	6.12	6.17	6.21	6.25	6.29	6.33	6.37	6.41	6.45	6.48	6.52
56	5.99	6.03	6.08	6.12	6.16	6.21	6.25	6.30	6.34	6.39	6.43	6.47	6.51	6.55	6.59
57	6.01	6.06	6.11	6.16	6.20	6.25	6.30	6.35	6.39	6.44	6.49	6.53	6.58	6.62	6.67
58	6.04	6.09	6.14	6.19	6.24	6.29	6.35	6.40	6.45	6.50	6.55	6.60	6.65	6.69	6.74
59	6.07	6.12	6.18	6.23	6.28	6.34	6.39	6.44	6.50	6.55	6.61	6.66	6.71	6.77	6.82
60	6.10	6.15	6.21	6.26	6.32	6.38	6.44	6.49	6.55	6.61	6.67	6.72	6.78	6.84	6.89
61	6.12	6.18	6.24	6.30	6.36	6.42	6.48	6.54	6.60	6.67	6.73	6.79	6.85	6.91	6.97
62	6.15	6.21	6.27	6.33	6.39	6.46	6.52	6.59	6.65	6.72	6.79	6.85	6.92	6.99	7.05
63	6.17	6.23	6.30	6.36	6.43	6.50	6.57	6.63	6.71	6.78	6.85	6.92	6.99	7.06	7.13
64	6.19	6.26	6.33	6.39	6.46	6.54	6.61	6.68	6.76	6.83	6.91	6.98	7.06	7.14	7.21
65	6.22	6.28	6.35	6.42	6.50	6.57	6.65	6.73	6.80	6.88	6.97	7.05	7.13	7.21	7.30
66	6.24	6.31	6.38	6.45	6.53	6.61	6.69	6.77	6.85	6.94	7.02	7.11	7.20	7.29	7.38
67	6.26	6.33	6.40	6.48	6.56	6.64	6.73	6.81	6.90	6.99	7.08	7.18	7.27	7.37	7.46
68	6.28	6.35	6.43	6.51	6.59	6.68	6.76	6.85	6.94	7.04	7.14	7.24	7.34	7.44	7.54
69	6.30	6.37	6.45	6.53	6.62	6.71	6.80	6.89	6.99	7.09	7.19	7.30	7.40	7.51	7.62
70	6.31	6.39	6.47	6.56	6.65	6.74	6.83	6.93	7.03	7.13	7.24	7.35	7.47	7.59	7.70
71	6.33	6.41	6.49	6.58	6.67	6.77	6.86	6.96	7.07	7.18	7.29	7.41	7.53	7.66	7.78
72	6.35	6.43	6.51	6.60	6.70	6.79	6.89	7.00	7.11	7.22	7.34	7.46	7.59	7.72	7.86
73	6.36	6.44	6.53	6.62	6.72	6.82	6.92	7.03	7.14	7.26	7.39	7.52	7.65	7.79	7.93
74	6.37	6.46	6.55	6.64	6.74	6.84	6.95	7.06	7.18	7.30	7.43	7.57	7.71	7.85	8.00
75	6.39	6.47	6.56	6.66	6.76	6.86	6.97	7.09	7.21	7.34	7.47	7.61	7.76	7.91	8.07
76	6.40	6.49	6.58	6.68	6.78	6.89	7.00	7.12	7.24	7.37	7.51	7.66	7.81	7.97	8.13
77	6.41	6.50	6.59	6.69	6.80	6.91	7.02	7.14	7.27	7.40	7.55	7.70	7.86	8.02	8.20
78	6.42	6.51	6.61	6.71	6.81	6.92	7.04	7.16	7.30	7.43	7.58	7.74	7.90	8.07	8.26
79	6.43	6.52	6.62	6.72	6.83	6.94	7.06	7.19	7.32	7.46	7.61	7.77	7.94	8.12	8.31
80	6.44	6.53	6.63	6.73	6.84	6.96	7.08	7.21	7.34	7.49	7.64	7.81	7.98	8.17	8.36
81	6.45	6.54	6.64	6.74	6.85	6.97	7.09	7.22	7.36	7.51	7.67	7.84	8.02	8.21	8.41
82	6.45	6.55	6.65	6.76	6.87	6.98	7.11	7.24	7.38	7.53	7.70	7.87	8.05	8.25	8.46
83	6.46	6.56	6.66	6.77	6.88	7.00	7.12	7.26	7.40	7.55	7.72	7.89	8.08	8.28	8.50
84	6.47	6.57	6.67	6.77	6.89	7.01	7.14	7.27	7.42	7.57	7.74	7.92	8.11	8.32	8.54
85	6.47	6.57	6.67	6.78	6.90	7.02	7.15	7.28	7.43	7.59	7.76	7.94	8.14	8.35	8.57

MALE AGE AT ISSUE	FEMALE AGE AT ISSUE														
	71	72	73	74	75	76	77	78	79	80	81	82	83	84	85
55	6.56	6.59	6.62	6.65	6.68	6.71	6.74	6.76	6.78	6.80	6.82	6.84	6.86	6.87	6.89
56	6.63	6.67	6.70	6.74	6.77	6.80	6.83	6.85	6.88	6.90	6.92	6.95	6.96	6.98	7.00
57	6.71	6.75	6.79	6.82	6.86	6.89	6.92	6.95	6.98	7.01	7.03	7.05	7.07	7.09	7.11
58	6.79	6.83	6.87	6.91	6.95	6.99	7.02	7.05	7.09	7.11	7.14	7.16	7.19	7.21	7.23
59	6.87	6.91	6.96	7.00	7.05	7.09	7.12	7.16	7.19	7.23	7.26	7.28	7.31	7.33	7.35
60	6.95	7.00	7.05	7.10	7.15	7.19	7.23	7.27	7.31	7.34	7.38	7.41	7.43	7.46	7.48
61	7.03	7.09	7.14	7.20	7.25	7.30	7.34	7.39	7.43	7.47	7.50	7.54	7.57	7.59	7.62
62	7.12	7.18	7.24	7.30	7.35	7.41	7.46	7.51	7.55	7.59	7.63	7.67	7.71	7.74	7.76
63	7.20	7.27	7.34	7.40	7.46	7.52	7.58	7.63	7.68	7.73	7.77	7.81	7.85	7.89	7.92
64	7.29	7.36	7.44	7.51	7.57	7.64	7.70	7.76	7.82	7.87	7.92	7.96	8.01	8.04	8.08
65	7.38	7.46	7.54	7.61	7.69	7.76	7.83	7.89	7.96	8.01	8.07	8.12	8.17	8.21	8.25
66	7.47	7.56	7.64	7.72	7.81	7.89	7.96	8.03	8.10	8.17	8.23	8.28	8.34	8.39	8.43
67	7.56	7.65	7.75	7.84	7.93	8.01	8.10	8.18	8.25	8.32	8.39	8.46	8.52	8.57	8.62
68	7.65	7.75	7.85	7.95	8.05	8.14	8.23	8.32	8.41	8.49	8.56	8.64	8.70	8.76	8.82
69	7.73	7.85	7.96	8.06	8.17	8.28	8.38	8.47	8.57	8.66	8.74	8.82	8.90	8.96	9.03
70	7.82	7.94	8.06	8.18	8.30	8.41	8.52	8.62	8.73	8.83	8.93	9.01	9.10	9.18	9.25
71	7.91	8.04	8.17	8.29	8.42	8.54	8.67	8.79	8.94	9.07	9.19	9.31	9.42	9.53	9.62
72	7.99	8.13	8.27	8.41	8.54	8.68	8.81	8.94	9.07	9.19	9.31	9.42	9.53	9.62	9.71
73	8.08	8.22	8.37	8.52	8.67	8.82	8.96	9.11	9.25	9.38	9.51	9.63	9.75	9.86	9.96
74	8.16	8.31	8.47	8.63	8.79	8.95	9.09	9.26	9.43	9.60	9.76	9.92	10.07	10.22	10.36
75	8.23	8.40	8.57	8.74	8.91	9.09	9.26	9.43	9.60	9.76	9.92	10.07	10.30	10.46	10.62
76	8.31	8.48	8.66	8.85	9.03	9.22	9.41	9.59	9.78	9.95	10.15	10.34	10.53	10.71	10.89
77	8.38	8.56	8.75	8.95	9.15	9.35	9.55	9.75	9.91	10.13	10.34	10.56	10.76	10.97	11.16
78	8.44	8.64	8.84	9.05	9.26	9.47	9.69	9.89	10.06	10.30	10.54	10.77	11.00	11.22	11.43
79	8.51	8.71	8.92	9.14	9.37	9.60	9.83	10.06	10.30	10.54	10.77	11.11	11.45	11.71	11.94
80	8.57	8.78	9.00	9.23	9.47	9.71	9.96	10.22	10.47	10.73	10.96	11.23	11.48	11.71	11.94
81	8.62	8.85	9.08	9.32	9.57	9.83	10.09	10.36	10.64	10.91	11.19	11.48	11.73	12.00	12.25
82	8.67	8.91	9.15	9.40	9.66	9.94	10.22	10.51	10.80	11.10	11.40	11.69	11.99	12.28	12.56
83	8.72	8.96	9.21	9.48	9.75	10.04	10.34	10.64	10.96	11.28	11.60	11.92	12.24	12.56	12.87
84	8.77	9.01	9.28	9.55	9.84	10.14	10.45	10.77	11.11	11.45	11.80	12.15	12.50	12.85	13.19
85	8.81	9.06	9.33	9.62	9.92	10.23	10.56	10.90	11.25	11.62	11.99	12.37	12.75	13.13	13.50

*Rates are based on age to last elapsed quarter

To find the monthly annuity payment obtained from a net purchase payment of $1,000, you enter the left-hand column entitled: Male Age at Issue, and find the husband's age of 79. Next you follow the column horizontally across to Female Age at Issue of 75. The answer found is $9.37. This is the monthly annuity for a *net purchase payment* of $1,000.

Since a sales charge of 8 percent has to be paid, plus a state premium tax (which is levied in approximately one-half of the states), 10 percent has to be deducted from the investment to take care of these charges. If a $10,000 annuity is being purchased, $1,000 has to be deducted, leaving a *net purchase payment* of $9,000; therefore $9.37 should be multiplied by 9, which is a result of $84.33. This is the amount of the monthly payment that would be paid to both of you, and to the survivor, for a $10,000 joint and survivor annuity, which is a guarantee of 10.01 percent ($84.33 × 12 months = $1,011.96 a year).

An annuity for 5, 10, or 15 years certain

This is simply a variation of the refund annuity. The beneficiary will receive payment for the number of years certain, *less* the number of years and months that were paid to the annuitant prior to his or her death.

Annuities for the Well-To-Do

Oddly enough, those who are well-off financially can also use annuities to their advantage. By buying non-refund annuities they can reduce death taxes and increase family income to a greater extent than would otherwise be possible.

At first glance, it would appear that a non-refund annuity would reduce rather than enhance the estate that would eventually pass to one's heirs because, as we have seen, the principal has been spent in exchange for a lifetime income. But this is not true if certain conditions exist in regard to the property that is used to purchase the contract, and the right kind of annuity is chosen.

Most wealthy people own assets that have tremendously increased in value since their original purchase. Such property can be common stocks, income real estate, or unimproved land. The income produced could be as low as 2 percent of the current market value or, in the case of growth stocks or land, no income at all. If such property is sold, it would be subject to the capital gains tax, which would reduce the amount of money that could be invested elsewhere and, therefore, the future income that could be obtained from it. Well-to-do property owners therefore tend to hold rather than sell such assets in their estates. If retained, however, the property eventually becomes subject to the upper brackets of the estate- and inheritance-tax tables, and to the expense of probate administration as well. This total can well represent a third or more of the property, an amount that will pass to profligate politicians to be spent in a manner that may be completely abhorrent to the testator.

On the other hand if $100,000 of low-income, appreciated property is given to a nonprofit educational institution or foundation, with instructions for them to sell it, no capital gains tax has to be paid, either by the donors themselves or by the institution or foundation to which the gift is made. This means that the entire $100,000 can be put to work elsewhere, not reduced by even one dollar. If this low-income property is placed in Grade A bonds paying 8 percent, reserving a life annuity for the donor, and in turn for his or her children, a decided family benefit can occur.

If the donated property is returning 2 percent, which is $2,000 a year on $100,000, an increase to $8,000 is a decided family income benefit, particularly considering the fact that the entire $8,000 can be tax-free income to the donor. Likewise, if it is properly arranged, no gift tax is incurred.

Mr. and Mrs. James Bailey had an estate of $3 million, and an income of $160,000 a year. One hundred thousand dollars of their money was invested in a common stock that had cost them only $20,000 many years before, and which was returning them a 2 percent dividend. They had two married sons in their late thirties.

After discussing the matter with the trustees of the university from which they had both graduated, they decided to give the $100,000 of common stock to their alma mater, reserving a life income of $8,000 a year for themselves, and upon their death, the same life income for their two sons.

They achieved several advantages from making this gift.

1. They had an allowable tax deduction (because of the $100,000 gift) of 30 percent of their adjusted gross income. This meant that $48,000 of their income would be tax-free (30 percent of $160,000). Since they received only $8,000 annually from the annuity, this was all they could use in any one year, but they could carry forward for five years the unused balance of $40,000. This resulted in the annuity being tax-free income to Mr. and Mrs. Bailey for a total of six years.

2. On an estate of $3,000,000 the top estate tax bracket is 53 percent, and the average state inheritance tax and probate administration costs exacts 12 percent more. This would result in the children inheriting only $35,000 of the $100,000. Mr. and Mrs. Bailey's respective ages were 70 and 65, and the average age of their two sons was 38. This resulted in a life expectancy of 40 years. The present value of $8,000 a year, payable for 40 years, is $158,000. This is the amount that would have to be paid to an insurance company in a lump sum for a non-refund annuity. This is four and one-half times what the sons would have inherited by allowing the $100,000 to pass through the normal probate process.

There could have been a drawback to this. If the Baileys had followed normal procedures, the life incomes reserved for their two sons would have constituted taxable gifts on which they would have had to pay a gift tax.

However, the Internal Revenue Service has ruled that a gift has to be complete at the time of the donation, or it doesn't constitute a taxable obligation. A gift of a reserved life income will remain incomplete if the following sentence is inserted in the non-refund annuity contract by the donee institution. "The donor reserves the right to revoke or terminate by his will any portion of the income to the beneficiaries named herein."

The Baileys had this clause inserted in their annuity contract and therefore not only received $8,000 a year for six years exempt from income taxes, but they didn't have to pay a gift tax either. In addition no federal estate tax would be paid on the $100,000 upon the death of Mr. and Mrs. Bailey, or upon the death of their two sons. The annuity would die with them, and therefore there would be nothing left to tax.

No charge is normally made by an institution for managing the assets in a reserved life income annuity. The advantage to the charitable or educational donee is their being the ultimate recipient of the charitable remainder upon the death of all of the income beneficiaries.

9

Social Security

Social Security is the nation's basic method of providing a continuing income when a family's earnings stop due to retirement, disability, or death.

Nine out of ten workers in the United States are paying Social Security taxes. Virtually the only groups excluded are government workers and railroad employees, and only because they have their own programs. More than one person out of seven is receiving a monthly Social Security check. Practically every family in the nation therefore has a stake in the program.

Of particular concern to retired people has been the attacks on the Social Security system claiming that it was basically unsound and headed for bankruptcy.

Was this true? It was, until Congress passed a Social Security bill in December 1977 that increased Social Security taxes by $227 billion, the largest peacetime tax increase in the nation's history.

As everyone knows, Social Security taxes, which are assessed against those who are currently employed, pay the benefits for those who are retired. The taxes paid by employees is matched dollar for dollar by their employers. Under the old law a worker making $17,700 or more in 1978 pays $1,070.85 at a tax rate of

6.05 percent. The huge new Social Security bill passed by Congress raised taxes and rates, starting in 1979, as follows.

In 1979, the bill requires a worker making at least $22,900 to pay $1,403.77 into the Social Security trust funds. In 1980, a worker earning at least $25,900 will have to pay $1,587.67. After that, the tax will continue to rise each year so that, by 1987, a worker making $42,600 or more will have to pay $3,045.90. In addition to raising the taxable wage base, the bill boosts the tax rate. In 1979 the rate goes up from 6.05 percent to 6.13 percent, and by 1981 to 6.65 percent. By 1986 it will be 7.15 percent, and in 1990 and thereafter, 7.65 percent.

For self-employed persons, the tax rate and the taxable earnings base will rise just as for employees and employers. The tax-rate for the self-employed for 1978 is 8.1 percent, and stays at this same rate through 1980. Under the new law, however, this rate increases to 9.3 percent in 1981, 9.35 percent in 1982 through 1984, 9.9 percent in 1985, and 10 percent in 1986 through 1989. Starting in 1990, the tax rate on the self-employed will be 10.75 percent, which imposes a tax of $4,579.50 on a person making $42,600 or more.

Incorporated in the higher taxable earnings base is the assumption by Congress that inflation will drive up earnings in coming years with the result that more and workers will be earning this kind of money, an unlikely event if the effect of inflation is ignored.

Besides raising taxes and increasing the tax-rate (in order to keep the Social Security system solvent), Congress also made other important changes in the law.

The bill increases the amount of money a person over 65 may earn without losing benefits. In 1978, a recipient between the ages of 65 and 72 may earn $4,000 without losing benefits. This amount increases to $4,500 in 1979, to $5,000 in 1980, to $5,500 in 1981, and to $6,000 in 1982. In that year another important change occurs. The age at which a recipient may receive benefits without regard to earnings drops from age 72 to 70.

Under the bill as passed by Congress remarriage no longer acts to reduce benefits of widows and widowers who are over 60 years of age. Also a divorced spouse can receive benefits after only 10 years of marriage, instead of 20 years, as under previous legislation.

The Social Security System provides for four different trust funds:

1. The Federal Old Age and Survivors Insurance Trust Fund (FOASI), which provides retirement and survivors benefits.
2. The Federal Disability Insurance Trust Fund, which provides monthly payments to a disabled covered worker, regardless of age.
3. The Federal Hospital Insurance Trust Fund, which provides hospital insurance for those 65 and over, popularly known as Medicare.
4. The Federal Supplementary Medical Insurance Trust Fund, which provides doctor benefits under Medicare.

Social Security first became law in 1935 and went into effect in 1937. At that time only the first $3,000 of wages was covered and the tax was 1 percent, or $30 a year, which provided a benefit from $15 to $84 a month. At first only the workers themselves were covered when they retired; but in 1939 the law was changed to pay the survivors of a deceased worker. In 1954 disability insurance was added, and in 1965 Medicare, which assures hospital and medical protection for those who are 65. Medicare benefits are so important they will be discussed separately in the next chapter.

The amount of earnings covered by Social Security for a forty-one-year period is shown in the following table.

Year	Amount
1937–1950	$3,000
1951–1954	3,600
1955–1958	4,200
1959–1965	4,800

1966–1967	6,600
1968–1971	7,800
1972	9,000
1973	10,800
1974	13,200
1975	14,100
1976	15,300
1977	16,500
1978	17,700

How much can a retired worker expect to receive in the form of a monthly retirement check? This depends upon how much he or she earned during working years, which in turn determined how much he or she paid in taxes. The higher the *average yearly earnings covered by Social Security*, the higher the payment. That's an important statement. It doesn't make any difference how much a worker made in earnings that were more than the amount in the above table. Only those earnings *that were covered by Social Security* are taken into account.

Example. If you earned $30,000 in 1977, only the first $16,500 was considered in computing your average yearly earnings because you paid Social Security taxes only on this amount.

The best way workers can determine the amount of their retirement check is to have the Social Security Administration calculate it for them, based on their record kept at its headquarters in Baltimore, Maryland. A person who will shortly retire should make application for a monthly benefit check ninety days in advance of his or her sixty-fifth birthday. This is important, for if the application is not made in time, it could delay the start of the benefit past age 65. A prospective beneficiary should take to the interview proof of age, his or her Social Security card, and his or her most recent W-2 form. If self-employed, the applicant should take to the interview his or her latest income tax return. And if the prospective beneficiary is married, and both spouses are making application for a retirement benefit, both should bring birth certificates, and they should have with them a copy of their marriage certificate as well.

Anyone who is still working can determine his or her *current* status by asking the Social Security Administration to calculate the amount credited to his or her account in accumulated earnings to date. All Social Security offices have free self-addressed postcards for this purpose. A sample one is reproduced here.

Under the Social Security system a worker is either *currently* or *fully* insured. A fully insured worker, as the name indicates, is entitled to all of the benefits under the program. A currently insured worker entitles only his or her *survivors* to receive benefits. If a worker has ten years of covered earnings, he or she is fully insured for life; if the worker has less than this (but at least six quarters of coverage in the three years preceding his death), he or she is currently insured.

A *fully insured* worker and his or her dependents are entitled to receive the following retirement benefits.

1. A monthly retirement check for the worker for life.
2. A monthly payment for a spouse if 62 or over, or if 65, 50 percent of a spouse's check, even though he or she has never worked under Social Security.
3. A monthly payment to unmarried children who are under 18 years of age (or to age 22, if full-time students). They receive 75 percent of the retired worker's benefit (subject to a family maximum).
4. A monthly payment to a fully disabled worker, regardless of age, which is computed as a retirement benefit.

A *currently insured* worker entitles the worker himself to nothing, only to *survivors benefits* that are paid to his or her qualified dependents. It should be emphasized, however, that *both* fully insured and currently insured workers have earned survivors benefits, paid as follows:

SOCIAL SECURITY MEANS . . .

MONTHLY BENEFITS TO

• Retired workers and their families

• Disabled workers and their families

• The families of deceased workers.

Benefits are based on the average earnings of the worker.

HEALTH INSURANCE BENEFITS FOR

• Men and women 65 and over.

YOU MAY CHECK THE SOCIAL SECURITY ADMINISTRATION'S RECORD OF YOUR EARNINGS.

Just tear off, fill in, stamp, and mail the attached post card.

You will then receive a statement showing the earnings credited to your social security record and a booklet explaining how social security works.

REQUEST FOR

STATEMENT

OF EARNINGS

SOCIAL SECURITY → NUMBER

DATE OF → BIRTH

MONTH	DAY	YEAR

Please send a statement of my Social Security earnings to:

NAME { MISS MRS. MR. _____

STREET & NUMBER _____

CITY & STATE _____ ZIP CODE _____

Print Name and Address In Ink Or Use Typewriter

SIGN YOUR NAME HERE
(DO NOT PRINT) _____

Sign your own name only. Under the law, information in your social security record is confidential and anyone who signs another person's name can be prosecuted.

If you have changed your name from that shown on your social security card, please copy your name below exactly as it appears on your card.

1. To a surviving spouse age 60 or older. If 65, the surviving spouse receives 100 percent of the deceased spouse's benefit.
2. To a spouse at any age, if the spouse is caring for a child under 18 who is entitled to receive a Social Security benefit check.
3. To an unmarried child under 18 (or 22, if a full-time student).
4. To dependent parents who are 62 or older.

The currently insured status is very important to young married couples with children. It is also not appreciated or understood by them. It is of course of no interest to retired people who are already receiving benefit checks. But for those older readers who have young working children or grandchildren, the following vital information should be passed along.

Too often young married couples feel that they are not receiving anything in return for their Social Security taxes but the dubious privilege of helping to support those who are now retired. This isn't true. Only 68 cents out of each Social Security dollar goes toward retirement benefits. Much of the difference provides insurance for the worker's dependents in the event of his death. This is of tremendous value to a young worker with small children if he or she should die at an early age.

Example. Let's assume a Social Security family benefit of $721.80 per month paid to a worker's survivors. The surviving children are 2 and 5 years old, and the deceased spouse was 29. This family benefit of $721.80 per month will be paid until the oldest child is eighteen, which is $8,661 a year. In thirteen years this amounts to over $112,500. All this for a minimum three-year Social Security deduction!

It's true that life insurance for this sum could be purchased from a private insurance company for less money than the amount paid in Social Security taxes—but only if a decreasing term policy is purchased, which many young couples won't buy (preferring a whole life policy with its cash surrender values), and which most life underwriters don't like to sell. The annual premium for a decreasing term policy for a male age 29, which will provide $700 per month for eighteen years, is only $283.90. But how many young married couples have this much insurance? Very few, according to life insurance statistics.

A working woman under Social Security has the same rights as a working man. A married woman when she retires may elect to receive her own monthly check, *or* a check as the spouse of a retired worker, whichever is greater. But she can't receive both.

What if a worker elects not to retire at age 65, but continues to work and earns more than the maximum allowed under the law? The worker will then continue to pay into Social Security and be taxed, but that individual will be given a special credit that will provide a greater retirement benefit. The credit will add 3 percent to his or her eventual benefit check for each year the worker delays retirement from age 65 to 72. This is not much of an increase, but at age 72 it will add 21 percent to a retirement check.

Income that you receive from royalties and patents, if such inventions and compositions were created prior to when you were 65, are not considered earnings and do not affect Social Security payments. Neither does income from investments or savings. You can be a millionaire and still receive a retirement check. Only *earnings from work* affect benefits.

A new service for Social Security recipients was added in 1975. A retired worker can now have a monthly benefit check deposited directly to his or her savings or checking account.

This direct deposit option was first offered on a test basis to Social Security beneficiaries in Georgia and Florida. It's now available nationwide because of the overwhelming favorable response in those two states. All but 20,000 of the 700,000 beneficiaries in Georgia, for example, signed up.

This direct deposit option has several advantages.

1. You don't have to stand in line at your financial institution each month in order to cash your check.
2. If you are out of town, or away from home for a day or two, your money is available in your account instead of sitting in your mailbox.
3. You don't have to worry about losing your check after you receive it, or having it stolen. Every year hundreds of thousands of checks are stolen or lost, some thieves making a living from stolen checks because they know they always arrive on the third of each month.
4. You don't have to apply for another check because it is lost or stolen. It takes several months before a new check is issued. This is because the Social Security Administration is not allowed by law to replace a check. It has to be drawn by the United States Treasury, and they have to wait until your stolen and forged check has been returned to them. After that you will receive a photocopy of the returned check, asking you to state that the signature isn't yours, and to prove that statement by your genuine signature on an application for replacement.

How do you arrange for a direct deposit?

The simplest way is to go to your favorite financial institution with your next monthly check and have them fill out the necessary form for you. Or you may fill it out yourself, if you prefer, for all financial institutions now have a supply on hand. Here is a copy of this form.

No charge is made by a financial institution for this service. Why? Because they have the use of the money until it is withdrawn, which means that they have millions at their disposal for at least a day or two, and some of it for a much longer period of time.

Shut-ins, by this direct deposit method, will no longer have to rely upon others to cash their checks, long lines on the third of each month at banks and savings and loan institutions will be virtually eliminated, and muggers will have to find other victims.

Standard Form 1199
April 1975

PLEASE PRINT

(SEE OTHER SIDE FOR INSTRUCTIONS)

AUTHORIZATION FOR DEPOSIT OF SOCIAL SECURITY PAYMENTS

PAYEE/BENEFICIARY TO COMPLETE ITEMS A THROUGH H

A NAME OF PAYEE(S)

I (we)_____ authorize and request the Social Security Administration to direct the net amount of the below indicated Federal recurring payment for crediting in my (our) account indicated at the financial organization designated below. This authorization is not an assignment of my (our) right to receive payment and revokes all prior payment direction notifications applicable to these payments. I (we) understand that the financial organization designated reserves the right to cancel this agreement by notice to me (us); however, this authorization will remain in effect with SSA until canceled by notice from me (us).

B NAME OF BENEFICIARY(IES) *(The person(s) entitled to receive benefits from the Social Security Administration.)*

C CLAIM NUMBER

SUFFIX

F TYPE AND NUMBER OF DEPOSITOR ACCOUNT TO BE CREDITED

Enter "C" if Checking Account or "S" if Savings Account

DEPOSITOR ACCOUNT NUMBER

D TYPE OF PAYMENT

E PAYEE'S TELEPHONE NO.

G MAILING ADDRESS OF PAYEE *(Number. Street, City. State, and Zip Code)*

H SIGNATURE OF BENEFICIARY(IES) OR AUTHORIZED REPRESENTATIVE PAYEE OR WITNESSES *(see instructions)*

DATE

SIGNATURE

SIGNATURE

FINANCIAL ORGANIZATION TO COMPLETE BELOW THIS LINE

We, the below designated financial organization, hereby agree to receive and deposit sums for the payee(s) named herein, in accordance with 31 CFR Parts 240, 209, and 210. We understand that our account number shown for the payee(s) named herein will be included as additional identification on individual payment credits to his (their) account. We understand that the payee(s) named above has (have) the right to cancel this authorization and we reserve the right to cancel this agreement by notice to the payee(s)

NAME OF FINANCIAL ORGANIZATION

CROCKER NATIONAL BANK

TYPE AND NUMBER OF DEPOSITOR ACCOUNT TO BE CREDITED

Enter "C" if Checking Account or "S" if Savings Account

DEPOSITOR ACCOUNT NUMBER

OFFICE ADDRESS *(Number. Street, City, State, and Zip Code)*

P. O. Box 38099, San Francisco, CA 94138

DEPOSITOR ACCOUNT TITLE

ROUTING NUMBER

| 1 | 2 | 1 | 0 | 1 | 0 | 2 | 0 |

CHECK DIGIT

9

BRANCH DESIGNATION, IF APPLICABLE

TELEPHONE NUMBER

AUTHORIZED SIGNATURE OF FINANCIAL ORGANIZATION OFFICER

TITLE

DATE

NOTARIZATION OPTION: NOTARIZATION SPACE IS PROVIDED IF REQUIRED. THERE IS NO FEDERAL NOTARIZATION REQUIREMENT. The payee(s)/beneficiary(ies) whose signature(s) appears above personally appeared before me, presented satisfactory identification. and, after being duly sworn, acknowledged this to be his (her) (their) freely given act and deed.

Notary Public

Date

Seal

SOCIAL SECURITY COPY

Supplemental Security Income

This is a federal program that pays monthly checks to people in financial need who are 65 or older, and to people in need at any age who are blind or disabled.

Who can qualify?

People who have little or no regular cash income, and who do not own much in the way of property or other things that can be turned into cash, such as stocks, bonds, and jewelry.

Because of these requirements we assume that most of the readers of this book won't qualify, but like survivor benefits for the young, this information should be passed along to friends and relatives. There are millions of people receiving Social Security retirement checks who are not taking advantage of the program.

Currently the basic cash income provided by SSI is $157.70 a month for an individual, and $236.60 per month for a couple. About half of the states supplement the federal program with money of their own. The maximum combined federal-state payment to a retiree in Massachusetts, for instance, is $269, and in California it is $235. California, in addition, will pay the entire cost of an extended care facility (rather than the monthly check), allowing the beneficiary to retain $25 per month for his own personal expenses.

In many states a recipient of an SSI gold check automatically qualifies for Medicaid, which pays for all of a beneficiary's hospital and doctors' bills. (Medicaid will be discussed along with Medicare in the next chapter.)

Supplemental Security Income benefits are not paid out of Social Security taxes. They come out of the general revenue of the United States Treasury. Because of this they are issued in gold color to differentiate them from the well-known green checks issued by the Social Security Administration.

How much in income and assets can a retired person have

and still be eligible to receive Supplemental Security Income? A person who is single can have assets worth up to $1,500 and still receive payments. The amount for a married couple is $2,250. This includes savings accounts, stocks and bonds, jewelry and other valuables. Not everything that is owned counts as an asset. A home with a market value of $25,000 or less ($35,000 in Alaska and Hawaii) doesn't count. Neither does $1,500 in household furnishings and personal effects, nor a car if its value is less than $1,200 (or any value if it is used to get to work or obtain medical care).

SSI is not applied for by the millions of Social Security retired beneficiaries who could obtain it because they don't realize that they can receive both Social Security and Supplemental Security Income at the same time.

How do you figure your net income to find out if you qualify? You must deduct the first $20 of any income you receive, earned or unearned, *including Social Security payments,* plus the next $65 of earned income, plus 50 percent of any earned income over and above that.

Example 1. As a retired individual you are receiving a Social Security check of $130 per month, which is your only source of income. First you deduct the $20, leaving you with $110 of net income. Subtracting this from the maximum SSI federal payment of $157.70 leaves $47.60. This is the amount to which you are entitled under SSI, which added to your Social Security check of $130 gives you an income of $177.60.

Example 2. As a retired individual you receive a minimum Social Security check of $104.40. You also earn $60 a month as a part-time street crossing guard for a school district. You must first deduct $20, then your earned $60, leaving you with a net income of $24.40. Subtracting this from $157.70 gives you a gold check every month of $133.30. Thus your total income would increase from $164.40 to $263.30 ($104.40 + $60 + $133.30).

The federal government is not allowed to impose a lien on

your property as a prerequisite for giving you an SSI benefit. To establish that you qualify, you have to fill out a form listing all of your assets and your income, which is no more information than you would have to supply to obtain a bank loan.

As with all programs there have been mistakes. Many people have been turned down for Supplemental Security Income who are entitled to the benefit. If you are one of them, we suggest that you apply again, this time filing a *written application* at your local Social Security office. You might very well be accepted the second time around.

In some states SSI beneficiaries are entitled to food stamps, in others they are not. The food stamp bonus has been eliminated for SSI recipients in five states—California, Massachusetts, Nevada, New York, and Washington—because these states increased their aid to take the place of it. In most of the other states SSI beneficiaries are eligible for food stamps so they should apply for them.

Conclusion

Practically all adult family members in the nation have a stake in Social Security, either because they are retired or disabled now, or because of eventual benefits as retirees or payments to their survivors.

Prospective beneficiaries, both men and women, should apply for their retirement benefit checks ninety days in advance of their sixty-fifth birthdays. When the application is approved each recipient will be issued a Certificate of Award which will state the monthly amount that will be received.

A currently insured status is of little interest to people who are already retired, but information about family survivor benefits for a currently insured beneficiary's dependents should be passed along to young people. It will make them happier about their admittedly high Social Security taxes. Also information about Supplemental Security Income should be given to those who might qualify for it.

All retired people should take advantage of the direct deposit option for their Social Security checks. This way there is no possibility of a benefit check being lost or stolen.

10

Medicare

Medicare is the health insurance portion of Social Security. It is an exceptionally important part when you consider that hospital costs alone amount to hundreds of dollars a day. A confinement of a few weeks can amount to thousands. Does hospital insurance under Medicare pay this much? Indeed it does!

Shown is a copy of a hospital bill presented to Tom Hogan (not his real name), a Medicare patient, for a continuous confinement from January 8, 1978 to March 15, 1978, a total of sixty-six days. The hospital charges were $16,051.52, which would be a financial catastrophe for most retired people if they were required to pay this sum themselves.

As can be seen from the bill, the patient was charged only $472.42. Medicare paid the balance.

One hundred and forty-four dollars was for the hospital insurance deductible which every Medicare patient has to pay for each benefit period. Forty-eight dollars and forty-five cents was for drugs that the patient took home with him, and $216 was the cost for six days of co-insurance at $36.00 a day. (This was because he was in the hospital longer than 60 days.) If Tom Hogan's hospital stay had been for just sixty days, he wouldn't have owed this additional $216 because

DATE: 3/28/78

STANFORD UNIVERSITY MEDICAL CENTER
STANFORD, CALIFORNIA 94305
REMIT TO: P.O. BOX 38140, SAN FRANCISCO, CALIFORNIA 94138

STATEMENT OF MEDICARE ACCOUNT

PATIENT:

BILL TO:

3/28/78

Medicare has paid its share on your bill. This statement is for the amount payable directly by you.

TO INSURE RECEIVING PROPER CREDIT PLEASE WRITE ABOVE ACCOUNT NUMBER ON YOUR CHECK AND RETURN WITH THIS STUB

ACCOUNT NUMBER	DATE ADMITTED	DATE DISCHARGED	TOTAL CHARGES	ROOM DIFFERENCE	ESTIMATED COVERAGE MEDICARE PLAN "A"
	1/8/78	1/15/78	$ 16,051.52	$	

YOUR PORTION TO PAY ON PLAN "A"

DEDUCTIBLE	BLOOD DEDUCTIBLE	PERSONAL SERVICES	OTHER	TOTAL
$ 144.00	+ $	+ $ 48.45	coinsurance + $ 216.00	= $ 408.45
		Take—home drugs		

LESS PAYMENTS TO DATE = $

PLAN "A" PART BAL. DUE = $ 408.45

TOTAL CHARGES PLAN "B" $ 831.60 Prof. fees for xrays, EKG

Medicare paid 767.63 CR

CPS PAYMENT PLAN "B" $

YOUR PORTION TO PAY PLAN "B"
Plan "B" will be billed to you when we receive notification of payment from Blue Shield (C.P.S.).

EXCLUDES X-RAY + PLAN "B" PART LIABILITY $ 63.97
+ EKG FEES

TOTAL BALANCE DUE $ 472.42

IF YOU HAVE ANY QUESTIONS PLEASE CALL
497-6061
STANFORD UNIVERSITY HOSPITAL
STANFORD, CALIFORNIA 94305

01-951 (Rev. 7/74)

Medicare doesn't charge the patient a per diem expense for the first two months.[1]

In addition, there was another charge included in the $472.42 of $63.97. This was for doctors' charges for X-ray and EKG fees, *performed in the hospital,* which were over and above the "reasonable charges" allowed by Medicare, which will be explained later.

The main point for retired people which should give them considerable peace of mind is that (because of Medicare) the patient had to pay only $472.42 out of a total hospital bill of $16,051.52! A truly remarkable Social Security benefit.

Medicare is for all people, both men and women, who are 65 and older. Everyone at age 65 automatically qualifies, *retired or not.* Therefore, even though a person doesn't intend to retire and take a retirement check, that individual should still make application for Medicare ninety days before his or her 65th birthday.

When approved, applicants will be issued a health insurance card by the Social Security Administration which will show their name, their claim number (which is the holder's Social Security number followed by a letter), and the dates their hospital insurance and medical insurance became effective. This date is almost always the first day of the month in which the applicant became 65 years old.

Medicare has two parts. One part is called hospital insurance (referred to as Part A). The other part is called medical insurance, which helps pay doctors' bills (referred to as Part B).

Medicare payments are handled by private insurance organizations that are under contract with the United States government. Those organizations that handle claims submitted by hospitals and skilled nursing facilities are called intermediaries;

1. This is the amount of the hospital insurance deductible, and the cost of co-insurance, in 1978. These amounts will probably increase in future years. But even if they do, they will still be only a small fraction of hospital costs.

those that handle claims for doctors' services are called carriers. We will consider the two parts of Medicare separately.

Medicare hospital insurance, Part A

Medicare will pay for sixty days of hospital care in each benefit period. During that time Medicare will pay for all covered services. After that the patient is charged a per diem expense, explained later.

A benefit period starts the first time you enter a hospital after your insurance is in effect. Once you have been released from the hospital, *and are out for sixty days in a row*, a new benefit period begins the next time you enter a hospital, even though you are being confined for the same sickness or injury. There is no limit to the number of benefit periods you may have.

Medicare's hospital insurance becomes effective only if all four of the following conditions are met.

1. A doctor must have prescribed inpatient hospital care for treatment of an illness or injury.
2. The patient requires the kind of care that only a hospital can provide.
3. The hospital is a participant in the Medicare program (a prerequisite that is almost automatic).
4. The Utilization Review Committee of the hospital does not disapprove the patient's stay. (This is to prevent a beneficiary from remaining in the hospital longer than is medically necessary, just because Medicare is paying the cost.)

If your stay in a hospital is covered by Medicare, you are responsible for the first $144.00 *in each benefit period.* If you are in the hospital twice in one year, for instance, and each stay by definition is for a benefit period, you will have to pay the $144.00 each time. This is called the hospital insurance deductible. Medicare will pay for *all other covered services* up to sixty days, if your medical condition requires that you stay in the hospital that long, as we have seen from Tom Hogan's bill.

What hospital charges are covered? Medicare's hospital insurance will pay for the following.

1. A semi-private room (two to four beds in a room).
2. All meals, including special diets.
3. Regular nursing services.
4. Intensive care unit costs.
5. Drugs furnished by the hospital *during your stay.* (As we have seen from the above bill, drugs that are taken home by the patient are not included. As a consequence the patient shouldn't take them home. They can probably be purchased cheaper at an outside drugstore.)
6. Laboratory tests that are included in your hospital bill.
7. X-rays and other radiology services, including radiation therapy, *billed by the hospital.*
8. Medical supplies, such as casts, surgical dressings, and splints.
9. Use of appliances, such as a wheelchair.
10. Operating and recovery room costs.
11. Rehabilitation services, such as physical therapy, occupational therapy, and speech pathology services.

Medicare's hospital insurance *cannot* pay for the following services.

1. Personal convenience items, such as a telephone or a television set in your room *if you have to request them.* (Most hospital rooms come equipped with them automatically.)
2. Private duty nurses.
3. Any extra charge for a private room.
4. The first three pints of blood you receive in any benefit period (unless replaced).
5. Any doctors' charges *which are included in the hospital bill* that are in excess of the reasonable charge set by the intermediary organization.

What happens if your stay in the hospital is for a period that is longer than sixty days?

Medicare continues to pay for all covered services from the sixty-first through the ninetieth day, *except for $36 a day.* This

per diem expense is called co-insurance, because the patient
has to pay part of the cost.

If your stay in the hospital is for longer than ninety days, all
Medicare coverage stops, unless you use your sixty hospital reserve days. If you elect to use them, Medicare will now pay for
all covered services for another sixty days, but your co-insurance costs will go up from $36 a day to $72 a day. These days
are lifetime reserve days—once you use any of them you never
get them back. Reserve days are not renewable like the other
ninety hospital days in each benefit period.

Example. Let's assume that Tom Hogan, who was billed for
a stay of 66 days in the above example, had to remain in the
hospital for a total of 120 days, and at the end of the 90th day
he elected to invade his lifetime reserve days. His co-insurance
costs would have been billed as follows:

1. 30 days at $36 a day, or		$1,080
2. 30 days at $72 a day, or		$2,160
	Total	$3,240

In addition, his lifetime reserve days would have been permanently reduced from 60 to 30 days.

Caution. If your stay in the hospital is for more than ninety
days, and you don't want to invade your lifetime reserve days,
you have to notify the hospital in writing of your decision,
otherwise they will use them automatically. You wouldn't want
to use them, for example, if you had a private hospitalization
insurance policy that would take care of the bill.

So patients will understand that the Medicare Program of
Social Security does not cover a hospital bill in full, and to avoid
a misunderstanding at a later date, many hospitals give a letter
to their Medicare patients shortly after they are admitted, and
ask them to sign it.

A copy of such a Notice to Medicare Patients is reproduced
here. It is a good review of the hospital portion of the health
insurance program.

STANFORD UNIVERSITY MEDICAL CENTER

STANFORD, CALIFORNIA 94305

MEDICAL CENTER FINANCE
Patient Services

Admitting/Patient Representatives
(415) 497-6221

Outpatient Registration
(415) 497-5442

Cashiering
(415) 497-5213

NOTICE TO MEDICARE PATIENTS

As a Medicare patient, you should be aware of the possibility that the Medicare Program may not cover your hospital bill. You will be responsible for any unpaid balance.

Stanford University Hospital is an acute care hospital and as such must follow Medicare rules as to the medical need for the services and facilities required for acute hospital care. Your hospital stay is reviewed from admission and throughout your stay by physicians on the Stanford Medical Staff. The purpose of this review is to assure that your care meets the Medicare guidelines for acute hospitalization.

If your care does not meet the Medicare guidelines, you and your doctor will be notified by letter. At that time, your Patient Representative will request a deposit to cover the balance of your hospital stay.

In order to avoid any misunderstanding at a later date, you and your doctor should be aware at the time of your admission that:

(A) As with any other hospital health insurance, Medicare makes the final decision to pay. Should Medicare determine that part of or all of your stay is not covered, you will receive a bill from the hospital for the non-covered portion. According to Medicare regulations, inpatient stays are covered only if they are medically necessary and if the care is reasonable for an acute hospital setting.

(B) If you have not been in a medical facility such as a Hospital or Nursing Home which was covered by Medicare for 60 days prior to this admission you:

(1) Are responsible for the first $144.00 of the hospital bill.

(2) Are responsible for the first three pints, should you need blood.

(3) Will be charged $36.00 per day from the 61st to the 90th day, should you be hospitalized for more than 60 days.

After 90 days of hospitalization:

(1) You will be responsible for the whole bill from the 91st day on, unless you elect to use your Lifetime Reserve days.

(2) Should you use your Lifetime Reserve days you will be charged $72.00 per day from the 91st day to the 150th day.

(3) Should you still be hospitalized after the 150th day, you will be personally responsible for the balance of your stay.

(C) You should know that when you are ready to be discharged and are awaiting post-hospital arrangements such as a nursing home or help at home, Medicare will not cover that portion of your stay at Stanford.

(D) If you have been hospitalized during the 60 days prior to this admission, inform your Patient Representative and she will give you a complete explanation of your benefits.

If you receive a letter stating that a portion of your hospital stay will not be covered by Medicare, you may appeal this decision by contacting the Santa Clara Valley Professional Standards Review Organization at (408) 294-2120 within two (2) months of your hospitalization.

Received _____

Date _____

01-520 (Rev. 12/77)   WHITE — PATIENT   YELLOW   ACCOUNT FILE

After paying a claim submitted by the hospital, the intermediary insurance company will send the patient a benefits record, which is clearly marked THIS IS NOT A BILL. This will show the services rendered, and which ones Medicare paid, and which they didn't pay. A filled-in copy of the three different statements that were sent to Tom Hogan for his sixty-six-day stay in the hospital is shown here.

The first copy shows that Stanford University Hospital of Palo Alto, California billed the intermediary, Blue Cross of Northern California, for an inpatient hospital stay from 1–08–78 through 2–03–78 and that Medicare paid for all covered services for twenty-seven hospital days, except for the $144.00 hospital insurance deductible.

The second copy shows that the inpatient hospital stay was for a period from 2–04–78 through 3–06–78 and that Medicare paid for all covered services with no exceptions for thirty-one days. There were no exceptions because, by this time, Tom Hogan had paid his $144.00 insurance deductible directly to the hospital.

The third copy shows that benefits were paid for an inpatient hospital stay from 3–07–78 through 3–15–78 and that Medicare paid for all covered services, except for $216.00. The period covered was for eight days, two of which were within the fully covered sixty-day period, and six that went beyond that time. These days had to be paid for by Tom Hogan at the co-insurance rate of $36 a day—total, $216 (6 × $36).

Current Rates for Medicare

According to the booklet entitled *Your Medicare Handbook* published by the Social Security Administration, Department of Health, Education and Welfare, the hospital insurance part of Medicare not only covers hospital costs, but will also pay for inpatient care in a skilled nursing facility, more commonly called a nursing home.

FORM **SSA-1533** (6-74)

U.S. DEPARTMENT OF HEALTH, EDUCATION, AND WELFARE / SOCIAL SECURITY ADMINISTRATION

MEDICARE HOSPITAL EXTENDED CARE AND HOME HEALTH BENEFITS RECORD

093550565C86A506

DATE: 4-01-78

HEALTH INSURANCE CLAIM NUMBER

Always use this number
when writing about your claim.

THIS IS NOT A BILL. This notice is to give you a record of the Medicare benefits you used during the period shown in Item 1. For important additional information please see the other side of this form.

1 OUR RECORDS SHOW THAT YOU RECEIVED THESE SERVICES

Type of Services	Services Were Provided By	Date
INPATIENT HOSPITAL	STANFORD UNIVERSITY HOSP 300 PASTEUR DR PALO ALTO CALIFORNIA 94304	01-08-78 THRU 02-03-78

2 MEDICARE HAS PAID FOR ALL COVERED SERVICES EXCEPT

$144.00 FOR THE INPATIENT DEDUCTIBLE.

IF YOU HAVE ANY QUESTIONS
ABOUT THIS RECORD
PLEASE GET IN TOUCH WITH:

BLUE CROSS OF NORTHERN CALIFORNIA
1950 FRANKLIN ST
OAKLAND CALIFORNIA 94659

3 OUR RECORDS SHOW THE FOLLOWING BENEFITS WERE USED THIS TIME

Inpatient Hospital Days	Lifetime Reserve Days	Extended Care Days	Home Health Visits Part A	Home Health Visits Part B
27				

FORM **SSA-1533** (6-74)

U.S. DEPARTMENT OF HEALTH, EDUCATION, AND WELFARE / SOCIAL SECURITY ADMINISTRATION

MEDICARE HOSPITAL EXTENDED CARE AND HOME HEALTH BENEFITS RECORD

B 39750995121A390

DATE: **5-02-78**

HEALTH INSURANCE CLAiM NUMBER

Always use this number
when writing about your claim.

THIS IS NOT A BILL. This notice is to give you a record of the Medicare benefits you used during the period shown in Item 1. For important additional information please see the other side of this form.

1   OUR RECORDS SHOW THAT YOU RECEIVED THESE SERVICES

Type of Services	Services Were Provided By	Date
INPATIENT HOSPITAL	STANFORD UNIVERSITY HOSP 300 PASTEUR DR PALO ALTO CALIFORNIA 94304	02-04-78 THRU 03-06-78

2   MEDICARE HAS PAID FOR ALL COVERED SERVICES EXCEPT

NO EXCEPTIONS.

IF YOU HAVE ANY QUESTIONS
ABOUT THIS RECORD
PLEASE GET IN TOUCH WITH:

BLUE CROSS OF NORTHERN CALIFORNIA
1950 FRANKLIN ST
OAKLAND CALIFORNIA 94659

3   OUR RECORDS SHOW THE FOLLOWING BENEFITS WERE USED THIS TIME

Inpatient Hospital Days	Lifetime Reserve Days	Extended Care Days	Home Health Visits Part A	Home Health Visits Part B
31				

FORM **SSA-1533** (6-74)

U.S. DEPARTMENT OF HEALTH, EDUCATION, AND WELFARE / SOCIAL SECURITY ADMINISTRATION

MEDICARE HOSPITAL EXTENDED CARE AND HOME HEALTH
BENEFITS RECORD

839750995121A390   DATE: 5-02-78

[   ]

[   ]

THIS IS   Me
in Item   oth

[1] OUR RECORDS SHOW THAT YOU RECEIVED THESE SERVICES

Type of Services	Services Were Provided By	Date
INPATIENT HOSPITAL	STANFORD UNIVERSITY HOSP 300 PASTEUR DR PALO ALTO CALIFORNIA 94304	03-07-78 THRU 03-15-78

[2] MEDICARE HAS PAID FOR ALL COVERED SERVICES EXCEPT

$ 216 .00 FOR   6   DAYS OF HOSPITAL CARE AFTER FIRST 60 DAYS.

IF YOU HAVE ANY QUESTIONS
ABOUT THIS RECORD   BLUE CRCSS OF NORTHERN CALIFORNIA
PLEASE GET IN TOUCH WITH: 1950 FRANKLIN ST
                             OAKLAND CALIFCRNIA 94659

[3] OUR RECORDS SHOW THE FOLLOWING BENEFITS WERE USED THIS TIME

Inpatient Hospital Days	Lifetime Reserve Days	Extended Care Days	Home Health Visits Part A	Home Health Visits Part B
8				

But don't you believe it.

This is a myth as far as the vast majority of patients are concerned. If you use such a facility, you had better be prepared to pay the bill yourself, with no help from Medicare.

Why?

Because Medicare will not pay for custodial care.

Care is considered custodial when it is primarily for the purpose of meeting personal needs which could be provided by persons without professional skills or training. For example, help in walking, getting in and out of bed, bathing, dressing, eating, and taking medicine. Most patients in a nursing home need help in most or all of these areas, but they don't need *skilled nursing or skilled rehabilitation services on a daily basis.* Yet it is only for this kind of care that Medicare's hospital insurance will make payment. If you need this kind of skilled nursing care on a daily basis, you are pretty sick and you had better be in a hospital, not a nursing home. Most people are. In addition, many nursing homes are so badly managed that doctors don't like to send a patient to one if he or she needs more than custodial care.

Therefore a person with hospital insurance under Medicare shouldn't count on any help from Part A of the health insurance program for bills incurred in a nursing home.

A skilled nursing facility is perfectly willing to send in a bill for payment to the intermediary organization in its area, but too frequently the claim for payment is denied. If denied, the beneficiary will receive the Medicare Notice shown here which notifies the applicant that "we are unable to make payment" for any one or several of the reasons stated on the form.

As this Medicare Notice demonstrates, a patient in a skilled nursing facility has to meet four conditions in order to qualify for Medicare payments.

MEDICARE NOTICE

	DATE

52280
Mutual of Omaha Insurance Company
Medicare Department
P.O. Box 456, Downtown Station
Omaha, Nebraska 68101

ALWAYS USE THIS
NUMBER WHEN
WRITING ABOUT
YOUR CLAIM ➝

DATE
April 28, 1975
YOUR HEALTH INSURANCE NUMBER

NAME AND ADDRESS OF PROVIDER

.ienlo Park Ext. Care Hospital
1275 Crane St.
ilenlo Park, CA.

PROVIDER NUMBER: 05-6221
TYPE OF SERVICE PROVIDED

☐ Hospital   ☐ Home Health
☒ Extended Care   ☐ Other
PART: **A**
NOTICE COVERS PERIOD

FROM   XXXX 3-25-75
Admission Date

This concerns the services you received from the facility shown above. We are unable to make payment for part or all of these services under Medicare health insurance for the following reason:

SNF 1 ☐ The extended care benefit is payable only for patients who need skilled nursing care on a continuing basis. Skilled nursing care is that type of service which must be performed by or under the direct supervision of a trained nurse to assure the safety of the patient and to achieve the medically desired result.

Since the services you required could have been safely and effectively rendered by a nonmedical person, the service may not be considered a skilled nursing service regardless of who actually performs or supervises the services. Therefore, no Medicare Part A payment can be made for your extended care facility stay.

SNF 2 ☒ Extended care services are covered only if a person has previously had a medically necessary inpatient stay in a qualified hospital. This stay must have been for a period of at least three consecutive days not counting the day of discharge from the hospital. The records show that you do not meet this requirement. Therefore, no Medicare Part A benefits can be paid for your extended care facility stay.

SNF 3 ☒ Extended care services can be paid for by Medicare only if the person required a covered level of care and was admitted timely to the skilled nursing facility. For an admission to be timely it must take place:

within 14 days after a qualifying hospital stay,

within 28 days if a bed was not available in the area in which he resides, providing a covered level of care was required within 14 days of discharge from the hospital and continued to be required through the time he was admitted to the skilled nursing facility, or

within such time as it would be medically appropriate to begin an active course of treatment where an individual's condition is such that skilled nursing facility care would not be medically appropriate within 14 days after discharge from a hospital.

The records show you do not meet any of these requirements. Therefore, no Medicare Part A benefits can be paid for your skilled nursing facility stay.

SNF 5 ☐ Your doctor could **not** medically certify your need for extended care.

If you have a question concerning this determination, you should first get a detailed explanation from the social security office. If you still believe that the determination is not correct, you may request a reconsideration for hospital insurance (or a review for medical insurance). You must file this reconsideration (or review) within 6 months from the date of this notice. You may make the request through your social security office.

FORM **SSA-1954** (9-71)   COPY - SSA-26 - PO - 24

1. The patient must have been in a hospital for at least three consecutive days before he or she was transferred to the skilled nursing facility.
2. The patient must have been transferred because he or she required care for a condition for which that individual was treated in the hospital.
3. The patient was admitted to the hospital within a short time, usually within the previous fourteen days.
4. A doctor certifies that the patient needs, and will actually receive, skilled nursing or skilled rehabilitation services on a daily basis.

As we have said the average patient is disqualified because of condition four—for all that he or she needs is custodial care.

Medicare medical insurance, Part B

This portion of the health insurance program under Social Security helps pay doctors' bills.

The patient has to pay the first $60, plus 20 percent. Medicare pays the balance, provided the doctor's charges are "reasonable." The insurance carrier for the area involved determines whether or not the submitted charges are reasonable.

The first $60 in covered expenses that the beneficiary is required to pay is called the medical deductible. It has to be paid *only once in a year*. In this respect it is different from the hospital insurance deductible of $144, which has to be paid for each and every benefit period.

Hospital insurance under Medicare is free. Medical insurance is not. It costs the beneficiary a premium of $7.70 per month which, if he or she is receiving a retirement check, is automatically deducted from it. If the person is not receiving a retirement check, but is still under Medicare, that individual will receive a bill each quarter for $23.10. If this isn't paid, the beneficiary's health insurance is canceled. If this happens, he or she may re-enroll only once.

A person has the right to refuse to take Part B of Medicare's health insurance program. If it's refused, it is usually because the beneficiary doesn't want to pay the premium. This is a serious mistake. Part B should never be turned down; the premium is very reasonable. Also the $7.70 charge is only a small part of the total premium; 72 percent of the cost is paid out of the general revenue of the United States Treasury.

If you elected not to take the medical insurance portion of your Social Security health insurance program when you became 65, you can sign up for it later in the first three months of any year. Generally speaking, for each year that you delay in taking it, the premium increases by 10 percent. When you sign up later, your protection won't start until July 1 of that year.

To demonstrate exactly how valuable Part B medical insurance is for a beneficiary consider the following example.

Henry Gorman became seriously ill with a series of heart attacks, plus emphysema and a kidney ailment. He was under treatment by several doctors for many months. His final total bill for his doctors was $6,000. Of this he had to pay the $60 medical deductible, plus 20 percent, or $1,260 ($60 plus $1,200). Medicare paid the balance. This amounted to $4,740, a benefit that was paid because Henry Gorman was covered by Part B of Medicare at a premium cost of only $7.70 per month!

How are Medicare claims paid under both Part A and Part B?

For most people this is the most confusing part of the health insurance program. Again let's consider each part separately.

Claims for hospital insurance, Part A

This is relatively simple compared to Part B.

When entering the hospital, all you have to do is show your health insurance card. The admission clerk will note down your name and Social Security number and ask you for your home address and telephone number. And that's it. You don't have to pay the $144 insurance deductible at that time, nor for that matter when you are later discharged from the hospital. You pay nothing, nor do you have to submit a claim to the intermediary insurance company. The hospital will do this for you.

After the hospital has been paid by the intermediary assigned to your area, they will mail you a statement of how much you owe. This will always include the $144 insurance deductible. If your stay in the hospital is for less than sixty days (which is normal), there will be no co-insurance charge, nor in-hospital doctors' services (if they were reasonable). In other words, for the usual hospital stay you will owe just the $144. This is why the admission office is not concerned about collecting any money. They know that the hospital will be paid.

Claims for medical insurance, Part B

This is the confusing part. It can also be a financial hardship for you, depending upon how the claim is handled. This is because the bill for doctors' services may be submitted to the carrier in two different ways.

By either method, a Request for Medicare Payment form must be filled out and submitted to the carrier in order for Medicare to pay for the services of doctors and suppliers who are covered by medical insurance. A copy of this form is shown here. All Social Security offices and most doctors' offices have copies, and instructions on how to fill out the form are on the reverse side.

The first way to submit a claim under Part B is for the doctor to agree to accept an assignment of his or her bill to Medicare, in which event (like the hospital) the doctor submits the claim. You complete and sign Part I of the form, which is a very simple procedure for basically it's just your name, address, and Social Security number, and the doctor completes Part II and sends it in. In the majority of cases, however, a doctor will not accept an assignment of his or her bill to Medicare.

Why not?

Because too often the doctor's charges are in excess of what the carrier in the area calls "reasonable." If he submits the claim, the physician can receive only the "reasonable" charge. If you submit it, you have to pay the excess.

REQUEST FOR MEDICARE PAYMENT

MEDICAL INSURANCE BENEFITS—SOCIAL SECURITY ACT (See Instructions on Back—Type or Print Information)

Form Approved
OMB No.
72–RO730

NOTICE—Anyone who misrepresents or falsifies essential information requested by this form may upon conviction be subject to fine and imprisonment under Federal Law.

PART I—PATIENT TO FILL IN ITEMS 1 THROUGH 6 ONLY

When completed, send this form to:

Blue Shield of California
P.O. Box 7968 Rincon Annex
San Francisco, California 94120

Copy from
YOUR OWN
HEALTH
INSURANCE
CARD
(See example
on back)

1 Name of patient (First name, Middle initial, Last name)

2 Health insurance claim number (Include all letters)

☐ Male   ☐ Female

3 Patient's mailing address   City, State, ZIP code   Telephone Number

4 Describe the illness or injury for which you received treatment (Always fill in this item if your doctor does not complete Part II below)

Was your illness or injury connected with your employment?
☐ Yes   ☐ No

5 If you have other health insurance or if your State medical assistance agency will pay part of your medical expenses and you want information about this claim released to the insurance company or State agency upon its request, give the following information.

Insuring organization or State agency name and address

Policy No.

Medi-cal Identification No.

6 I authorize any holder of medical or other information about me to release to the Social Security Administration or its intermediaries or carriers any information needed for this or a related Medicare claim. I permit a copy of this authorization to be used in place of the original, and request payment of medical insurance benefits either to myself or to the party who accepts assignment below.

Signature of patient (See instructions on reverse where patient is unable to sign)

SIGN HERE ▶

Date signed

PART II—PHYSICIAN OR SUPPLIER TO FILL IN 7 THROUGH 14

7 A. Date of each service	B. Place of service (*See Codes below)	C. Code surgical or medical procedures and other services or supplies furnished for each date given	D. Nature of illness or injury requiring services or supplies	E. Charges (If related to unusual circumstances explain in 7C)	Leave Blank
		Code		$	

8 Name and address of physician or supplier (Number and street, city, State, ZIP code)

Telephone No.

Physician or supplier code

9 Total charges $

10 Amount paid $

11 Any unpaid balance due $

12 Assignment of patient's bill
▶ ☐ I accept assignment (See reverse) ☐ I do not accept assignment.

13 Show name and address of facility where services were performed (If other than home or office visits)

14 Signature of physician or supplier (A physician's signature certifies that physician's services were personally rendered by him or under his personal direction)

▶

Date signed

*O—Doctor's Office
IL—Independent Laboratory

H—Patient's Home (If portable X-ray services, identify the supplier)
IH—Inpatient Hospital

ECF—Extended Care Facility
OH—Outpatient Hospital

OL—Other Locations
NH—Nursing Home

FORM SSA-1490D (CA) (8-72)

Department of Health, Education, and Welfare
Social Security Administration

HOW TO FILL OUT YOUR MEDICARE FORM

There are two ways that Medicare can help pay your doctor bills

One way is for Medicare to pay your doctor.—If you and your doctor agree, Medicare will pay him directly. This is the assignment method. You do not submit any claim; the doctor does. All you do is fill out Part I of this form and leave it with your doctor. Under this method the doctor agrees to accept the charge determination of the Medicare carrier as the full charge; you are responsible for the deductible and coinsurance. Please read Your Medicare Handbook to help you understand about the deductible and coinsurance. (Because Medicare has special payment arrangements with group practice prepayment plans these plans handle all claims for covered services they furnish to their members.)

The other way is for Medicare to pay you.—Medicare can also pay you directly—before or after you have paid your doctor. If you submit the claim yourself, fill out Part I and ask your doctor to fill out Part II. If you have an itemized bill from him, you may submit it rather than have him complete Part II. (This form, with Part I completed by you, may be used to send in several itemized bills from different doctors and suppliers.) Bills should show who furnished the services, **the patient's name and number,** dates of services, where the services were furnished, a description of the services, and charges for each separate service. It is helpful if the diagnosis is also shown. Then mail itemized bills and this form to the address shown in the upper left-hand corner. If no address is shown there, use the address listed in Your Medicare Handbook—or get advice from any social security office.

SOME THINGS TO NOTE IN FILLING OUT PART I
(Your doctor will fill out Part II.)

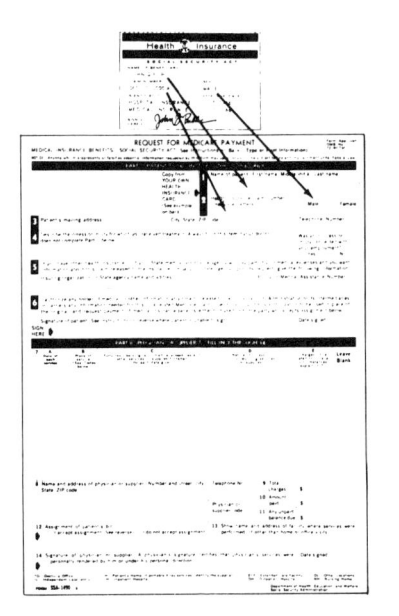

1 & 2 Copy the name and number and indicate your sex exactly as shown on your health insurance card. Include the letters at the end of the number.

3 Enter your mailing address and telephone number, if any.

4 Describe your illness or injury. Be sure to check one of the two boxes.

5 If you have other health insurance or expect a welfare agency to pay part of the expenses, complete item 5.

6 Be sure to sign your name. If you cannot write your name, sign by mark (X), and have a witness sign his name and enter his address on this line.

If the claim is filed for the patient by another person he should enter the patient's name and write "By," sign his own name and address in this space, show his relationship to the patient, and why the patient cannot sign. (If the patient has died, the survivor should contact any social security office for information on what to do.)

IMPORTANT NOTES FOR PHYSICIANS AND SUPPLIERS

Item 12: In assigned cases the patient is responsible only for the deductible, coinsurance, and non-covered services. Coinsurance and the deductible are based upon the charge determination of the carrier if this is less than the charge submitted.

This form may also be used by a supplier, or by the patient to claim reimbursement for charges by a supplier for services such as the use of an ambulance or medical appliances.

If the physician or supplier does not want Part II information released to the organization named in item 5, he should write "No further release" in item 7C following the description of services.

☆U.S.GPO-1975-0-584-980/4

The second way a medical insurance claim is submitted is for you to mail in the request for payment because the doctor refuses to do so. Payment by the Medicare carrier is now made directly to you, and you pay the doctor.

Again you must complete Part I of the Request for Medicare Payment. You then ask the doctor to complete Part II, *or* ask the doctor's nurse to give you an itemized bill to send in with the form. The latter method is preferable, for then you only have to deal with the nurse or the billing office. If you wait for the doctor to fill out Part II you might wait for several weeks —for many doctors are lax in such matters, and too busy besides that.

The doctor's itemized bill that you attach to the completed Request for Medicare Payment form *must* show the following:

1. The date you received the services
2. The place where you received them
3. A description of the treatment
4. The nature of your illness or injury (the doctor's diagnosis, in other words)
5. The charge for each service
6. Your name *and* your health insurance claim number, *including* the letter at the end of the number

If the bill doesn't include all of this information, your payment will be delayed.

If you are sending in several itemized bills, you may submit any number of them with a single Request for Medicare Payment. It doesn't make any difference whether all the bills are from one doctor or supplier, or from different people who gave you services.

Before any payment can be made, however, your record must show that you have paid that year's medical deductible of $60. Therefore as soon as your *paid* bills amount to this much, send them in with the request form. All future bills should be mailed to the carrier as soon as you get them, so that the

Medicare payment can be made to you promptly. A list of the carriers for all fifty states, with their addresses, is in Appendix 2.

This payment-to-you method of submitting a claim for doctors' bills under Part B of the health insurance program of Medicare is a lot of work for retired people, and beyond the physical and/or mental capacity of many who are 65 and still counting. This method should not be used if at all possible.

Those who are under the Social Security's health insurance program should not use the services of a doctor who refuses to accept an assignment of his bill to Medicare. This is not, however, as flat a statement as it appears to be. If a retired person trusts a certain doctor (or doesn't mind paying an extra charge), it is up to the patient which method of payment is chosen. But for most retired people the statement still holds. Don't use the services of a doctor who refuses to accept an assignment of his or her bill to Medicare.

Charles Beckwith was seriously ill, and in and out of a hospital for months. At one time he had ten doctors treating him simultaneously, trying to keep him alive. They succeeded, but his doctors' bills were staggering. They totaled $5,254.83. After recovering sufficiently to be up and around at home, but still too weak to handle his own affairs, he asked a friend of his to go to the cashier's office of the clinic and find out what could be done about the bill. He was under Medicare, and gave his friend his health insurance card.

The young female clerk at the window of the cashier's office stated flatly that it was against the policy of the clinic to accept an assignment to Medicare.

Fortunately Charles Beckwith's friend understood the two payment methods.

"Why won't the clinic accept an assignment?" he asked.

"Like I told you. It's against the clinic's policy."

"I'm sorry," said the friend patiently. "That answer isn't good enough."

"Then you'll have to ask the patient to come in and talk to us about it personally."

"That he can't do. He's not well enough."

"Then you'll have to submit a claim for him."

"I'm not willing to do that."

"Well," replied the clerk, somewhat nonplussed, "you'll have to ask his doctor about it."

"He has ten doctors. Which one would you suggest that I see?"

"I don't know."

"Let's put it this way, miss," said the friend. "This is a very large bill. You tell me that the clinic won't submit a request for Medicare payment, and I'm not going to either. This way nobody will get paid. I would say it would be better for the clinic to accept the reasonable charges allowed by Medicare than to get nothing."

At this point the clerk was completely at a loss. "All right," she said. "I'll have to ask the boss."

After quite a while she returned all smiles. "We'll accept an assignment," she said.

Mr. Beckwith's friend was mildly surprised. He had expected to be confronted with the manager and another argument.

"What do I have to do?"

"Just have Mr. Beckwith sign Part 1 of this Request for Medicare Payment and return the form to me."

"Thank you, miss."

And that was the end of it. Charles Beckwith only had to pay the $60 medical deductible charge and the 20 percent co-insurance.

A Medicare patient should know not only what services and supplies are covered by medical insurance, Part B, but should also know those that are not. The following items are *not* covered.

Acupuncture

Christian Science practitioners' services

Custodial care

Drugs and medicines you buy yourself, with or without a doctor's prescription

Eyeglasses, and eye examinations for prescribing, fitting, or changing eyeglasses

Hearing aids, and hearing examinations for prescribing, fitting, or changing hearing aids

Homemaker services

Injections that can be self-administered, such as insulin

Meals delivered to your home

Nursing care on a full-time basis in your home

Services which are not reasonable and necessary

Physical examinations that are routine and tests directly related to such examinations

Private duty nurses

Services performed by immediate relatives or members of your household

Services paid by workmen's compensation

Naturopath's services

The following services *can* be covered by Medicare, Part B, *but only under the conditions stated.*

Chiropractic services

The only treatment that can be covered is manual manipulation of the spine to correct a subluxation that can be demonstrated by X-ray. A subluxation is loss of stability of a joint due to injury causing stretching of the ligaments. The surfaces of the bones are no longer held closely together. Many times, on the first visit to a chiropractor, X-rays are necessary. This does not mean that the expense is automatically covered by Medicare. There has to be a subluxation involved.

Dental care

Only if it involves surgery of the jaw or related structures, or setting fractures of the jaw or facial bones

Foot care that is routine

Only if you have a medical condition affecting the lower limbs

(such as severe diabetes) that requires that such care be administered by a podiatrist or a doctor

Immunizations
Unless required because of an injury, or because of immediate risk
of infection

Orthopedic shoes
Unless part of a leg brace

Private room
Unless you need it for medical reasons

During a hospital stay covered by hospital insurance, a Medicare patient may also receive services *by doctors* who are responsible for radiology and pathology services provided by the
hospital. Charges for these services (even though billed by the
hospital) are paid for by medical insurance, Part B, without
the beneficiary having to meet the $60 medical deductible. For
these services medical insurance pays 100 percent of the reasonable charges, not just the usual 80 percent.

Medicaid

Both Medicare and Medicaid help the elderly (and the blind
and disabled) pay their medical bills. Both are a part of the
Social Security Act, and they work together, but they are by no
means the same.

Medicare, as we have seen, is for everyone 65 or older, retired
or not, rich or poor. Medicaid is part of the federal-state welfare
program.

In most states qualifications for Medicaid assistance and for
Supplemental Security Income (SSI gold checks) are the same.
These qualifications were discussed in the last chapter. To repeat, an applicant must have little or no cash income, and not
much in the way of property that can be turned into cash. In
some states the qualifications for Medicaid assistance are
stricter than for SSI.

Because Medicaid is granted only to needy and low-income people it will probably not apply to most people who read this book. But like SSI and Social Security survivors benefits for the young, this information should be passed along to those who need it.

Generally speaking, if an individual has less income than $157.60 per month, and a couple less than $236.60 (including Social Security), they qualify for Medicaid assistance from an income standpoint. Applicants may also own a home valued up to $25,000, have personal cash assets (or their equivalent, such as stocks) up to $1,500, and own a car worth up to $1,200.

Medicaid is of vital importance to the needy because it pays for *all* of a beneficiary's hospital and medical bills. There are no exceptions.

We have seen the numerous exceptions in the Medicare program. The Medicare patient has to pay the first $144 to take care of the hospital insurance deductible, and $36 a day of co-insurance after the first sixty hospital days. The patient has to pay $60 a year for the medical insurance deductible, and 20 percent of all doctors' bills, plus everything that is over and above a "reasonable" charge if the patient is the one who submits the claim to the insurance carrier. Patients also have to pay a $7.70 monthly premium charge for Part B. If a patient qualifies, Medicaid will pay for all of these charges.

In addition, many states will pay bills incurred for dental care, eyeglasses, and hearing aids, all prescription drugs, and for clinic services and intermediate care facilities.

It can't be emphasized too strongly that the person who qualifies for Medicaid normally pays nothing when he or she becomes ill or injured.

Money from Social Security taxes pays the medical bills for those who are insured under Medicare. Money from federal, state, and local taxes pays the medical bills for people under Medicaid. If people are covered under both programs, Medicare is used first, then Medicaid is billed for those services that the Social Security health insurance program does not provide.

The various states design their own Medicaid programs (within federal guidelines); therefore the covered services vary from state to state. Medicaid is now in effect in forty-nine states, the District of Columbia, Guam, Puerto Rico, and the Virgin Islands. Arizona is the only state that doesn't have it.

The following thirty-two states and territories have Medicaid programs for those who qualify for Supplemental Security Income, *plus for some other low-income people.*

Arkansas	Massachusetts	Puerto Rico
California	Michigan	Rhode Island
Connecticut*	Minnesota*	Tennessee
District of Columbia	Montana	Utah*
Guam	Nebraska*	Vermont
Hawaii*	New Hampshire*	Virgin Islands
Illinois*	New York	Virginia
Kansas	North Carolina*	Washington
Kentucky	North Dakota	West Virginia
Maine	Oklahoma*	Wisconsin
Maryland	Pennsylvania	

The following twenty-one states have Medicaid programs *only* for those who are receiving Supplemental Security Income.

Alabama	Indiana*	New Mexico
Alaska	Iowa	Ohio*
Colorado*	Louisiana	Oregon
Delaware	Mississippi*	South Carolina
Florida	Missouri*	South Dakota
Georgia	Nevada	Texas
Idaho	New Jersey	Wyoming

In addition, all of the above states and territories extend Medicaid assistance to those who qualify for Aid to Families

---

*These states don't use national Supplemental Security Income standards to determine Medicaid eligibility. Instead they use their own qualifications, which are usually stricter.

with Dependent Children, a discussion which is outside the scope of this book.

The best way to understand how Medicaid assistance operates is to give an example. This case history shows how persistence is sometimes necessary in order to obtain aid, even though the patient qualifies. It also demonstrates the benefits Medicaid provides.

Warren Baxter, age 67 and living in California, was covered by Medicare. He became seriously ill and was in the hospital for five months. Medicare paid for the first sixty days, less the $144 deductible, and for all but $36 a day for the next thirty days. After that he was on his own, because he elected not to use his sixty hospital lifetime reserve days.

He was a bachelor and lived alone, and upon being released from the hospital his doctor decided that he wasn't well enough to go home, so the physician recommended that Warren Baxter enter an intermediate care facility. This type of facility, in contrast to a nursing home, admits only those people who are ambulatory, and thus able to take care of their daily needs usually provided by custodial care, and who can get to a dining room without help even though they might have to use crutches or a walker. The cost to Mr. Baxter was $400 per month and, fortunately for him, California's Medicaid program paid for such an intermediate care facility, allowing the patient to retain from his income $25 for his personal needs.

After five months in the hospital, Mr. Baxter's medical expenses amounted to $33,000.

At the end of the first sixty days of his five-months stay, having exhausted his own resources, and also run out of free Medicare benefits, the patient representative of the hospital recommended that he apply immediately for Medicaid. Since Warren Baxter was still confined and very ill, he elicited the help of his first cousin, Glen Curtis, who made application for him at the local Social Security office for an SSI gold check and Medicaid assistance. They assured him that there should be no difficulty, and when approval was granted for a monthly Supplemental

Security Income gold check, a Medicaid card would be automatically issued as well. However, there would be a delay of a month or two in order to give the state of California time to verify all of the financial information on the application.

But three months later, when Warren Baxter was released from the hospital, he was still waiting for approval.

At this point his cousin, Glen Curtis, again went to the local Social Security office, inquiring about the long delay. He was informed that it was a computer problem in the state capital in Sacramento, and that there might be a further delay of a month or two.

"But my cousin can't wait that much longer," objected Glen Curtis. "His application is already three months old. He doesn't have any money except his Social Security check, and he has been released from the hospital."

"Where is he living now?"

"At an intermediate care facility where it is costing him $400 per month. The cashier told me that as long as he had applied for Medicaid assistance, they would be willing to wait for two or three weeks to be paid, but no longer."

"In that case," said the Social Security interviewer, "your cousin qualifies for emergency assistance. But this isn't granted by Social Security. You'll have to go to the county welfare office."

However, this presented a problem. Warren Baxter had become ill when visiting his cousin and was rushed to a hospital in Santa Clara county, but his permanent residence was in San Francisco City and County, thirty miles away. Which county had jurisdiction?

After much discussion at the Santa Clara welfare office, it was decided that the application for an emergency Medicaid card would be accepted, but the forms would have to be mailed to the San Francisco County office for processing and approval. However, this office, when the application was mailed to them, proceeded to lose the file!

After filling out new forms, and spending the better part of two days at the San Francisco welfare office, Glen Curtis was informed they could do nothing for Warren Baxter.

"You see," explained the welfare clerk, "a Medicaid card can't be issued by both Social Services and Social Security. It has to be awarded by one office or the other, otherwise an applicant could be issued two cards. Since you have already applied to Social Security, our hands are tied."

But Glen Curtis wasn't satisfied with this answer, so he asked to see a supervisor. Finally after several days of arguing, a temporary Medicaid card was issued. The original application to Social Security was made in late June—it was by this time August. So Social Services (because the application was made in June) issued a current card not only for August, but retroactive cards for June and July as well, so Glen Curtis's persistence finally paid off.

The final result was that Medicaid paid all of Warren Baxter's back hospital costs, including the $36 a day of co-insurance. All that he had to pay was his $144 hospital insurance deductible. They also paid his doctors' bills except for the first month. For this period it cost him the $60 medical insurance deductible, plus 20 percent—but no more, because his doctors had accepted an assignment to Medicare.

Warren Baxter had to pay only $404 out of a total medical expense of $33,000! Medicaid also paid in full for the $400-per-month cost of the intermediate care facility, where he was confined for several more months before his doctor said he was well enough to go home.

Conclusion

Medicare is of tremendous financial assistance to retired people in helping to pay for their medical expenses. It relieves them of the worry that a serious illness might deplete their life savings. And if a supplemental hospital and medical insurance policy is carried (at an average cost of about $25 per month), even the expenses that Medicare doesn't pay will not present a problem.

For those who have little or no income or property, Medicaid is the supplemental health insurance part of Social Security that will step in and pay all medical expenses, including (in many states) bills for dental care, eyeglasses, hearing aids, all prescription drugs, and even charges incurred for clinic services and intermediate care facilities.

11

Income Planning for Retirement: Keogh, IRA, and Pensions

As people approach retirement their main concern is how they are going to solve the problem of living on a reduced income after they stop working. They begin to realize that the monthly income from a man or woman at work is not going to be there anymore. So then what? Very simply stated, property at work has to take its place.

Income upon retirement must come from the following sources:

Social Security
A pension
Insurance policies
Savings
Investments
Part-time work

The most that many people can achieve in financial security for their retired years is a free and clear home and a modest savings account. These, along with their monthly Social Security check and Medicare, comprise their financial independence.

Many others, however, as can be seen from the above list,

have their retirement income considerably increased by receiving in addition to Social Security a monthly corporate or government pension check. Sometimes income from this source can be substantial.

Jack Bennett was one of those fortunate ones, well-off because of *four* different pensions. By careful planning he received a Navy pension, a federal employee pension, a state pension, and Social Security. The four combined checks gave him a lifetime income of $1,900 per month! When this was coupled with a free and clear home and $40,000 in stocks and bonds, he was well-off indeed.

Another government employee of a small suburban town was equally unconcerned when he had a heart attack, and was faced with sudden retirement due to disability at the age of 55.

"We have nothing to fear, Mother," he said to his anxious wife from his hospital bed. "After all, because of disability, I am retired on 95 percent of my salary for life. So what's the problem?"

But for those who don't have an adequate pension from their company or the government, the problem becomes more acute, particularly if they don't have adequate savings or investments. These people facing retirement should realize where their money goes. A recent study of household expenditures disclosed that out of every $1.00, working Americans spend on the average the following amounts.

```
        .29  for food
        .28  for home operation or rent
        .14  for automobile expenses
        .12  for clothing
        .07  for goods and services
        .05  for medical and personal care
        .05  for recreation
      ------
      $1.00
```

As this demonstrates, food, clothing, and shelter take a large part of each dollar. These three necessities have always been a problem since people lived in caves, for the main concern of living is how to have a roof over one's head, clothing to keep warm, and food to eat. And in addition to these three, in this modern day and age, there has to be added another essential, transportation.

What can you do about these costs when facing retirement? You will have more left over for travel and recreation if you can spend less for these essentials. But how can you do that? First, by clearing the mortgage on your home. It's surprising how little it costs for a roof over your head, when your home is free and clear.

Second, let's realize that older people eat less, and that the monthly food bill sinks like a stone once the kids are grown. You will also have the leisure time to shop more carefully in order to reduce food costs.

Third, you should drive a recent vintage car, and have it paid for. Along with this thought, you should also pay off all install-ment debts. Installment payments are murderous when you are retired.

After these steps have been taken, you can breathe a lot easier about how you are going to make ends meet, at age 65 and still counting.

For those who have enough time left before retirement, and by this we mean that they will be working for at least another ten years, there are basic rules to follow that will make them more financially independent.

The road to financial security is a long and narrow one, with many pitfalls along the way, not the least of which is procrasti-nation. When we are young there always seems to be plenty of time left. Mañana is a very convenient word when planning for the future, so why start today when there will always be a tomorrow?

But if the following rules are followed, they will keep one on that narrow and admittedly difficult road to financial indepen-dence, and even eliminate most or all of the stumbling blocks that seem to be so cleverly placed to make one fall prostrate on the path. They are:

1. *There are only seven places to put a dollar.*

Where and how to save, or invest, is therefore not as difficult a problem as it would at first seem to be. You can learn about the seven places without going to too much trouble.

The first five are fixed dollars:

   a. Bank deposits
   b. Savings and loan accounts
   c. Credit unions
   d. Government bonds
   e. Life insurance

The last two are fluctuating dollars:

   f. Real estate
   g. Stocks and bonds

Most people attempt to become financially independent by using one or two, or all, of the first five. If they start early enough, it can be done, but they will never become wealthy. For those who want to achieve better-than-average results, they must invest most of their excess dollars in one or both of the other two.

2. *There are just six basic money problems.*

By knowing what they are you will have a better chance for financial success. They are the following:

   a. Not enough money
   b. Too much money
   c. The risk of inflation
   d. The risk of deflation
   e. Dying too soon
   f. Living too long

If you save part of your money, learn where and how to invest your excess dollars, and realize the importance of a balanced program so that you don't put all you have into fixed dollars, nor for that matter all into investments, you will solve the first four problems.

If the young head of a family realizes the importance of an adequate life insurance program, consisting mainly of term insurance, he or she can leave the family dollars, not debts, which is what he or she intended if death occurs too soon.

And if you don't procrastinate too long in getting your savings program started, you can solve the last money problem, which is living too long because you died broke.

3. *In building for the future, you should use a four-cornerstone philosophy.*

You should have the following:

   a. A cash reserve for everyday needs and small emergencies
   b. Adequate life insurance
   c. An automatic savings program adhered to during working years
   d. A lump sum investment in a sound ownership (i.e., stocks and bonds or real estate)

4. *Thrift is the foundation stone on which all estates are built.*

It is an unfortunate, mundane, simple fact that you cannot become financially successful without first learning how to save.

5. *When you have decided to start saving, pay yourself first.*

The first check you write each month should be to yourself, then let the other people get theirs. If you have to make some creditor wait a month or two, let that person wait. But get yours *first*.

6. *Don't spend the income from your saved, excess dollars.*

It's remarkable how much more you will have after a period of years if you will follow this simple rule. One hundred dollars per month set aside for thirty years is $36,000 saved, but if you compound it at 5 percent it will be worth $83,713!

7. *Don't put all of your savings into fixed dollars.*

Money in a bank or in a cookie jar is too easily available. These put-and-take dollars are too easy to put in and take out. They are also fixed dollars and cannot increase in value. You will never meet anyone who has accumulated a sizable estate who did it by simply saving dollars. They invested their money instead.

8. *You should realize there is no such thing as a risk-proof investment.*

Investments fluctuate, and many people don't like this. But dollars in a bank or a savings and loan institution will lose their purchasing power. So where is the lack of risk?

9. *Buy a home. It's a sound investment, and a tax shelter as well.*

A house will go up in value with time, and you can deduct the interest on the mortgage and the property taxes every year on your income-tax return. It will also give you a cheap roof over your head when you are retired.

Pensions

We have already mentioned (and given two examples) of the importance in retirement planning of having a pension check each month in addition to receiving a monthly check from Social Security.

A pension from the armed services or the government— federal or state—is secure. The government worker or the service man or woman can count on it because the check comes from taxes.

But far too often in the past, pensions that were promised to employees by private industry have proven to be a snare and an illusion. They were illusory because in far too many cases they were never paid to anyone, and they were a snare because it lulled the prospective pensioner into a false sense of financial security for his or her older years.

In 1974 the United States Congress made a major move in the direction of making private pensions more dependable for their beneficiaries. On Labor Day of that year President Ford signed into law the most comprehensive pension legislation since Social Security was enacted, called the Employee Retirement Income Security Act. The number of workers affected has been estimated at approximately thirty-five million. Two of the most important provisions of this law concern vesting and portability.

Vesting in pension lexicon is simply another word for ownership. Formerly ownership by an employee of his pension account depended upon the whims of his corporate employer. No more. Under the new law employers have only three choices.

1. Ten-year vesting. Full ownership of his or her account by the employee after ten years of service.

2. Fifteen-year vesting. Twenty-five percent of his or her pension account must be owned by the employee after five years. After that it increases by 5 percent a year for the next five years, and then 10 percent a year for the final five.

3. The Rule of 45. Under this method of vesting, the employee must own 50 percent of his or her account when (a) the employee has completed at least five years of service and the employee's age plus years of service equal or exceed forty-five;

or (b) the employee has completed ten years of service regardless of age. The vesting then increases 10 percent per year during the next five years.

Too often in the past an employee couldn't enter a company pension plan until the worker had been employed for ten years, and just before that event occurred he or she would be fired. In other plans, the employee had no ownership of a pension account until the worker was 55 years of age, and again he or she would be fired. In either event, the employee not only lost a pension, but a job as well.

Portability. Formerly pensions could not be carried from job to job. When a person left the company with a partial, or 100 percent, ownership of a pension account, the employee was paid his or her pension in cash in a lump sum. Then it became fully taxable, and if the employee were a poor money manager he or she might spend it all, or lose it all through poor investments.

No more. Pensions can now be transported from job to job, without losing their tax-free status. Exactly how this can be done will be explained later.

Until the passage of the Pension Reform Act of 1974, if your corporate pension plan went bankrupt, it was just too bad for you. Your pension check went out the window. The Treasury Department estimated in 1973 that 750,000 workers who had vested pension benefits would not receive one penny during the succeeding twenty years because their pension plans had failed.

Now corporate pension plans are backed up by government insurance, similar in operation to the Federal Deposit Insurance Corporation that insures bank accounts up to $40,000. The new federal agency is called the Pension Benefit Guarantee Corporation. Trustees of the fund are the secretaries of the Departments of Labor, Treasury, and Commerce.

If a corporate pension plan fails, the Pension Benefit Guarantee Corporation is authorized to pay up to $750 per month to each individual covered by the bankrupt plan (less, of course, if an employee is entitled to less). All pension plans regardless of size must contribute to the plan termination insurance. Priority in payment will be given to those who are already retired and currently receiving benefits.

Unfortunately the law has also had an adverse effect. Many pension plans of smaller companies have been terminated because of the higher costs caused by the new vesting and funding rules, and because of the cost of the plan termination insurance.

For those workers who have had their pension plans terminated by their employers, the pension reform legislation gives them a break. When their employer pays them their vested interest, they may take this lump sum and establish their own pension account.

But what is even more important, *it allows those millions of workers who are not covered by a qualified plan where they work* to also have their own individual pension account. This is because major changes were made in the Self-employed Individuals Retirement Act, which was originally passed in 1962. This legislation granted tax-deferred pension and profit-sharing plans to the self-employed, occasionally called HR-10 plans (after the title of the law), or more often simply Keogh Plans (after the author of the bill).

Now not only can a self-employed person have his or her own tax-free pension account, but under the new regulations, everyone can if he or she is qualified.

IRA

For the tax years beginning on or after January 1, 1975, if you are an eligible individual, you can establish your own individual retirement account, called an IRA. You are allowed to make contributions to your own pension program equal to 15 percent of your earned income, or $1,500, whichever is less.

An individual retirement account, with a maximum contribution of $1,500 for twenty-five years, compounded at 6 percent, will amount to $87,234! When this is paid out in the form of a 6 percent pension, the monthly check would be $436.17, a truly wonderful addition to a Social Security check. When such a plan is available, it is no longer necessary for an individual to retire broke.

The Treasury Department states that you may contribute to an individual retirement savings program if you are not an active participant, during any part of the tax year, in any of the following:

1. A qualified pension, profit-sharing, or stock bonus plan of an employer, or a qualified annuity plan or bond purchase plan of an employer

2. A retirement plan established by a government for its employees (such as the Civil Service Retirement System, or one of the military retirement plans)

3. An annuity contract purchased by certain tax-exempt organizations or public schools

4. A qualified plan for self-employed individuals (HR-10 or Keogh)

If you are already receiving retirement benefits, that fact will not prohibit you from establishing your own pension account; however, you must meet all of the requirements.

Your contribution to your individual retirement savings program reduces your gross income; therefore, even if you don't itemize your deductions and use the standard deduction instead, you still don't pay taxes on this amount.

Since an IRA is a bona fide retirement plan, thereby making your contribution and the earnings on it nontaxable, the law prohibits you from being eligible to receive distributions until you are 59½ years of age. Your account is locked in until then, and distributions must start no later than when you are 70½ years of age. This mandatory starting date makes sense. After all, the Internal Revenue Service wants to tax your pension benefits sometime before you die!

If you receive a premature distribution from your pension account (i.e., before you are 59½ years old) you will be subject to a penalty. The premature distribution must be included in your gross income for that year and becomes 100 percent taxable. In addition your income tax liability is increased by an amount equal to 10 percent of the premature distribution. This 10 percent penalty is not imposed, however, if a distribution is made to your beneficiary because you die, or is paid to you because you are permanently disabled.

You may place your IRA account money in any place you choose—a bank or a savings and loan account, life insurance, stocks and bonds, mutual funds, or special U.S. Individual Retirement Bonds.

Of all the changes that were made in the Pension Reform Act of 1974, IRA is the least understood and the most neglected despite massive attempts by banks, savings and loan associations, insurance companies, and mutual funds to promote it. This is a shame when there is no finer method to provide for a continuing income after retirement. So let's take a look at the other major provisions of the law.

Since a tax deduction is available to each individual, marital status, or election to file a joint return, does not affect eligibility. Both husband and wife can claim the deduction if each of them is eligible and each adopts a separate IRA. If they do, the deduction is computed separately for each spouse, whether or not they file a joint return. If one spouse doesn't work, each consort may have an IRA account of $875 a year, which increases the maximum yearly contribution from $1,500 to $1,750.

An individual retirement account is a trust, or custodial, account organized in the United States for the exclusive benefit of the taxpayer and his or her beneficiaries. It must be created by a written document. The trustee or custodian must be a bank, a federally insured credit union, a savings and loan association, or another person who is eligible under the regulations to act as trustee or custodian. Practically all financial institutions have the necessary forms to set up an IRA.

When the taxpayer is eligible to start receiving his or her benefits the distribution may be made in a single sum, or he or she may receive periodic distributions, just as long as the entire interest in the trust is distributed over any of the following periods:

(a) For life
(b) For the lives of the taxpayer and his or her spouse
(c) For a certain period that does not exceed the taxpayer's life expectancy
(d) For a certain period that does not exceed the life expectancy of the taxpayer and his or her spouse

If contributors to IRAs die before their entire interest is distributed to them, the remaining amount will, within a maximum period of five years after their deaths, be paid in a single sum to their beneficiaries, or before that time if the taxpayers would have been 70½ years of age. Or the undistributed interest may be applied toward the purchase of an immediate annuity. A distribution to the beneficiary of an IRA is included in the taxpayer's estate for federal estate-tax purposes, and a tax will be imposed if one is due.

Many people, rather than use any one of the other avenues for investment, may prefer to buy U.S. Individual Retirement Bonds, which were specifically created as a vehicle of investment for an IRA. These bonds earn 6 percent interest, compounded every six months, and are issued in demoninations of $50, $100, and $500. A person who buys them does not have to have a custodian or trustee, or a written agreement of any kind. The bonds cease earning interest on the first day of the month in which the individual who purchased them attains the age of 70½ years. Distribution from an individual retirement account, as we have seen, must start no later than this date.

U.S. Individual Retirement Bonds can be purchased at any

Federal Reserve bank or branch, or from the Bureau of the Public Debt, Securities Transactions Branch, Washington, D.C. 20226. They may be registered in the names of individuals, whether they are adults or minors, either in single ownership or beneficiary form. However, only one beneficiary can be named. Application for them must be made on Form PD 4345, ABC of the Department of the Treasury.

Workers who receive their vested interest in a qualified pension plan because they leave their employer voluntarily, or because their plan has been terminated, may rollover this money into an IRA. This permits the portability of pension benefits that we mentioned earlier. Only the taxable portion of the vested interest can be transferred, and the rollover contribution must be completed within sixty days after the employee receives it. If property other than cash is distributed (i.e., stocks), that same property must be reinvested in the new program.

After the worker has rolled over the lump sum distribution into an IRA, he may subsequently transfer it, if he desires, into a new employer's qualified pension plan. It should be emphasized that the entire taxable portion must be rolled over; the pensioner cannot transfer just a portion of the distribution.

A self-employed individual who terminated his or her Keogh Plan (explained later), and rolls it over into an IRA, may not subsequently roll these assets over into a qualified employer's pension plan. However, an individual retirement savings plan may be rolled over into another IRA without suffering any adverse tax consequences. This may be done only once every three years. The law recognizes the fact that workers may be dissatisfied with their investment in their current IRA and want to transfer it.

When retirees receive a distribution from their IRA in a lump sum, it is taxed as ordinary income in the year received, or they may elect to compute their tax liability under the regular income averaging provisions of the Internal Revenue Code.

Keogh Plans

As we mentioned earlier, an individual retirement savings program was made possible through major changes in the Self-employed Individuals Retirement Act, originally passed in 1962. It also made major changes in Keogh Plans for the self-employed.

The amount that can be invested in a Keogh Plan remains at 15 percent of earned income, but the maximum amount that can be contributed in any one year has been increased from $2,500 a year to $7,500. This is a real boon.

A self-employed person who contributes the maximum of $7,500 every year for twenty years, and compounds his account at the rate of 6 percent, will have a distribution of $282,447.50! Furthermore, like an IRA, all of it is tax-deferred, not only the $7,500 annual contribution, but the earnings on this money as well. This is without question one of the finest tax deductions available and a tremendous boost in pension benefits for the self-employed. No longer do they have to complain about being discriminated against compared to the pension benefits paid by large corporations to their employees who are in comparable tax brackets.

It should be pointed out that self-employed individuals do not have to have Keogh Plans, they may have IRAs instead, but if they do they are limited to the maximum yearly contribution of $1,500. If self-employed persons are making more than $10,000 they should therefore consider a Keogh Plan instead of an IRA. For example, if they are making $30,000 a year, they may contribute to their own pension plan $4,500 (15 percent of $30,000), not just $1,500.

The same restrictions apply to Keogh Plans as those established for an IRA in that HR-10 plans must be bona fide pension arrangements. Distributions cannot be made before the contributor is 59½ years of age; if a premature distribution is made the same penalty applies, and withdrawals must commence by the time the pensioner is 70½ years of age. But in addition there are many other rules that apply that are peculiar to the self-employed. This is because if they have employees the owners generally must include them in their Keogh Plans.

The best way to clarify this important subject is by questions and answers that have been partly provided by the Internal Revenue Service.

Q. Under what circumstances am I considered an owner-employee?

A. You are an owner-employee if you are a self-employed individual (whether you have employees or not), and you are a sole proprietor, or a partner who owns more than a 10 percent interest in either the capital or the profits of a partnership.

Q. I am in a partnership with three other individuals. May I set up my own plan?

A. No. An individual partner may not set up his or her own plan. The plan must be set up by the partnership.

Q. I am covered under a corporate pension (or profit-sharing) plan. I also operate a little business on the side in the evening. Can I set up a Keogh Plan for my self-employed income?

A. Yes, you can. And because of a change in the law, you are not limited to 15 percent of earned income. You may put into a Keogh Plan a minimum of $750, regardless of how much you earn. Let's assume that as a moonlighter you make $750 a year in taxable income; the whole amount— 100 percent, not just 15 percent—can be put into a tax-free pension fund. Or let's assume that you make $2,000 a year. Under the old rules you could set aside only 15 percent, or $300. Under the new law you can set aside $750, which is close to 40 percent of your earnings.

Q. Some time ago I took into my practice a dental graduate who wanted to obtain experience before opening his own office. Must I include him in my self-employed plan?

A. You must include him if he is a full-time employee who has worked for you for three years or more. A full-time employee is one who normally works more than twenty hours a week for more than five months a year.

Q. I have been in business one year. May I require my employees to wait three years before I cover them under my plan?

A. No. You may not require a longer waiting period for your present or future employees than you do for yourself.

Q. May I reduce my common-law employees' compensation to offset my additional expenses because of the contributions I make for them under my qualified plan?

A. No.

Q. I am a sole proprietor and have employees who participate in a union-negotiated pension plan. May I set up a HR-10 plan for myself only?

A. Yes, if the union plan is at least comparable to yours in every respect, such as the rate of benefits and vesting.

Q. What must I do to set up a Keogh Plan?

A On or before the last day your return is due (usually April 15), sign a plan that meets the applicable requirements for qualification, or a prototype trust agreement that has already been approved. You must also inform your employees (if any) of the plan, and pay your contributions for the year.

Q. If I contribute less than the maximum allowed in one year, may I make it up by contributing more than the maximum limit in the next year?

A. No. There are no carryover provisions. All contributions are on a year-to-year basis.

Q. Am I, as an owner-employee, entitled to a capital-gains tax treatment if I receive a lump-sum distribution when I retire?

A. No. However, you may apply a five-year special averaging method to a lump-sum distribution if it includes your entire interest in the plan, and if it is distributed to you in one year.

Q. I understand that distributions cannot be made before age 59½, except in case of disability or death, and that there is a

penalty for premature distributions. But if I should need the money before that time, and I am willing to pay the penalty, may provision be made for an earlier payment?
A. No. No benefits (including those attributable to voluntary contributions) may be paid. Voluntary contributions, if you have an employee, may be made up to 10 percent of earned income, whether or not your employee elects to take advantage of this privilege. This is in addition to the normal 15 percent. Voluntary contributions, however, are not tax deductible; only the earnings from them can be deducted from gross income.

Contributions to a Keogh Plan, just like an IRA, may be made to a custodian bank or savings and loan association, to a credit union, to an individual retirement annuity, or to special U.S. government bonds. They may also be invested in stocks and bonds and mutual funds.

However, despite this detailed explanation of Keogh Plans and Individual Retirement Accounts, approximately one-half of all workers are not entitled to invest in these plans. This is because they are covered by a qualified plan where they work, or they are not self-employed. These workers are therefore faced with providing for a continuing income after retirement by saving and investing without the benefit of a tax shelter.

Millions of these people invest in common stocks, or they would like to, because they want protection from the serious inroads of inflation. They feel they can afford to take the risks involved, but they also realize they can't just mount their horse and ride off in all directions. They would like to have some rules to follow for investing in the stock market. These guidelines are the following:

1. *Buy a stock only when it is going up in price, never at any other time.*

No matter how sold you may be on a company and its growth potential, never buy a stock that is just holding its own, or when the price is going down. Remember that risk in the stock market is all on the down side.

2. *You will never go broke taking a profit.*

Too many investors become married to stocks that have done well for them. You must have an open mind toward your investments at all times. It is admittedly difficult to sell a stock that has justified your faith in it by going up handsomely over the years. But remember there comes a time when a stock becomes fully valued, and you should sell.

3. *Diversify your holdings.*

"Don't put all of your eggs in one basket" is a rule that we have all heard from infancy. But how much diversification should you have? Four or five stocks are enough. You should not spread yourself so thin that it becomes impossible for you to manage your portfolio intelligently.

4. *Set your sights high.*

Try for a 100 percent increase in one year. You probably won't get it, but you certainly won't if the stock doesn't have a ghost of a chance of doing that well. If you do only half as well as 100 percent, you will still double your money in two years, and if you do only half as well as that, you will double your money in four years, which is 25 percent per year.

5. *If you are not close to retirement, buy stocks for growth, not for dividends.*

You can't have both. Those companies that pay out most of their net profits to their shareholders in the form of high dividends have very little left in retained earnings for expansion. You should try for increased values, not for dividends, for growth can be the larger of the two.

6. *Reinvest all of the dividends while you are still working.*

Normally investors spend their dividends. All corporations mail their dividends to their shareholders, and human frailty being what it is, most investors spend them. Money that we receive is easily dissipated, especially if it comes in small amounts at various times during the year, like dividends on stock. But the investor who is building for his own retirement should not do this.

There are two ways that dividends can be automatically saved. Increasingly many corporations, upon instruction from their shareholders, are willing to reinvest the dividends automatically in additional shares and send a notice to their stockholders instead of a check. The other way is to hold your stock in a street name with your broker. This way the dividends will be mailed to the brokerage firm and not to you. You can then instruct your registered representative to hold them in your account until you have decided where to invest them. Either way you, the investor, will not receive the dividends and spend them, which is the main thing.

7. *No investment that is a good speculation should be considered safe.*

If you are deliberately speculating, you should stand ready to lose everything. Therefore this kind of money should be invested only by young people. If they lose, they have the time to save some more money and invest again.

8. *Buy on facts, not on rumors or hunches.*

There is no better rule to follow than this for success in the stock market. No matter what your objective may be, do not invest until you have the facts. Anyone who buys and sells thousands of dollars in securities on the basis of a two-minute telephone conversation with his or her stockbroker deserves to lose.

9. *Don't buy on margin.*

Buying stocks on margin is borrowing money, usually from your broker, in order to buy more shares than you could if you paid cash. It isn't recommended because the price of stocks is too volatile. They go up and down in price too rapidly. In addition, nobody can predict what the market is going to do tomorrow. Banks also lend money on stock portfolios. If your stocks seriously go down, and you can't put up more money or collateral, Mr. Banker will insist upon selling you out, and you will have lost the amount that your stocks declined. There is no worse pessimist in a bear market than a banker; the current economic conditions are a disaster as far as he is concerned, and even though two years later you might have a wonderful portfolio of stocks if you could only hang on, he or she will insist that the bank has to be protected from this terrible situation from which the country will apparently never recover.

10. *Never commit all of your excess funds in the market.*

You should have a reserve of cash. An unforeseen emergency may arise that is greater than you anticipated, and that cannot be met with your Number 1 cornerstone, your cash reserve. If you have too little cash, and your stocks are down when this occurs, you would have to sell at a loss.

11. *Have the courage to sell if you are wrong.*

Everyone makes a bad investment once in a while. To err is human, and this is never more true than in the marketplace. You will definitely make mistakes. You should reconcile yourself to this, and sell when you do. Never for any reason ride a bad stock down. It will kill you.

12. *Long-term trading is a must.*

The days are gone when you can just buy blue-chip stocks and hold them, putting them away in your safe-deposit box and forgetting about them. The economy has become far too complex for this.

13. *Short-term trading is only for the professional.*

Those amateurs who every day sit in stockbrokers' board rooms watching the market, trading in and out when a stock moves a few points, are kidding themselves.

14. *Dollar cost average when a stock is going up, never when it is going down.*

Many stockbrokers advise doubling up on a stock when the price has gone down, in order to reduce the average cost. Example:

You as an investor purchased in the past one hundred shares of a stock priced at $40 per share. It is now selling at $30 per share. Your broker suggests that you should dollar cost average and buy another one hundred shares.

The arithmetic looks like this:

One hundred shares at $40 equals	$4,000
One hundred shares at $30 equals	3,000
Total investment	$7,000
Average cost of all two hundred shares	$35 each

So now you own two hundred shares, and have invested another $3,000, in a stock that is going down. This doesn't make sense. The theory is that you are better off owning two hundred shares at an average cost of $35 than you are owning one hundred shares that cost $40. If a stock is going down, it is—temporarily at least—a bad investment. You should sell a stock under these conditions, not buy more.

15. *Sell high and buy low.*

This is the most obvious rule and something that every investor in the stock market would like to do. Unfortunately no one can sell at the absolute high of a bull market and buy in again at the low of a subsequent bear market. The best that you can hope to accomplish is to avoid doing the opposite. Be satisfied and get out of the market into cash after you have a good profit in a bull market. If the market goes higher after you have sold, you would have made more if you had waited, but be content with less.

At the same time, don't try to reinvest at the absolute low of a bear market. Wait until the market starts up. There is still plenty of appreciation left. Many careful investors were caught napping in the big bear market of 1969–70. They thought the market had hit bottom when the Dow Jones Industrial Average declined to 800. It had not, for it went down in the spring of 1970 to below 650 in late May. Those who went back in at 800 bought back too soon.

Conclusion

Income planning for retirement should include paying off all debts, particularly installment payments, and if possible the mortgage on a home. It also means the early establishment of a habit of thrift, for savings is the foundation stone on which all estates are built.

If possible, have a pension to supplement Social Security. Formerly the promise of a corporate pension from an employer was a snare and an illusion. Far too often it was never paid because the employee did not own his or her account soon enough, or because of bad investments, or worse yet because the plan or the company went broke. Now with the changes incorporated in the Pension Reform Act of 1974 these pensions are more of a reality.

If you are not covered by a qualified plan, establish your own pension account, either with an IRA, or if you are self-employed with a Keogh Plan. No longer is it necessary to retire without a pension. The benefits from an IRA or a Keogh Plan are worth repeating.

An individual retirement account, with a maximum contribution of $1,500 per year for twenty-five years, compounded at 6 percent, will amount to $87,234!

A Keogh Plan, with a maximum contribution of $7,500 per year for twenty years, compounded at 6 percent, will amount to $282,447.50.

Now that such plans are available, no one should ever retire broke.[1]

---

1. For those who want more information on accumulating for retirement, see John Barnes, *How to Have More Money* (New York: Morrow).

12

How to Solve Your Income Tax Problems

Judge Learned Hand said:

There is nothing sinister in so arranging one's affairs to keep taxes as low as possible. Nobody owes any public duty to pay more than the law demands; taxes are enforced exactions, not voluntary contributions. To demand more in the name of morals is mere cant.

One of the major objectives for all people in the management of their finances should be to keep their income taxes as low as possible. Despite this, most people overpay them. This is particularly true of those who are retired. This is not an idle statement. It is the considered opinion of the Special Committee on Aging of the United States Senate expressed in a February 1974 committee report on the special tax problems of older persons, after hearing testimony of many expert witnesses over a period of months.

No one should pay more in income taxes than the law demands. To pay more in taxes than the law requires is not only a deterrent to financial independence, but it could be courting financial disaster as well. Contrary to popular opinion, the Internal Revenue Service does not want anyone to pay more than he or she owes, but on the other hand they will not tell the taxpayer how to pay less. Paying less is entirely up to the individual. That person who is filing an income tax return must know how to take all of the deductions allowed under the law. These deductions make for a significant difference between an individual taxpayer's gross income and the *taxable income* on which that person actually pays his or her income tax. Within reasonable limits, this variation is intended by Congress and is inherent in our income tax system. It's only net income that is subject to the income tax, after recovery of the expenses and capital consumed in earning it, and after setting aside a basic sum for personal expenditures of the taxpayer and his family.

One needs to know, therefore, when a return has to be filed, when to itemize deductions rather than take the standard deduction, and what the tax rates are. Investors need to know how to report capital gains and losses, and how stocks and bonds, mutual funds, and real estate are taxed. So let's consider in turn each one of these problems.

How to File an Income Tax Return

Approximately 80 million persons file an income tax return every year. It's a chore and a financial obligation. Nevertheless, it has to be done.

A person must file a federal income tax return if he or she is a United States citizen or resident, and has a gross income in excess of a fixed sum for the particular category in which he or she falls—mainly whether single, married filing a joint return, or filing as the head of a household. This minimum fixed sum that requires a person to file an income tax return changes from year to year.[1]

In addition, if you are self-employed, you must file a return if you had net earnings from self-employment of $400 or more.

---

1. Currently it is $2,950 for a single person, and $4,700 for a married couple filing a joint return.

You should also file a federal income tax return if you had income taxes withheld from your pay, even though you didn't have enough income that required you to file a return. By filing a return, and claiming your personal exemption, you can get a refund even though you may be claimed as a dependent by another taxpayer.

The two most commonly used forms for filing individual federal income tax returns are the Short Form 1040A and the regular Form 1040. Most taxpayers have a choice as to which form to use.

Short Form 1040A may be used if all of the taxpayer's income came from wages, salaries, and tips, and that individual did not have more than $400 in dividends and $400 in interest. Short Form 1040A may not be used if the taxpayer elects to itemize his or her deductions. It may not be used if the taxpayer can be claimed as a dependent on his or her parent's return and had $750 or more of dividend and interest income.

Regular Form 1040 should be used, and deductions itemized, if expenses for such items as medical and dental care, interest, taxes, contributions, casualty and theft losses, and miscellaneous deductions exceed the standard deduction for the year involved.

In most cases the Internal Revenue Service will mail the taxpayer either Short Form 1040A or the regular Form 1040, with related instructions, including the Tax Table and the Tax Rate Schedules that are used to determine the amount of income tax that person owes. If the forms are not received, they may be obtained from offices of the IRS, all post offices, and most banks.

If Short Form 1040A is used, no additional schedules are required. If Form 1040 is used, the taxpayer must attach the following schedules as necessary.

Schedule A to itemize deductions.

Schedule B to report dividends and interest income if either one exceeds $400.

Schedule C to report a profit (or loss) from a business or a profession.

Schedule D to report gains and losses on selling capital assets.

Schedule E to report income from pensions, annuities, rents, royalties, partnerships, estates, trusts, and small business corporations.

Schedule F to report farm income and expenses.

Schedule G for income averaging.

Schedule R to claim a retirement income credit.

Schedule SE to compute self-employment tax.

Schedule TC to compute your tax if you cannot use the Tax Tables.

The income tax return must be signed, and if it is a joint return, both spouses must sign even if only one had income. Social Security numbers must be shown. All money items appearing on the return may be rounded off to whole dollars. This means that amounts under fifty cents are eliminated and amounts from fifty cents to ninety-nine cents are increased to the next dollar. Copy B of the taxpayer's W-2 form, which is a statement from the employer of the employee's wages and the taxes withheld, must be attached to the return. Copy C of the W-2 form should be retained for the taxpayer's records.

How to determine the income tax

The taxpayer determines the amount of his or her income tax by using the Tax Tables or by using the Tax Rate Schedules. The amount of the tax owed is based on taxable income, which is adjusted gross income minus deductions and the $750 personal exemption. The final tax is further reduced by the $35 tax credit. Each one is discussed below.

The Tax Tables. The average taxpayer enters the Tax Tables with the amount of his or her taxable income to determine the tax that he or she owes. The Tax Tables are used if the taxpayer's taxable income does not exceed $20,000 if single or an unmarried head of household, or $40,000 if married and filing a joint return.

The Tax Rate Schedules. There are three Tax Rate Schedules: Schedule X for single taxpayers, Schedule Y for married taxpayers, and Schedule Z for unmarried taxpayers who qualify as heads of households. The taxpayer uses the Tax Rate Schedules if unable to use the Tax Tables. These schedules demonstrate that the income tax is a progressive tax. As taxable income increases, so does the tax rate.

Deductions. There are two ways to take deductions: (1) The taxpayer may claim the Zero Bracket Amount (also referred to as the standard deduction), or (2) the taxpayer may itemize deductions using Schedule A.

The Zero Bracket Amount (ZBA) is currently $2,200 for single persons and $3,200 for married couples filing a joint return. When using either the Tax Tables or the Tax Rate Schedules, these deductible amounts ($2,200 or $3,200) are automatically included in them.

Itemized deductions that are listed on Schedule A are personal deductions that are individually listed because they are large enough to result in the taxpayer paying a lower tax than if he or she automatically used ZBA only. Ordinarily a homeowner who pays interest and taxes, or a taxpayer who has unusually large medical and dental expenses during the year, would benefit by using Schedule A. Since our income tax system is one of individual self-assessment and voluntary compliance, each taxpayer determines how much he or she owes, and voluntarily files his or her income tax return by April 15. This self-assessment requires the taxpayer to know what deductions can be taken on Schedule A, and if they are high enough to warrant the trouble of itemizing them. There are six deductions on Schedule A.

Medical and dental expenses. These expenses must exceed 3 percent of adjusted gross income or no deduction can be taken. Of this 3 percent, prescription medicine and drugs must exceed 1 percent of annual gross income (AGI), or no deduction can be taken for these items. There is one medical expense that does not come under the overall 3 percent limitation. One-half of the premium for hospitalization insurance, up to a maximum of $150, can be deducted *first* without having to consider the 3 percent rule. Many persons, with little or no medical and dental bills for the year because they were healthy, erroneously assume that they are not entitled to a deduction under this heading. They therefore pass up this opportunity for a $150 deduction.

Taxes. Most taxes are deductible. If the investor is a homeowner, the biggest deductible item under this heading is for property taxes. To qualify, a tax must meet three conditions.

1. It must be a tax imposed by a state or local government and fall into one of five categories. It must be an income tax, a real estate property tax, a personal property tax, a general sales tax, or a gasoline tax. Federal taxes do not qualify as a deduction. Neither does an inheritance tax, although this is a tax imposed by a state government.
2. It must be imposed upon the taxpayer. For instance, real property taxes can be deducted only by the property owner.
3. The tax must be paid during the tax year.

Optional general sales tax tables for all of the fifty states are included in the instructions for Form 1040, based on the taxpayer's adjusted gross income and the number of dependents the taxpayer has claimed on his or her income tax return. In addition to the general sales tax deduction, there are four additional sales taxes that may be deducted. If you purchase a car, a boat, an airplane, or a mobile home, the sales tax imposed on these sizable purchases is deductible. For instance, if you bought a boat during the year for $6,000, and a sales tax was assessed of 6 percent, you paid a tax of $360. This is a legitimate sales tax deduction in addition to the amount you deducted from the optional general sales tax tables.

Interest. Most interest charges incurred on loans are deductible. The most common interest deduction is for the interest on a home mortgage. Careful records have to be maintained in regard to interest charges because of the widespread use of credit cards, revolving charge accounts at stores, and borrowing to pay for the cost of a college education. All of these interest charges are deductible, but the taxpayer must keep the proof.

Contributions. All contributions to schools, churches, and hospitals, and to other qualified charitable, religious, educational, scientific, and literary organizations are tax deductible. They can be sizable and still come within the law. They shouldn't be given in cash, unless a receipt is obtained.

Casualty and theft losses. As a result of hurricanes, fires, storms, floods, and other disasters, many people suffer losses from damage to grounds, dwellings, automobiles, boats, furniture, and other property. Insurance for this type of loss is for a small amount at best, and quite often not available at all. If the property is covered by insurance, the deduction allowed is the amount of the loss that is in excess of the insurance proceeds. If the loss is a personal one (as against a business loss), it is deductible only to the extent that it exceeds one hundred dollars.

A casualty loss is defined by the IRS as a complete or partial destruction of property resulting from an event that is (1) identifiable, (2) damaging to property, and (3) sudden, unexpected, and unusual. A "sudden" event is one that is swift and precipitous and not gradual and progressive. An "unexpected" event is one that is ordinarily not anticipated and that occurs without the intent of the one who suffered the loss. An "unusual" event is one that is extraordinary and nonrecurring.

A theft is the unlawful taking and removing of money or property with the intent to deprive the property owner of it. The mere disappearance of money or property from one's person or home is not a theft.

If a taxpayer knows these definitions, he or she is able to take the deductions under this heading of casualty and theft losses with little difficulty.

Miscellaneous deductions. There are many deductions under this heading. They may or may not apply to the individual taxpayer, but when one or more of these deductions are available, they can help to reduce taxes. Deductions that should not be overlooked fall into three main categories. They are obvious and require no explanation.

1. Employee expenses
   Uniforms not adaptable to general use
   Employment agency fees to secure employment
   Subscriptions to professional journals
   Dues to professional societies
   Union dues and initiation fees
   Physical examinations required by your employer
   A college professor's research, lecturing, and writing expenses
   Amounts a teacher pays a substitute
   Surety bond premiums
   Malpractice insurance premiums
   A research chemist's laboratory breakage fees
   Small tools and supplies
   Educational expenses to keep your job or maintain your skills

2. Income-producing expenses
   Gambling losses (to the extent of winnings)
   Expenses of an income-producing hobby

3. Other expenses
   Certain appraisal fees

Tax counsel and assistance
Political contribution not in excess of $100 ($200 if married and filing a joint return)

It is also well to know the personal expenses that are not deductible under the miscellaneous classification in Schedule A. They are the following:

Home repairs, insurance, rent
Personal legal expenses
Insurance (except medical)
Burial expenses
Lost or misplaced cash or personal property
Fines and tax penalties

A filled-in Schedule A is shown here. The taxpayer should take note that after the deductions are totaled, he or she *must subtract the standard deduction,* otherwise this amount is taken twice because it is already included in the Tax Tables and the Tax Rate Schedules.

The personal exemption. Every taxpayer is allowed a personal exemption of $750. Each taxpayer is also allowed an additional $750 exemption for a spouse, and for each person who qualifies as his or her dependent by meeting the dependency tests below. The taxpayer may qualify for an additional exemption for himself and a spouse because of age or blindness. Thus a married taxpayer with three small children has five personal exemptions for a total of $3,750 (5 × $750). Or a married taxpayer with no children, with both spouses over 65, qualifies for four exemptions for a total of $3,000 (4 × $750), one exemption for each spouse, and two because of age. Once again, however, no computation is necessary by the taxpayer because the personal exemption is incorporated in the Tax Tables and the Tax Rate Schedules, unless he or she is required to use Schedule TC.

Schedules A&B—Itemized Deductions AND
(Form 1040)   Interest and Dividend Income

1977

Department of the Treasury
Internal Revenue Service
▶ Attach to Form 1040. ▶ See Instructions for Schedules A and B (Form 1040).

Name(s) as shown on Form 1040   Frank B. and Evelyn H. Jones

Your social security number

Schedule A Itemized Deductions (Schedule B is on back)

Medical and Dental Expenses (not compensated by insurance or otherwise) (See page 14 of Instructions.)

1 One-half (but not more than $150) of insurance premiums for medical care. (Be sure to include in line 10 below) . . .	69	00
2 Medicine and drugs	300	00
3 Enter 1% of line 31, Form 1040 . . .	210	30
4 Subtract line 3 from line 2. Enter difference (if less than zero, enter zero) . .	89	70
5 Enter balance of insurance premiums for medical care not entered on line 1 . .	69	00
6 Enter other medical and dental expenses:		
a Doctors, dentists, nurses, etc.	589	00
b Hospitals	240	35
c Other (itemize—include hearing aids, dentures, eyeglasses, transportation, etc.) ▶		
7 Total (add lines 4 through 6c) . . .	988	05
8 Enter 3% of line 31, Form 1040 . . .	630	91
9 Subtract line 8 from line 7 (if less than zero, enter zero)	357	14
10 Total (add lines 1 and 9). Enter here and on line 33 . . . . . . ▶	426	14

Taxes (See page 14 of Instructions.)

11 State and local income	677	88
12 Real estate	285	36
13 State and local gasoline (see gas tax tables)	74	00
14 General sales (see sales tax tables) . .	244	86
15 Personal property	141	04
16 Other (itemize) ▶		
17 Total (add lines 11 through 16). Enter here and on line 34 . . . . . . ▶	1,423	14

Interest Expense (See page 16 of Instructions.)

18 Home mortgage	537	04
19 Other (itemize) ▶	4	90
	60	00
20 Total (add lines 18 and 19). Enter here and on line 35 . . . . . . ▶	601	94

Contributions (See page 16 of Instructions for examples.)

21 a Cash contributions for which you have receipts, cancelled checks or other written evidence	529	50
b Other cash contributions. List donees and amounts. ▶		
22 Other than cash (see page 16 of instructions for required statement)		
23 Carryover from prior years		
24 Total contributions (add lines 21a through 23). Enter here and on line 36 . . ▶	529	50

Casualty or Theft Loss(es) (See page 16 of Instructions.)

25 Loss before insurance reimbursement .	see	
26 Insurance reimbursement	attached	
27 Subtract line 26 from line 25. Enter difference (if less than zero, enter zero) .	Form 4684	
28 Enter $100 or amount on line 27, whichever is smaller		
29 Casualty or theft loss (subtract line 28 from line 27). Enter here and on line 37 . ▶	929	50

Miscellaneous Deductions (See page 16 of Instructions.)

30 Union dues.	150	00
31 Other (itemize) ▶		
safe deposit box rental	7	50
small tools	35	00
correspondence course	40	00
32 Total (add lines 30 and 31). Enter here and on line 38 . . . . . . ▶	232	50

Summary of Itemized Deductions   A
(See page 17 of Instructions.)

33 Total medical and dental—line 10 . .	426	14
34 Total taxes—line 17	1,423	14
35 Total interest—line 20	601	94
36 Total contributions—line 24	529	50
37 Casualty or theft loss(es)—line 29 . .	929	50
38 Total miscellaneous—line 32	232	50
39 Total deductions (add lines 33 through 38). ▶	4,142	72
40 If you checked Form 1040, box: 2 or 5, enter $3,200 1 or 4, enter $2,200 3, enter $1,600	3,200	00
41 Excess itemized deductions (subtract line 40 from line 39). Enter here and on Form 1040, line 33. (If line 40 is more than line 39 see "Who MUST Itemize Deductions" on page 11 of the Instructions.) . . ▶	942	72

The dependency test. The following five tests must be met for a person to qualify as a taxpayer's dependent.

The support test. The taxpayer must furnish over one-half of the dependent's total support during the calendar year. This total support includes any pensions the dependent received, including Social Security and Railroad Retirement benefits.

The gross income test. Generally you cannot claim a person as a dependent if that individual had a gross income of $750 or more. The gross income test does not apply to a taxpayer's child who is less than nineteen years of age, or to a child who is a full-time student, *regardless of age.*

Relationship test. The dependent must be related to the taxpayer. These relations are child, grandchild, great-grandchild, legally adopted child, and stepchild. Brother, sister, half-brother, half-sister, step-brother, step-sister, parent, grandparent, stepfather, stepmother. Uncles, aunts, and first cousins. The taxpayer's father-in-law, mother-in-law, son-in-law, daughter-in-law, brother-in-law, and sister-in-law. Such relations don't have to live in the taxpayer's household to qualify as a dependent. For example, a taxpayer may claim an exemption for his or her mother-in-law, if she qualifies in all other respects, even though she does not live with the person who is claiming the exemption. Once any of the above relationships have been established by marriage, they are not terminated by death or divorce.

Citizenship test. The taxpayer's dependent must be a citizen or resident of the United States, or a resident of Canada or Mexico.

The joint return test. The taxpayer is not allowed an exemption for a dependent if that person files a joint return.

Example. You supported your daughter for the entire year while her husband was in the armed forces. The couple files a joint return. Even though your daughter meets all the other tests, you may not claim her as a dependent. However, if your son-in-law files a separate return, he may not claim an exemption for your daughter, but you can because she now qualifies as your dependent.

Exception. You may claim an exemption for your married dependent, if neither the dependent nor the dependent's spouse is required to file a return, but they file a joint return anyway in order to claim a refund of tax withheld.

The tax credit. The tax credit is $35 for each personal exemption that the taxpayer claims on his return. In lieu of the $35 tax credit per exemption, the taxpayer may take 2 percent of his or her adjusted gross income up to a maximum of $180, if this is greater. This alternative method of calculating the amount of the tax credit benefits low-income taxpayers with a small family, or no family. For example, a married couple with no children has an adjusted gross income of $8,000. Since they have only two personal exemptions, they have a $70 tax credit by the normal method of computation (2 × $35). By the alternative method, they can take a tax credit of $160 (2% of $8,000). If the regular method of a $35 credit for each personal exemption is used, the taxpayer does not have to make any computation or entry on the tax forms because this tax credit (like the ZBA) is *automatically included* in the Tax Tables and the Tax Rate Schedules.

In addition to filling out Schedule A, there are various other computations that are necessary to properly file an income tax return. One of the most confusing is how to compute the capital gains tax. This is a problem for anyone who sells a capital asset at a profit or a loss, retired or not. However, older persons quite often encounter this tax for the first time. This is because throughout life, so far, they have retained all of their capital assets. But now, because of a change in life-style (the children are grown), or because more income is required (the breadwinner has retired), they need to sell securities or real estate. They are, therefore, faced with (to them) a brand new application of the income tax law.

The Capital Gains Tax

The capital gains tax is a tax imposed on the profit realized from selling a capital asset that a person bought, held for a certain period of time, and later sold. For income tax purposes, any property that is not used in the operation of a business is considered to be a capital asset. Examples of capital assets are stocks and bonds, mutual funds, and real estate.

The selling or exchange of capital may result in either gains or losses. These gains and losses on stocks and bonds and similar investments, and gains (but not losses) on a home owned and occupied by the seller as a residence, must be reported on Schedule D at the time the federal income tax return is filed.

First, let's consider the taxation of capital gains (as against losses).

A capital gain is a *long-term gain* if the asset sold was held for more than one year.[2] If a long-term gain is incurred, the taxpayer gets a break because only one-half of the profit needs to be reported on the federal income tax return; the other one-half is tax-free. The tax liability on the half that is reported as income varies according to one's income tax bracket.

For example, assume that you are a married taxpayer and you bought in the past 100 shares of XYZ Corporation for $5,000.

2. For taxable years beginning after 1976, the Tax Reform Act of 1976 increased the holding period necessary to qualify a capital asset for a long-term capital gain or loss treatment. For the taxable year beginning in 1977, the holding period increased from "more than six months" to "more than nine months." For taxable years beginning after 1977, the period was increased to "more than one year."

More than one year later you sell these shares for $6,000. One-half of the profit, or $500, is yours tax-free. The remaining $500 is assessed according to your income tax bracket. If your tax bracket is 32 percent, you must pay an income tax of $160 on the $500 profit. On the other hand, if you earn $1,000 of interest income from your savings account and are in the same 32 percent bracket, you must pay a tax of $320, for you are assessed on the entire $1,000. In either case the extra $1,000 is equally important to you, but it is how you made it that makes the difference. The $1,000 of long-term profit from the sale of a capital asset would leave you with $160 more to save or to spend.

A capital gain is a *short-term gain* if the asset was held for one year or less. In this case the entire gain is taxed at ordinary income tax rates; that is, the short-term capital gain is treated as though it were ordinary income, such as derived from wages, salary, or interest.

Second, let's consider the taxation of capital losses.

A capital loss is incurred when a capital asset (except a home) is sold at a loss. Capital losses (like capital gains) are classified as either long-term losses or short-term losses.

A capital loss is a *long-term loss* if the asset was held for more than one year. Only one-half of a long-term loss is deductible, up to a maximum of $3,000.[3] Any long-term loss in excess of this amount must be carried forward to future years, but it can be carried forward indefinitely until it is exhausted.

For example, assume that you bought a piece of real estate for $50,000 and more than one year later sold it for $44,000. You incurred a long-term loss of $6,000. Thus, you can take the maximum deduction of $3,000 (one-half of $6,000) against ordinary income in the year you report the loss.

A capital loss is a *short-term loss* if the asset was held for one

3. For the 1977 taxable year the maximum long-term loss increased from $1,000 to $2,000. For the 1978 taxable year it increased to $3,000.

year or less. A short-term loss is fully deductible dollar for dollar against ordinary income, subject to the three limitations mentioned below concerning the capital loss deduction.

If you have both capital gains and capital losses during the year, they must be balanced against each other. After the net short-term gain (or loss) is entered on Schedule D, and the net long-term capital gain (or loss) is also entered on Schedule D, the two results are merged. If the result is a net gain, one set of rules applies. If the result is a net loss, a different set of rules is used.

How to take a capital gain deduction. If the net long-term capital gain exceeds the net short-term capital loss, a deduction equal to 50 percent *of the excess* may be claimed on Schedule D. If there is no net short-term capital loss, the capital gain deduction is 50 percent of the net long-term capital gain.

How to take a capital loss deduction. If the capital losses exceed the capital gains, a capital loss deduction may be claimed. The deduction is limited to the smallest of the following: (a) the taxable income for the year, computed without regard to either capital gains and losses or deductions for personal exemptions, (b) $3,000, or (c) the net capital loss as described below.

As we mentioned earlier, net short-term capital losses can be used to reduce ordinary income dollar for dollar, subject to limitations (a) and (b) above.

However, only 50 percent of net long-term capital losses can be used to reduce ordinary income. For example, it takes $2,000 of net long-term capital losses to produce a $1,000 deduction. Thus, it takes $6,000 in net long-term capital losses to take the maximum deduction of $3,000, according to limitation (b) above.

For example, assume that for the tax year you had wages of $8,000, a net long-term capital loss of $1,600, and you claim the standard deduction. Your capital loss serves to reduce your ordinary income by $800 (one-half of $1,600).

In another example, assume that you had wages of $8,000 but a net long-term capital loss of $600, and in addition, you had a $500 net short-term capital loss. Your capital loss deduction of $800 is computed as follows:

Net short-term capital loss	$500
One-half of net long-term capital loss (½ of $600)	300
Total capital loss deduction	$800

If you have both a gain and a loss in one year, or a combination of a long-term loss and a short-term loss, you need to know how to compute your net capital loss for the year. You calculate it by using one of the three following rules.

1. If you had a net *short-term capital loss* and a net *long-term capital gain,* your capital loss is the excess of your net short-term capital loss over your net long-term capital gain.
2. If you had a net *long-term capital loss* and a net *short-term capital gain,* your capital loss is one-half of the excess of your net long-term capital loss over your net short-term capital gain.
3. If you had both a net *short-term capital loss* and a net *long-term capital loss,* your capital loss is your net short-term capital loss plus one-half of your net long-term capital loss.

For example, assume that you had the following gains and losses for the year.

	Short-Term	Long-Term
Gains	$700	$ 400
Losses	800	2,000

Your net capital loss would amount to $900, computed as follows:

Short-term capital loss	$800	
Less: Short-term capital gain	700	
Net short-term capital loss		$100
Long-term capital loss	$2,000	
Less: Long-term capital gain	400	
Net long-term capital loss	$1,600	

Less: One-half of net long-term loss		
(½ of $1,600)	800	800
Net capital loss		$900

Capital loss carryover. If the net capital loss is greater than that allowed under the three limitations on taking a capital loss deduction (normally the $3,000 limitation), the excess may be carried over to subsequent years until it is completely used up.

When a loss is carried over, it retains its original character as either a short-term capital loss or a long-term capital loss. That is, a long-term capital loss carried over from a previous year will offset long-term gains of the current year *before* it offsets short-term gains of the current year. Also, when carrying over an unused long-term capital loss, 100 percent of the loss is carried over to the following year and is treated as if it had been incurred in that year.

Computation of the alternative capital gains tax. Computing the alternative capital gains tax may result in a lower tax liability than computing the tax liability at regular tax rates. This is because the maximum capital gains tax is 25 percent on the first $50,000 ($25,000 for a married person filing a separate return) of long-term capital gains in any one year. This holds true no matter how high a taxpayer's bracket may be. Therefore, if there is any question in your mind about which method to use in computing your capital gains tax, you should try both the regular and the alternative methods and then elect the one which produces the lower tax.

There are two conditions under which the alternative tax method will yield a smaller tax liability than the regular method. These situations are explained below.

When the long-term capital gain exceeds $50,000. Under this condition, the alternative capital gains tax is computed as follows:

1. Compute the regular tax on the ordinary income.
2. Add the maximum tax (25 percent) on the first $50,000 of net long-term capital gain.

3. Add the difference between the regular tax on the total taxable income and the regular tax on the ordinary income, plus $25,000.

To illustrate, assume that you are single and your total taxable income is $150,000, which includes $38,000 of ordinary income and a $112,000 net capital gain deduction (which is one-half of your total long-term gains of $224,000). The two methods of computing your total tax liability are shown below for purposes of comparison.

Regular Method

Ordinary taxable income	$38,000
50% of long-term gains	122,000
Total taxable income	$150,000
Regular tax rates:	
On $100,000	$53,090
70% of amount in excess of $100,000	35,000
Total regular tax	$88,090

Alternative Tax Method

Regular tax on $38,000 of ordinary income		$13,290
Maximum tax of 25% on the first $50,000 of long-term capital gains		12,500
Regular tax on total taxable income	$88,090	
Less: Regular tax on $38,000 + $25,000 (one-half of the first $50,000 of long-term gains)	38,310	
Difference		59,780
Total alternative tax		$85,570

By using the alternative capital gains tax method, you save $2,520 ($88,090 less $85,570). The effect of this computation is to tax the first $50,000 of your long-term capital gain at the maximum rate of 25 percent, and the balance of your income at the higher rates.

When the long-term capital gain is less than $50,000. When this condition exists (even though your capital gain is low), it is also advantageous to use the alternative tax, *but only if your*

income tax bracket is above 50 percent. The alternative capital
gains tax is then computed as follows:

1. Reduce the taxable income by the amount of the capital gain
deduction (i.e., one-half of the total capital gain).
2. Compute the regular tax on the amount obtained from (1) above.
3. Add one-half of the capital gain deduction to the tax computed
in (2) above.

To illustrate, assume that you are single and have a total
taxable income of $44,000 (which places you in a 55 percent tax
bracket). Your total taxable income includes a $2,000 capital
gain deduction (which is one-half of your total long-term gain
of $4,000). The regular tax on $44,000 of taxable income is
$16,590. Your alternative tax is computed as follows:

Total taxable income	$44,000
Less: Capital gain deduction	2,000
Reduced taxable income	$42,000
Regular tax on $42,000	$15,490
Plus: One-half of the capital gain deduction	1,000
Total alternative tax	$16,490

Again, by using the alternative capital gains tax method, you
save $100 ($16,590 less $16,490). The effect of this computation
is to tax a long-term gain of less than $50,000 at the maximum
of 25 percent no matter how high a taxpayer's bracket may
be.

There are five conditions under which a taxpayer who has
made a long-term capital gain can reduce the capital gains tax
or not pay it at all. Two of these conditions were discussed in
the chapter on real estate and involved selling a home. When
the three other situations occur the capital gains tax can be
avoided entirely.

When a property is exchanged for another of similar kind, no
capital gains tax is imposed provided both properties were held
for business or investment purposes. The investor who is on his
or her way up, i.e., acquiring a larger piece of property each

time a trade is made, should have no difficulty in avoiding the capital gains tax. How long can this go on? It can go on until the owner sells or dies. If the owner sells, then the deferred capital gains tax must be paid. If he or she dies before selling, and the heir in turn sells, then the heir will have to go back to the testator's original cost basis. Exchanging one property for another enables an investor to build up equity over a period of years through a series of tax-deferred exchanges. It's true that if cash is needed the equity that is locked up in the property won't buy groceries or finance a trip to Europe. The answer: the owner can refinance the property. The money obtained through refinancing is spendable cash that can be used for any purpose, including financing additional investments. It is tax-free, since it represents neither income nor capital gain—the money obtained from the proceeds is a loan, nothing more. And what is also advantageous, it enables the investor to retain ownership of the property.

When real estate is sold because of an involuntary conversion, no capital gains tax is imposed on the profit. An involuntary conversion takes place when property is taken by the government (federal, state, or local) under its right of eminent domain. A government exercises the right in order to build a school or a highway, for instance. The property owner need not pay the capital gains tax in this case provided that the money received for the involuntarily converted property is used to buy similar property. That is, if the property involuntarily converted was not used for business purposes, the individual must buy replacement property similar or related in service or use; by the same token, if the involuntarily converted property was used for business purposes, the replacement property also must be of like kind.

When an individual transfers ownership of property by giving it to someone else, rather than by selling it, he or she does not have to pay a capital gains tax. For example, if you transfer ownership of a ranch to your son, no tax is imposed on this transaction. However, if your son should later sell the ranch, the cost basis upon which to determine any profit he makes is based on what the ranch cost you.[4]

Dividends from stocks are taxed at ordinary income rates. However, every taxpayer is allowed a dividend exclusion of $100 ($200 if married and filing a joint return). If a married couple would like to have a little tax-free income (an advantage they don't now have), they could invest $4,000 in a sound common stock that pays a 5 percent dividend and thus receive $200 that is tax-free. In addition, they would have an opportunity for profit, thus giving them a chance for protection against the inroads of inflation.

Sometimes a corporation declares a stock dividend instead of paying a cash dividend. Stock dividends, which are distributions by a corporation of its own stock to its shareholders, are not taxable when received. In effect, stock dividends reduce the cost basis of all the shares owned by the shareholder. However, if the shares are subsequently sold, the difference between the reduced cost basis and the sale price must be treated by the shareholder as a capital gain (or loss).

For example, assume that you own 100 shares of the XYZ Corporation which cost you $2,000. If the XYZ Corporation subsequently issues a 50 percent stock dividend, this means that you now own 150 shares instead of 100. The additional 50 shares do not constitute taxable income. However, the cost basis of all 150 shares is reduced from $20 a share ($2,000/100) to $13.33 a shares ($2,000/150). If you subsequently sell the shares, the price you must use to determine your capital gain (or loss) is $13.33.

Stock rights are not to be confused with stock dividends when computing taxable income. Stock rights are issued to stockhold-

4. If the value of the gift property exceeds the annual exclusion of $3,000, the donor is subject to the federal (and possibly a state) gift tax. See the discussion on gift taxes on pages 244–247.

ers when a corporation wants to raise money via a new stock issue. For instance, one stock right might be given to buy one new share for each ten shares already held by a stockholder. These stock rights have a value in the market, and they may or may not be exercised by the stockholder. At the time the stock rights are received, they are nontaxable. However, if the rights are exercised or sold, the stockholder must know how to compute the cost basis of the rights, as well as the cost basis of the new and old shares.

The value of one right is computed by the following formula:

$$\text{One right} = \frac{\text{Market value of stock less subscription price}}{\text{Number of rights required to purchase one share plus 1}}$$

For example, assume that you own 100 shares of the ACE Corporation that you bought at $22 a share, or for a total of $2,200. Also assume that the current market price of ACE stock is $30 and that the corporation issues you ten stock rights that entitle you to purchase ten additional shares of ACE stock at a subscription price per share of $26. According to the formula given above, the value of one right is $2, computed as follows:

$$\frac{\$30 - \$26}{1 + 1} = \frac{\$4}{2} = \$2$$

Thus, if you sell the ten rights, the cost basis that you must use to determine your capital gain (or loss) is $2 per right, or $20 for all 10 rights.

On the other hand, if you decide to purchase new shares when exercising your rights, the cost bases of both the new and the old shares are computed in different ways. The cost basis of the new stock is equal to the subscription price plus the value of one right ($26 + $2), or $28 per share. The cost basis of the 100 shares of the old stock is reduced by the cost basis of the 10 rights to $2,180 ($2,200–$20).

The distribution of a realized gain by a mutual fund at the end of its fiscal year is the result of shifting the fund's investment portfolio during the year at a net profit. This realized gain distribution is treated as a long-term gain by the shareholder. All realized gain distributions, *regardless of the length of time the shareholder has owned shares of the fund,* are taxed at the capital gains tax rate. That is, the shareholder does not have to own the shares for more than one year in order to have a long-term gain.

A mutual fund shareholder who is on a withdrawal plan receives a check monthly or quarterly from the sale of his or her shares. The shareholder on such a plan must know whether the shares were sold at a long-term gain or a long-term loss. The mutual fund's year-end financial statement to the shareholder will give the amount of the gain (or loss) for income tax purposes. The amount of gain (or loss) is determined by a computer, using the average cost of the shares in the shareholder's account.

The ownership of real estate has decided tax advantages.

No matter what kind of real estate is owned (including your home) the interest on the mortgage and the property taxes are deductible. If real estate is sold, the gain (or loss) is subject to the rules concerning capital gains and losses (except no loss deduction can be taken on your home).

The biggest tax deduction on real estate is depreciation, which can be taken on property that is owned for investment or business purposes. Depreciation is a loss in value of an asset due to deterioration, obsolescence, or use. Depreciation may be taken as a deduction over a period of years on the improvements and the buildings of income property. Just how much depreciation is allowed by the Internal Revenue Service on income-producing property depends upon its interpretation of an asset's useful life. For example, a new house purchased as an investment can be depreciated over a period of fifty years, or at the rate of 2 percent a year. A new apartment house can be depreciated over a period of forty years, or at the rate of 2½ percent a year. An older building, such as an old house or an old apartment building, is considered by the IRS to have a useful life of twenty years and can be depreciated at the rate of 5 percent a year.

Depreciation is a bigger tax deduction than most people realize because it is taken against the entire value of the property, not just on the amount of the property owner's down payment. As a result of this inherent advantage, income-producing property that is actually operated at a profit can often be shown as operating at a loss on the owner's income tax return. For example, assume that an investor bought an old apartment house for $200,000 with a down payment of 25 percent and financed the balance of the purchase price with a $150,000 mortgage at 8 percent. Assume also that the gross rental income is $30,000 and that operating expenses are $14,000.

Gross rental income	$30,000
Less operating expenses	14,000
Income after operating expenses	$16,000
Less interest on the mortgage	
(8% × $150,000)	12,000
Net income	$ 4,000
Less depreciation	
(5% of $200,000)	10,000
Net loss	($ 6,000)

The above example demonstrates how a net income of $4,000 actually turned into a net loss of $6,000 because of the $10,000 depreciation deduction. The net income of $4,000 was cash in the investor's pocket because depreciation is not an out-of-pocket expense. Ideally the investor should put this money aside every year so that some day, when the apartment house wears out, he or she will have the money available to buy or build a new structure. In reality, however, no real-estate owner sets this money aside. The depreciation deduction means income to the investor, and it is excluded income as far as federal income tax returns are concerned.

There are several applications of the income tax law that apply to people for the first time because they are retired. This is because they receive payments or income that are different from any that they have received before. These include lump-sum payments from an insurance policy, lump-sum payments from a pension or profit-sharing plan, income from annuities, or installment proceeds from life insurance.

The normal settlement of a life insurance policy is payment of the face amount in a lump sum to the named beneficiary because the insured died. This lump-sum payment is not income to the beneficiary. The insurance proceeds are a capital asset, and like other capital assets, they are simply a transfer of property from one individual to another, which may subject the funds to death taxes, depending upon the size of the estate and state law, but not to income taxes. In addition, a life insurance death benefit is different from any other type of property. The proceeds are not a transfer by the insurance company of the deceased's already existing funds. They are a benefit which became due and payable only because the insured died.

A lump sum may also be paid to the insured himself, because he or she surrendered the policy while still alive, in order to receive the cash surrender value. This lump-sum payment is also not subject to federal or state income taxes for it comes under the cost-recovery rule, meaning that the insured is allowed to recover the cost before an income tax is due. The cost of a life insurance policy is the sum of the premiums paid. In a whole life policy the cash surrender value is always less than the total premiums, unless the insured is one of the lucky ones who lives to be one hundred years old.

If the life insurance involved is a participating policy and dividends are earned, these are also not subject to income taxes, because the IRS has ruled that dividends from a mutual policy are not income to the insured but the return of an overpayment. If the dividends have been left to compound with the insurance company, and then cashed for a lump sum, this amount is not subject to tax, except for any interest that the dividends may have earned.

When a person retires and receives a lump-sum payment from a qualified pension or profit-sharing plan, it is treated for tax purposes in three different ways.

1. The employee's contribution portion will not be taxed, for he or she paid taxes on these payments at the time that they were put into the plan.
2. The employer's contribution portion that was accrued before 1970 will be taxed as a capital gain.
3. The employer's contribution portion that was paid into the plan *after 1969* is ordinary income. (This was inserted into the Tax Reform Act of 1969.)

Example. During 1974 you retired from your job and received a lump-sum distribution of $20,000 from your employer's pension plan. Included in this amount was $3,000 that you paid into the plan and $17,000 of employer contributions, of which $2,000 was contributed after 1969. The tax treatment of the distribution looks like this:

Total distribution	$20,000
Less: Return of your contribution tax-free	3,000
Balance	$17,000
Employer's post 1969 contributions—	
taxed as ordinary income	2,000
Remainder taxed as capital gain	$15,000

Let's suppose in the above example that you didn't want to retire in 1974. You wanted to work beyond retirement age, and your employer agreed. You are considered to have received no income under the plan until you actually retire if, *before you reach retirement age,* you irrevocably agree to forego your right to withdraw your vested interest until after you terminate your employment. It is important to realize that you must make this election before you retire if a favorable capital gain treatment of the lump-sum distribution is to be obtained.

Annuities are normally paid to people who are 65 and over. The income tax computation that must be made in regard to them is therefore almost exclusively the province of those who are retired.

Annuities are not life insurance policies. A lump-sum immediate annuity purchased by a retired person, which guarantees to pay a fixed number of dollars per month, is simply a return to him or her (in a series of payments) of the annuitant's own money plus some interest. They are sold solely by life insurance companies for one reason only—the payments are guaranteed for life.

Since most of each payment is the annuitant's own money, the greater proportion of it is nontaxable. The percentage that is excluded from income is determined by dividing the investment in the contract by the expected return. This percentage remains the same for the entire period of the annuity, even though the total payments exceed the investment. The investment in the contract is its cost; the expected return is the total payments that will be received.

Carol Lucas, a widow age 70, purchased a non-refund annuity for $22,000 that guaranteed her a payment of $200 per month for life. The life expectancy of a female age 70 is twelve years —therefore her expected return from the contract was $28,800 ($200 × 12 × 12). Her investment in the contract of $22,000 divided by her expected return of $28,800 equals 76 percent. She could exclude from each monthly payment $152.00 (76 percent of $200), no matter if she lived to age 100.

A joint and survivor annuity. This type of annuity is usually purchased by a married couple for it guarantees the same payment for life to both annuitants. The multiple percentage that is used can be obtained from the Internal Revenue Service and depends upon the age of each of them.[5]

A joint annuity, with one-half to the survivor. Married peo-

5. Internal Revenue Service, Publication 76.

ple who buy this type of annuity want the payment to be larger while they are both alive, on the theory that the survivor can live for less. When the survivor receives less, a different calculation of the expected return has to be made.

Example. You and your wife purchased a joint annuity providing for payments to you of $100 per month for life, but after your death, $50 per month to your wife. If you are 70 and she is 67, the expected return is computed as follows:

The combined life expectancies of both annuitants	19.7 years
Life expectancy for age 70	12.1 years
Difference	7.6 years
Portion of expected return age 70 (12.1 × $1,200)	$14,520
Portion of expected return age 67 (7.6 × $600)	4,560
Total expected return under the contract	$19,080

If your investment in the contract is $14,310, then 75 percent of each payment is a return of your own capital and is nontaxable ($14,310/$19,080). Twenty-five dollars ($100–$75) is taxable income. After your death your wife continues to use the same percentage; only $12.50 of each $50.00 payment will be taxable income to her.

A refund life annuity.[6] When this type of an annuity is purchased, the investment in the contract has to be reduced by the amount of the possible refund, which is expressed as a percentage of the investment. Once again tables are provided by the Internal Revenue Service so the taxpayer can determine the percentage that applies to her or him, which in turn depends upon age.

Example. You are a male, age 65, and you purchased for $12,000 an immediate refund annuity that pays you $100 per month for life, ten years certain to your beneficiary. The contract provides that if you do not survive the full ten years, the same monthly payment will be made to your beneficiary, but

6. For an explanation of a refund annuity, the reader is referred to Chapter 8.

only, of course, for the number of months that you did not live to receive it.

Because of the refund feature, your investment in the contract has to be reduced by the dollar value of the refund. This is computed as follows:

Total investment in the contract	$12,000
Amount to be received annually	$ 1,200
Number of years payment is guaranteed ($12,000/$1,200)	10
Rounded to nearest whole number of years	10
Percentage of cost reduced by refund feature (IRS Publication 76, page 52)	24%
Value of the refund feature (24% of $12,000)	$ 2,880
Investment in the contract	$ 9,120

You may exclude from income 76 percent of your $100 monthly payment ($9,120/$12,000). The other $24 ($100 less $76) is taxable income.

Many times an annuitant does not purchase a contract from an insurance company, but the monthly installments are paid to him or her as part of a company pension plan. If the employee has partly contributed to the pension cost, a special three-year rule applies that makes the payment in the early years nontaxable.

If an employee will recover his or her cost within three years after receiving the first payment, all of the monthly payments are tax-exempt until the cost is recovered. Thereafter, all payments are income.

If the taxpayer recovers his or her cost in the annuity in less than three years, the annuitant is faced with a special computation.

Example. James Smith, age 66 and retired, received $300 a month from his company in the form of an annuity. He had contributed during his working years a total of $9,000 toward its cost. He received his first annuity check in 1972, and recovered $7,200 of his contribution within two years. In the first six months of 1974 he recovered the balance of his investment in the contract of $1,800. Up to this point, because his investment was returned to him in less than three years after he retired, his $300 a month annuity income was tax-free. In July, however, his annuity became fully taxable. He therefore had to report $1,800 on his return in 1974, and thereafter had to pay a tax on the full $3,600 each year.

As we have previously stated, a life insurance death benefit that is paid in a lump sum is not subject to income taxes.

If, however, the beneficiary receives the death benefit in installments, the payments are treated as an annuity and taxed like an annuity. If the beneficiary is a surviving spouse, he or she is given a tax break. The Internal Revenue Code provides that, each year, up to $1,000 of the interest portion of such payment may be excluded.

However, if a surviving spouse elects to leave the insurance proceeds on deposit with the insurance company under an agreement to pay interest only, then the interest is income to the beneficiary. The "surviving spouse" rule does not apply.

The Tax Credit for the Elderly

This is the tax benefit that is least understood by those who are retired.[7]

You may qualify for the credit if you are 65 before the close of the year. This is the only requirement. However, if you receive either Social Security or Railroad Retirement benefits you probably won't qualify because the amount you receive from this source would exceed the initial amount on which the credit is based. This means that the tax credit is mainly for those who have little or no benefits from Social Security or Railroad Retirement.

The tax credit is 15 percent of the allowable amount. This

7. This was formerly called The Retirement Income Credit.

amounts to a maximum credit of 15 percent of $2,500, or $375, if single; and 15 percent of $3,750, or $562.50, if married filing a joint return, both spouses 65 or over. This is a sizable tax credit; therefore it is important for retired people to understand the regulation.

The initial amount on which the credit is based is the following:

a. $2,500 if single, 65 or over
b. $2,500 if married filing a joint return, only one spouse 65 or over
c. $3,750 if married filing a joint return, both spouses 65 or over
d. $1,875 if married filing a separate return, 65 or over, and have not lived with your spouse at any time during the taxable year

However, this amount is reduced by:

a. Social Security or Railroad Retirement benefits
b. Tax-free pension or annuity income, and
c. One-half of your adjusted gross income exceeding $7,500, if you are single; and $10,000, if you are married and filing a joint return.

No reduction has to be made for tax-free payments from the cost portion of an annuity payment, life insurance proceeds, military disability pensions, payments for injury or sickness, and workmen's compensation benefits.

Example. Both you and your spouse are over 65. Your Social Security benefits amount to $2,000. Your adjusted gross income from a part-time job and dividends and interest is $12,000. You would figure your tax credit for the elderly as follows:

Initial amount		$3,750
Less: Social Security	$2,000	
Reduction for excess adjusted gross income (½ of $2,000)	1,000	
Total reductions		3,000
Balance equals credit base		$ 750
Amount of credit (15% of $750)		$ 112.50

While this may not seem like much of a tax advantage, a retired couple should realize that this is not just a tax deduction, but a tax credit against their final income tax computation. A couple with an adjusted gross income of $12,000 would be in a 19 percent tax bracket. A *tax deduction* of $112.50 reduces their taxes by $21.38 ($112.50 × 19%). A *tax credit* deducted from the tax itself saves the entire $112.50. A filled-in form for Schedule R, using this example is shown here.

Tax Aid for the Elderly

Many older people are simply unable to comprehend all of the deductions, credits, and exemptions allowed by the Internal Revenue Code. The tax provisions discussed in this chapter present formidable challenges, and to some they are hopelessly confusing. To an aged widow, who has had no previous experience in tax matters, the tax law seems to present innumerable pitfalls.

Proper tax counseling, however, can overcome many of these difficulties. In 1969 the American Association of Retired Persons set up a Tax Aide program for those who are 65 and over. It has proven to be tremendously successful. Tax Aide provides helpful advice to several hundred thousand elderly taxpayers every year, many of whom are not members of the AARP, for the program is open to all older retired persons as a public service of the association. Under this program, the local chapters of the American Association of Retired Persons (and the National Retired Teachers Association, for they are affiliated) select coordinators each year who organize and supervise Tax Aide for their particular area. Working under the coordinator, counselors volunteer their services and undergo intensive training by the Internal Revenue Service. Being retired people themselves, they are uniquely qualified to win the confidence and handle the tax problems of those who are retired.

The counselors *do not* make out tax returns. They counsel

Schedules R & RP—Credit for the Elderly

(Form 1040)
Department of the Treasury
Internal Revenue Service

(Public Retirees Under 65 See Schedule RP on Back)

▶ **Attach to Form 1040.** ▶ **See Instructions for Schedules R and RP (Form 1040).**

1977

Name(s) as shown on Form 1040	Your social security number
Frank B. and Evelyn H. Jones	

Important:

- Use Schedule R if you are 65 or over (or if married filing jointly and either spouse is 65 or over) and have any type of income.
- Use Schedule RP (on back) if you are under 65 and have pension or annuity income from a public retirement system such as a federal, state, or local government system.
- You may elect to use Schedule RP (on back) if you are married filing jointly, one of you is 65 or over and the other is under 65, and the one who is under 65 has pension or annuity income from a public retirement system. Unless you both elect to use Schedule RP, you must use Schedule R.

Schedule R Credit for the Elderly—Individual(s) 65 or Over Having Any Type of Income   **R**

Filing Status and Age (check only one)	A ☐ Single, 65 or over
	B ☐ Married filing joint return, only one spouse 65 or over
	C ☒ Married filing joint return, both spouses 65 or over
	D ☐ Married filing separate return, 65 or over, and have not lived with your spouse at any time during the taxable year

1 Initial amount of income for credit computation: If box A or B checked—enter $2,500 / If box C checked—enter $3,750 / If box D checked—enter $1,875			**1**	3,750 | 00
2 Deduct:				
a Amounts received as pensions or annuities under the Social Security Act, the Railroad Retirement Acts (but not supplemental annuities), and certain other exclusions from gross income (see instructions)	2,000 | 00			
b Enter one-half the excess of your adjusted gross income (Form 1040, line 31) over: $7,500 if box A checked; $10,000 if box B or C checked; or $5,000 if box D checked	1,000 | 00			
3 Total of lines 2a and 2b			**3**	3,000 | 00
4 Balance (subtract line 3 from line 1). If line 3 is larger than line 1, do not file this schedule			**4**	750 | 00
5 Tentative credit. Enter 15% of line 4			**5**	112 | 50
6 Amount of tax shown on Form 1040, line 37			**6**	630 | 00
7 Credit for the Elderly. Enter here and on Form 1040, line 39, the amount on line 5 or 6 whichever is smaller ▶			**7**	112 | 50

about various sections of the tax law, such as the Tax Credit for the Elderly, for example. They make computations when necessary and try to ensure that each taxpayer interviewed is taking all of his or her deductions. Thousands of counselers are appointed each year, trained by IRS officials using resource material prepared especially for assisting those who are 65 and over.

This service is becoming increasingly important as inflation robs the older retired person's limited pocketbook.

13

Watch Out—The Internal Revenue Service Could Be Your Biggest Heir

There is nothing sure in life except death and taxes, as the old saying goes.

And you agree. But since you've always paid your income taxes, and you're not dead yet, you might well say: "What's the problem?"

The problem is death taxes, both federal and state, which may be assessed against your estate when you die. It's true, if you're not worth much, you won't owe anything. But you are probably worth more than you think. The way prices of houses have gone up, your home has probably doubled in value the last few years. If, to the increased value of your home, you add the death benefit of your life insurance, and the amount of your savings and investments, you may be surprised to find that your estate is large enough to be taxed at your death.

Even if you find you are not worth enough to subject your estate to death taxes, it might be advisable to know all about these taxes anyway just to satisfy yourself and your spouse (or your other heirs) that you don't have a problem.

The first and foremost assessment against your estate is the federal estate tax. This is not an inheritance tax as such, but a tax levied by the Internal Revenue Service on a testator's right to transfer his property to his heirs. Most people, when they learn about this for the first time, are outraged. After paying income taxes all of their lives, they now have to pay again on what they thought was a tax-free estate. Why should they have to pay an additional tax on the right to transfer their death estate to their heirs! The fact that they do has been true since 1916, and it is still true, despite the fact that the estate and gift tax laws were changed and liberalized (at least as far as the amount of the personal exemption is concerned) by the passage of the Tax Reform Act of 1976.

This act established a combined federal estate and gift tax schedule.[1] When a person dies, the estate tax applies to (1) all property passing to heirs, (2) all taxable gifts made since January 1, 1977,[2] and (3) all gifts made within three years of death. The legal representative of the deceased enters the combined rate schedule with this total to find the amount of the tentative tax. The actual tax is found by subtracting any gift taxes paid by the decedent since January 1, 1977.

This actual tax, however, is further reduced by the amount of the unified credit, which is $30,000 for 1977 (the first year of the new law). The unified credit increases every year to a maximum of $47,000 for the year 1981 and thereafter. A copy of the combined rate schedule is shown. Below the schedule is a table illustrating the unified credit, and the amount of the exemption "equivalent" that this credit produces in dollars. The dollar amount that is exempt from the estate tax was approximately doubled by the Tax Reform Act of 1976, which put into effect the first changes in the estate and gift tax laws in over thirty years.

Many people don't know how to use the combined rate schedule, or how the exemption "equivalent" is computed.

Let's assume that a testator dies in 1978, leaving an estate

1. Formerly, the estate tax and the gift tax had separate schedules, with the gift tax rate equal to about 75 percent of the estate tax rate.
2. A taxable gift is the amount by which a gift to a donee in a calendar year exceeds the $3,000 annual exclusion.

COMBINED
██████ ████ Rate Schedule for Federal Estate and Gift Taxes

If the amount with respect to which the tentative tax to be computed is:	The tentative tax is:
Not over $10,000	18 percent of such amount
Over $10,000 but not over $20,000	$1,800, plus 20 percent of the excess of such amount over $10,000.
Over $20,000 but not over $40,000	$3,800, plus 22 percent of the excess of such amount over $20,000.
Over $40,000 but not over $60,000	$8,200, plus 24 percent of the excess of such amount over $40,000.
Over $60,000 but not over $80,000	$13,000, plus 26 percent of the excess of such amount over $60,000.
Over $80,000 but not over $100,000	$18,200, plus 28 percent of the excess of such amount over $80,000.
Over $100,000 but not over $150,000	$23,800, plus 30 percent of excess of such amount over $100,000.
Over $150,000 but not over $250,000	$38,800, plus 32 percent of the excess of such amount over $150,000.
Over $250,000 but not over $500,000	$70,800, plus 34 percent of the excess of such amount over $250,000.
Over $500,000 but not over $750,000	$155,800, plus 37 percent of the excess of such amount over $500,000.
Over $750,000 but not over $1,000,000	$248,300, plus 39 percent of the excess of such amount over $750,000.
Over $1,000,000 but not over $1,250,000	$345,800, plus 41 percent of the excess of such amount over $1,000,000.
Over $1,250,000 but not over $1,500,000	$448,300, plus 43 percent of the excess of such amount over $1,250,000.
Over $1,500,000 but not over $2,000,000	$555,800, plus 45 percent of the excess of such amount over $1,500,000.
Over $2,000,000 but not over $2,500,000	$780,800, plus 49 percent of the excess of such amount over $2,000,000.
Over $2,500,000 but not over $3,000,000	$1,025,800, plus 53 percent of the excess of such amount over $2,500,000.
Over $3,000,000 but not over $3,500,000	$1,290,800, plus 57 percent of the excess of such amount over $3,000,000
Over $3,500,000 but not over $4,000,000	$1,575,800, plus 61 percent of the excess of such amount over $3,500,000.
Over $4,000,000 but not over $4,500,000	$1,880,800, plus 65 percent of the excess of such amount over $4,000,000.
Over $4,500,000 but not over $5,000,000	$2,205,800, plus 69 percent of the excess of such amount over $5,000,000.
Over $5,000,000	$2,550,800, plus 70 percent of the excess of such amount over $5,000,000.

The tentative tax applies to the sum of (a) the amount of the taxable estate and (b) the amount of the adjusted taxable gifts.

Year	Estate Appraisal	Tentative Tax	Tax Credit	Amount of Estate Tax
1977	$120,666	$30,000	$30,000	00
1978	$134,000	$34,000	$34,000	00
1979	$147,333	$38,000	$38,000	00
1980	$161,563	$42,500	$42,500	00
1981	$175,625	$47,000	$47,000	00

valued at $134,000. According to the combined rate schedule, the federal estate tax is computed as follows:

For the first $100,000	$23,000
30% of the amount in excess of	
$100,000 (30% × $34,000)	10,200
Tentative tax	$34,000
Gift taxes paid since 1–1–77	0
Actual tax	$34,000
Less unified credit	34,000
Federal estate tax	$ 0

Since no federal estate tax is due in the above example the entire value of the estate, $134,000, is the exemption "equivalent" provided by the 1978 unified credit of $34,000.[3]

So, as we previously stated, if you're not worth much you don't have an estate tax problem. Therefore, if you like, you can ignore the balance of this chapter. But for those of you with estates in excess of the above exemption "equivalents," we suggest that you read on.

The Marital Deduction

The purpose of the marital deduction rule, as passed by Congress many years ago, is to allow only one-half of the combined estate of a husband and wife to be taxed upon the death of the first spouse. This is the biggest estate tax deduction available to the average couple.

To understand the marital deduction rule, let's review the history of the common law in these United States. In the eight community property states, as we discussed in Chapter 4, the common law goes back to Spain. In these states the deceased spouse owns one-half of the community property; therefore only one-half of the total estate is taxed upon the first death.

3. For those who are familiar with the old law that was in existence prior to January 1, 1977, a comparison between the old and new law might be enlightening. Under the old law only the first $60,000 was exempt. On the same $134,000 appraisal, this resulted in an estate tax of $13,148 ($9,340 + $3,808).

In the other forty-two states the common law goes back to England where the husband dies possessed of everything; therefore not one-half but the entire estate of the two spouses is taxed upon the husband's death.

When residents of the non-community property states became aware of this discrimination many years ago, they objected vociferously, especially with the escalation of the federal estate tax during World War II.

In order to render all fifty states equal, despite the difference in origin of the common law, Congress passed the marital deduction rule. Now in all fifty states only one-half of a married couple's combined estate is taxed, providing the surviving spouse inherits his or her one-half by will or trust agreement, *with no strings attached.* This is where a competent attorney is important. He must draw the will so that one-half of the joint estate which is left to the surviving spouse meets five conditions.

1. The survivor is entitled to all of the income from the entire property (i.e., one-half of the joint estate).
2. Such income shall be paid annually, or at more frequent intervals.
3. She has the power, exercisable in favor of herself or of her estate, to appoint the entire interest, which means she has the legal right to leave her one-half to whomever she pleases.
4. Such power must be exercisable by her alone.
5. No part of the marital interest is subject to a power in anyone else (but the spouse) to leave the property to any person other than the *surviving* consort.

If these five conditions are met, only one-half of a joint estate will be taxed. The tax saving is substantial.

The amount of the marital deduction in both the eight community property states and the forty-two common law states is $250,000, or one-half of the adjusted gross estate, whichever is larger.[4] If $250,000 is the amount of combined estate of a hus-

---

4. Formerly only one-half of the adjusted gross estate was deductible. This meant that on a $250,000 estate only one-half, or $125,000, qualified for the marital deduction. The other one-half was taxed.

band and wife, the surviving spouse may be left the entire property and no federal estate tax will be imposed. This is a tremendous boon for married couples. However, there is a catch to it, for the reduction of the estate tax to zero is only an "interim" saving. This is because the surviving spouse will now own the entire $250,000, and when he or she in turn dies, the whole $250,000 is subject to the combined rate schedule.

Assume that you and your wife live in a non-community property state with an estate of $250,000, and that your will provides that your spouse inherits everything, with your lawyer inserting in your testamentary disposition the necessary five conditions of the marital deduction rule. Also assume that you have children.

When you die, the federal estate tax will be zero. When your wife dies in 1978 (using that year as an example) and leaves the $250,000 to your two children the federal estate tax is computed as follows:

Tentative tax on $250,000	$70,800
Gift taxes since 1–1–77	0
Actual tax	$70,800
Less unified credit for 1978	34,000
Federal estate tax	$36,800

This is a sizable sum to be paid on the death of the second spouse, and most married couples with children (or even other heirs) would like to avoid it, if possible.

There are two ways this can be accomplished. One way is to leave your spouse only $134,000. Since this is the amount of the exemption "equivalent" in dollars, the tax would be zero when he or she in turn dies. The balance of $116,000 ($250,000–$134,000) you can leave outright to your children. Since in 1978 your estate would also qualify for the $34,000 unified tax credit, which is the exemption "equivalent" of $134,000, the $116,000 you leave your children would not be taxed. Thus, upon the death of each of you, a federal estate tax would not be imposed at all against your respective estates.

This looks great, and the tax saving is substantial. But most people don't do this. Why? For several reasons.

First, because an estate of $250,000, even if it is entirely in assets earning 6 percent (which most estates are not) produces an income of only $15,000 a year, or $1,250 a month. Adequate, but not sumptuous, in these days of high living costs. The surviving spouse, therefore, needs the income from the entire estate.

Second, most couples have worked hard for their money and, therefore, feel it should be theirs to enjoy until they are both dead. The children will simply have to inherit less.

Finally, the children could squander the part that is left directly to them. Maybe they would dissipate all of the money anyway when they eventually inherit the entire estate, but at least their parents would be spared the knowledge of it.

No, most people won't go this route of leaving $116,000 directly to the children (out of a combined estate of $250,000), despite the federal estate tax saving of $36,800.

Fortunately there is a way, however, to avoid paying this estate tax, with the income from the entire estate, and the control of it, remaining in the hands of the surviving spouse. This is by the creation of a marital deduction trust. This way the $116,000 is still left to the children, but they do not inherit it now. The deceased spouse's portion, which is not left to the survivor, is left *in trust* for the children, with all of the income from the entire estate being paid to the surviving spouse. The children receive none of the income, nor do they come into possession of the property, until their parents are gone. The surviving spouse can not only receive all of the income, but the survivor can also be given the right in the trust agreement to withdraw $5,000, or 5 percent of the principal of the trust (whichever is greater), and still the remainder will pass tax-free to the children upon the second death.

The reason for this fortuitous result is because leaving an estate *in trust* for someone does not change its death tax status. A chart of a combined estate of $250,000, with $116,000 left in trust, looks like this:

Total Combined Estate—$250,000

HIS	HERS
$116,000	$134,000
31,300 tentative tax	34,000 tentative tax
34,000 unified credit	34,000 unified credit
$ 0 estate tax	$ 0 estate tax

$5,000 or 5% of the principal per year to the surviving spouse all income, plus

By this alternative method of leaving the $116,000 in trust, the survivor is not hurt financially in any way. The widow or widower, for it operates the same way for either spouse, has complete access to the capital of the marital deduction portion of the estate, and may draw an additional $5,000 of capital each year, or 5 percent, from the trust.

We have used an example of a combined estate of a married couple that amounts to $250,000. Larger estates can also employ the same principle, of course, and to an even greater advantage.

Assume that Mr. and Mrs. Albert Rodriguez have a combined estate of $400,000. With no marital deduction, Mr. Rodriguez's estate tax after deducting the $34,000 unified credit would be $87,800. However, if the full $250,000 marital deduction is taken, his estate is reduced to $150,000, resulting in an estate tax of $4,800 ($38,800 − $34,000). This results in an interim saving to Mrs. Rodriguez of $83,000, from which she can either spend the income or enjoy the capital, rather than giving this sum to the Internal Revenue Service. The $83,000 is called an interim saving, rather than a true ultimate saving, because full use of the marital deduction of $250,000 escalates the tax in the heirs' estate when Mrs. Rodriguez dies.

There is a danger of miscalculation here. It's not possible for Mr. Rodriguez to leave $384,000 to his wife free of the federal estate tax. This faulty reasoning assumes that Mr. Rodriguez can make full use of the marital deduction of $250,000 *and* the $134,000 exemption "equivalent" in his estate, thereby leaving both parts to Mrs. Rodriguez tax-free. This can't be done. The only way he can leave both parts tax-free is to leave the $134,000 to someone else, either outright to his children (or other heirs), or in trust for them.

Let's take one more example of an even larger estate.

Assume that Mr. and Mrs. Joseph Cleveland have a combined estate of $800,000. Now the marital deduction can be $250,000, or 50 percent of the adjusted gross estate, whichever is greater. Therefore, $400,000 can be left tax-free to Mrs. Cleveland because of the marital deduction, with the other $400,000 held in trust.

There can be also, in an estate of this size (or larger), a further tax saving. The trustee should realize that the income from the $400,000 that is held in trust (which will not be taxed again) can be compounded for the benefit of the eventual heirs. Thus, the tax-free portion of the estate will be increased. This is possible because an adequate cash flow can be provided to the survivor by spending not only the income from the marital deduction portion but part of the principal (up to the whole of it) as well. Principal dollars are 100 percent spendable dollars since no portion of them has to be taken for income taxes. Also, the more Mrs. Cleveland's estate can be reduced before she dies, the less will be taxed. If her estate is reduced from $400,000 to

$250,000, the estate tax saving will be $51,000 ($87,800 versus $36,800).

It should be emphasized that use of the marital deduction trust is not restricted to marriages that have lasted most of the adult lives of the two spouses involved. In these days of increasing longevity hundreds of thousands of people are marrying a second time, and they, too, can make use of the marital deduction trust. It should be understood by these couples, however, that the eventual disposition of the marital deduction portion must be left up to the survivor. The surviving consort must be given the absolute right to leave the marital deduction part of the combined estate to anyone that he or she chooses.

There is an additional problem encountered with all marital deduction trusts. This is created by the attorney who draws the trust agreement. Most attorneys want to name a bank as trustee, placing the entire estate in trust, calling the residuary trust portion Trust A and the marital deduction portion Trust B. This should not be allowed by the testator. It is frustrating for the survivor to have to deal with a bank trustee on the entire estate, possibly for a period of many years. This is avoided by naming the survivor as trustee instead of a bank. This way the survivor may revoke Trust B (which the bank won't do) and thereby be in sole possession of this portion of the estate. Only the deceased's portion is irrevocable and must be held in trust for the eventual remaindermen, who are the children or other heirs.

Of course, if the estate assets are difficult to manage, or the surviving spouse is completely inexperienced in money matters, then there is no alternative but to name a bank trustee on the entire estate.

A marital deduction trust is seldom used when the couple have no children. The sole purpose in creating such a trust is to reduce estate taxes upon the death of the surviving spouse. Most couples will agree there is slight object in holding part of a combined estate in trust, maybe for years, in order to save money for distant relatives. Let the death taxes fall where they may, for who cares? The heirs, whoever they may be, will be fortunate enough to inherit what is left, after taxes.

When a marital deduction trust is created, growth assets should not be used for the marital deduction portion. The testator should remember that marital deduction assets will be taxed in the survivor's estate to the extent that they are retained until his or her death. Further, they will be taxed at their fair market value upon the survivor's death. For this reason high income assets should be used for marital deduction purposes, with growth assets left in trust.

Gift Taxes

Gifts are made to heirs during a testator's lifetime for many reasons, but one of the most compelling is to reduce death taxes. A property owner may make gifts each year of $3,000 (or less) to as many donees as he or she likes, relatives or not, without paying a gift tax, or having the property that was transferred subject to death taxes, federal or state. If the spouse joins in the gifts, they may give $6,000 to each donee completely tax-free. No taxes of any kind will have to be paid—income taxes, gift taxes, or estate taxes—by either the donor or the donee. Definitely the donee, as the recipient of the gift property, should understand that he or she does not have to pay income taxes on the gift. The amount of the gift is not income to the donee—it is simply a transfer of capital.

Mr. and Mrs. Philip Carlyle had three children and were wealthy enough to have a death tax problem. Upon the advice of their investment representative they started giving $6,000 a year to each one of their children, or $18,000 a year, under their combined annual exclusion. At the end of ten years they had given away $180,000, completely free of taxes. Since their top combined rate schedule was 39 percent, they saved $70,200 in federal estate taxes by making these gifts.[5]

The above example assumes that Mr. and Mrs. Carlyle survived their tax-free gifts by three years. This is known as the three-year rule. If they did not survive the gifts by that length of time, the gifts they made within three years of death would have to be included in the estate appraisal for federal estate tax purposes.[6]

There is a gift tax marital deduction as opposed to an estate tax marital deduction. For many years a *gift tax marital deduction* has been allowed for 50 percent of gifts to a spouse. Under current law the first $100,000 of qualifying lifetime gifts to a spouse are deductible; none of the second $100,000 are deductible; then 50 percent of such gifts in excess of $200,000 are deductible.[7] Also under the law there is a close interplay between the gift tax marital deduction and the estate tax marital deduction. This is because the estate tax marital deduction is reduced by an amount equal to 50 percent of any gift tax marital deduction that is taken. This makes the first $100,000 of tax-free lifetime gifts to a spouse only an interim saving.

Andrew Dowd in 1978 gave $100,000 to his wife, and as a consequence did not pay a gift tax. But by so doing, he reduced the amount of the marital deduction available to his estate by $50,000—an amount that is equal to one-half of the $100,000 of lifetime gifts to his wife.

If Mr. Dowd's top combined rate schedule is 39 percent, the loss of $50,000 of his marital deduction will cost his estate eventually $19,500 in estate taxes when he dies.

If a testator gives away in any one calendar year in excess of

5. The $30,000 lifetime gift exemption per individual that was available prior to the Tax Reform Act of 1976 has been abolished.
6. The three-year rule supplants the old three-year contemplation of death rule, which gave the legal representative a chance for rebuttal. Under current law the donor must live three years, period.
7. The net result of this rule is to tax one-half of the first $200,000 of lifetime gifts to a spouse at the combined rate schedule.

his or her $3,000 annual exclusion per donee, the donor is subject to the combined estate and gift tax schedule. Referring to this schedule, if $10,000 is given away, this amount is subject to a gift tax of $1,800. However, at the donor's death this $10,000 taxable gift must be included in the appraisal of the estate. After the tentative tax is calculated, the $1,800 in gift taxes is then deducted to arrive at the actual estate tax.

Mrs. Elmo Eaton, a widow, was worth $500,000 and had already given $3,000 to her only son under the annual exclusion. She decided to give him an additional $10,000 that same year and pay the gift tax. The computation looks like this.

Without the gift

Value of the estate	$500,000
Tentative tax	155,800
Gift tax	0
Actual tax	$155,800
Unified tax credit in 1978	34,000
Estate tax	$121,800

With the gift

Value of the estate	$490,000
Plus the taxable gift	10,000
Total estate	$500,000
Tentative tax	155,800
Gift tax	1,800
Actual tax	$154,000
Unified tax credit in 1978	34,000
Estate tax	$120,000

The result of including the taxable gift in the appraisal of Mrs. Eaton's estate, and then deducting the gift tax paid, is to tax the estate the same, with or without the gift. Without the gift the total tax paid would have been $121,800. With the gift the total tax was the same, $121,800 ($120,000 estate tax + $1,800 gift tax).

Since there is no tax advantage in making taxable gifts why should well-to-do people make a taxable gift at all? They should (and do) for three reasons.

1. Any appreciation in the gift property from the time of the gift to the time of the donor's death is not taxed. If a growth asset is used as the gift property (and it usually is) it could double in value (or more) by the time of the donor's death. If it does, the appreciation is not included in the donor's estate.
2. The gift property will be free of probate. Although the amount of the gift has to be included in the appraisal of the estate for tax purposes, title to the property rests with the heirs; therefore it will not be tied up in probate court.
3. The *income* from the gift asset will now be reported on the income tax return of the donee, who in most cases is in a lower tax bracket than the donor.

If a taxable gift is made, the donor has to file a gift tax return with the Internal Revenue Service. A copy of this return is shown. No gift tax return has to be filed until the end of the year as long as the total taxable gifts for the year do not exceed $25,000. If they do exceed $25,000, a gift tax return has to be filed for the calendar quarter in which the donor's taxable gifts first exceed $25,000. Thereafter an additional return has to be filed for any quarter in which taxable gifts are made.[8]

Gifts should be made with caution. No estate planning decision should be made solely with the objective of saving estate taxes. Careful calculations should be made to ensure that the donor's future financial security will not be jeopardized in any way. Normally the property owner should be at least well-to-do, if not wealthy. He or she must have enough capital and income, after the gifts, so that the donor will remain financially independent.

The Carryover Provision

Assets in a testator's estate that have appreciated in value since he or she acquired them, and which have not been sold, are not

8. Before 1977 a gift tax return had to be filed within forty-five days of the end of any quarter in which taxable gifts were made, regardless of their amount.

Form 709
(Rev. June 1977)
Department of the Treasury
Internal Revenue Service

United States Quarterly Gift Tax Return

(Section 6019 of the Internal Revenue Code) (For gifts made after December 31, 1976)
Calendar quarter(s) ending (month and year) ▶ ....
For "Privacy Act" notification, see the Instructions for Form 1040.

Donor's first name and middle initial	Donor's last name	Social security number		
Address (number and street)		Residence (domicile)		
City, State, and ZIP code		Citizenship	Yes	No

If you (the donor) filed a previous Form 709, has your address changed since the last Form 709 was filed? . . . .

A Gifts by husband or wife to third parties.—Do you consent to have the gifts by you and by your spouse to third parties
during the calendar quarter(s) considered as made one-half by each of you? (See instruction 8.) . . . .
(If the answer is "Yes," the following information must be furnished and the consent shown below signed by your spouse.)

1(a) Name of spouse	1(b) Social security number

2 If the consent is effective for gifts made in a previous quarter(s) of the calendar year and no return was filed for such
previous quarter(s) (see instruction 1) and such gifts are being reported on this return (see instruction 10), write the
previous quarter(s) ending (month and year) in addition to the current quarter ending (month and year).

3 Were you married during the entire calendar quarter(s)? . . . .

4 If the answer to 3 is "No," check whether ☐ married, ☐ divorced, or ☐ widowed, and give date ▶

5 Will a gift tax return for this calendar quarter(s) be filed by your spouse? . . . .

Consent of Spouse—I consent to have the gifts made by me and by my spouse to third parties during the calendar quarter(s) considered as made one-half by each of us. We are both aware of the joint and several liability for tax created by the execution of this consent.

Spouse's signature ▶   Date ▶

1 Enter the amount from Schedule A, line (j)	**1**	
2 Enter the amount from Schedule B, line (c)	**2**	
3 Total (add amounts on lines 1 and 2)	**3**	
4 Tax computed on amount on line 3 (See Table A in separate instructions.)	**4**	
5 Tax computed on amount on line 2 (See Table A in separate instructions.)	**5**	
6 Balance (subtract amount on line 5 from amount on line 4)	**6**	
7 Enter the amount of unified credit from Table B	**7**	
8 Enter the amount of unified credit against gift tax allowable for all prior quarters	**8**	
9 Balance (subtract amount on line 8 from amount on line 7)	**9**	
10 Enter 20% of the amount allowed as specific exemption after September 8, 1976	**10**	
11 Balance (subtract amount on line 10 from amount on line 9)	**11**	
12 Unified credit (enter the smaller of (i) amount on line 6 or (ii) amount on line 11)	**12**	
13 Credit for foreign gift taxes (see instruction 20)	**13**	
14 Total (add amounts on line 12 and line 13)	**14**	
15 Tax due (subtract amount on line 14 from amount on line 6)	**15**	

Computation of Tax

Please attach the necessary supplemental documents; see instruction 15.

Under penalties of perjury, I declare that I have examined this return, including any accompanying schedules and statements, and to the best of my knowledge and belief it is true, correct, and complete. Declaration of preparer (other than donor) is based on all information of which preparer has any knowledge.

Donor's signature ▶   Date ▶

Preparer's signature
(other than donor) ▶   Date ▶

Preparer's address
(other than donor) ▶

Please attach Check or Money Order here

235-271-1

Form 709 (Rev. 6–77)   Page **2**

Schedule A	Computation of Taxable Gifts			
Item number	Donee's name and address and description of gift. If the gift was made by means of a trust, attach a copy of the trust instrument	Donor's adjusted basis of gift	Date of gift	Value at date of gift
1				

(a) Total gifts of donor . . . . _____

(b) One-half of items _____ to _____ attributable to spouse (see instruction 11) . . . . _____

(c) Balance (subtract amount on line (b) from amount on line (a)) . . . . _____

(d) Gifts of spouse to be included (from line (b) of spouse's return) (see instruction 11) . . . . _____

(e) Total gifts (add amounts on lines (c) and (d)) . . . . _____

(f) Total exclusions not exceeding $3,000 for the calendar year for each donee (except gifts of future interests) . . _____

(g) Total included amount of gifts (subtract amount on line (f) from amount on line (e)) . . . . _____

(h) Deductions (see instructions 16 and 17):

(1)(a) Gift of qualified interests to spouse for this period (before annual exclusion, based on items _____ to _____ from Schedule A) . . . . _____

(b) Annual exclusion attributable to gifts on line (h)(1)(a) . . . . _____

(c) Net amount (subtract amount on line (h)(1)(b) from amount on line (h)(1)(a)) . . _____

(2)(a) First $100,000 marital deduction $100,000

(b) Marital deduction for prior periods after December 31, 1976 . . . . _____

(c) Balance of first $100,000 marital deduction available (subtract amount on line (h)(2)(b) from amount on line (h)(2)(a) but not less than zero) . . . . _____

(3)(a) Excess over first $100,000 marital deduction (if total of amount on line (h)(1)(c) plus amount on line (h)(2)(b) is $100,000 or less enter zero. Otherwise, enter amount on line (h)(1)(a) less amount on line (h)(2)(c)) . . . . _____

(b) Excess over first $100,000 for prior periods (after December 31, 1976) . . . . . _____

(c) Total excess over first $100,000 (add amounts on lines (h)(3)(a) and (h)(3)(b)) . . _____

(4)(a) Second $100,000 . . . . $100,000

(b) Gifts qualifying for additional marital deduction (subtract amount on line (h)(4)(a) from amount on line (h)(3)(c) but not less than zero) . . . . _____

(5)(a) Enter 50% of amount on line (h)(4)(b) . . . . _____

(b) Enter 50% of amount on line (h)(1)(a) but not more than amount on line (h)(1)(c) . _____

(c) Enter the lesser of the amount on line (h)(1)(c) or the amount on line (h)(2)(c) . . _____

(6) Marital deduction (if amount on line (h)(4)(b) is zero, enter amount on line (h)(5)(c). Otherwise, enter amount on line (h)(5)(c) plus the lesser of the amounts on line (h)(5)(a) or line (h)(5)(b)) . . . . _____

(7) Charitable, public, and similar gifts (based on items _____ to _____, less exclusions) . . . . _____

(i) Total deductions (add amounts on lines (h)(6) and (h)(7)) . . . . _____

(j) Amount of taxable gifts (subtract amount on line (i) from amount on line (g)) . . . . _____

Schedule B	Did you (the donor) file gift tax returns for prior periods? (If "Yes," follow instruction 19 in completing Schedule B below.) . ☐ Yes ☐ No			
Calendar years (prior to 1971) and calendar quarters (1971 and subsequent years)	Internal Revenue office where prior return was filed	Amount of unified credit against gift tax for periods after December 31, 1976	Amount of specific exemption for prior periods ending before January 1, 1977	Amount of taxable gifts

(a) Totals for prior periods (without adjustment for reduced specific exemption) . . . . . _____

(b) Amount, if any, by which total specific exemption, line (a), exceeds $30,000 (see instruction 19) . . . . . _____

(c) Total amount of taxable gifts for prior periods (add amount, last column, line (a), and amount, if any, line (b)) . _____

(If more space is needed, attach additional sheets of same size.)

subject to the capital gains tax at death. If the heir should later sell these assets, however, that person is subject to this income tax. In other words the decedent's cost basis is "carried over" to the recipient of the estate property. Thus, some portion or all of the appreciation that took place on estate assets during the owner's lifetime, may be subject to the capital gains tax when the property is ultimately sold by the heirs. In the long run this can prove very costly the longer in time we get away from December 31, 1976, as we shall see in a moment.

This carryover concept of a decedent's cost basis is not new. It has been applied for years to lifetime gifts. If John Doe gave a ranch to his son, and his son in turn gave it to his son, no capital gains tax had to be paid at the time of either transfer. But when the grandson sold the ranch many years later, he had to go back to the cost basis of his grandfather. If John Doe paid $30,000 for the ranch, and his grandchild sold it for $230,000, a capital gains tax had to be paid on the $200,000 appreciation ($250,000 sale price − $30,000 cost basis).

Under existing law, this carryover provision of appreciated assets applies to all property that passes to heirs, not just to gifts made during a testator's lifetime. The assets in a decedent's estate no longer take on a stepped-up cost basis at death equal to the value at which they here appraised in the estate. The cost basis of estate assets (for determining the capital gains tax, if any, when the heirs sell) is the fair market value of the property on December 31, 1976.

Samuel Fairchild died on October 10, 1977. His estate consisted of securities, real estate, and cash. On December 31, 1977 his heirs decided to sell all of the property. The amount of their long-term profit was the appreciation in the assets (if any) which had occurred since December 31, 1976.

The fair market value of the securities on that arbitrary date was easily determined by the heirs from the published prices of securities in the *Wall Street Journal.* The fair market value of the real estate presented a different problem. When passing the

Tax Reform Act of 1976, Congress recognized that it wasn't practical to require property owners to have their real estate appraised on December 31, 1976 to determine its fair market value. So the law provides a different method of calculation. Mr. Fairchild's heirs had to go back to the price at which the decedent originally bought the property to determine the amount of appreciation from that date up to when the heirs sold it. It's then assumed that the appreciation took place at a constant rate during the intervening period. Therefore they had to pay a capital gains tax on the amount of the profit that this constant rate of appreciation attributed to the property from December 31, 1976 to December 31, 1977.

If we assume that Mr. Fairchild bought his real estate on December 31, 1965 for $150,000, and that his heirs sold it for $300,000 on December 31, 1977, the appreciation over that twelve-year span was $150,000. This is at a constant rate of appreciation of $12,500 a year ($150,000 − 12). The amount of the appreciation was therefore $12,500 from December 31, 1976 to December 31, 1977, one year later. It makes no difference how much of the appreciation actually took place before or after December 31, 1976.

It's important to realize that the longer in time that we get removed from December 31, 1976, the more costly this new carryover provision is going to be to heirs who sell assets that have appreciated in value.

For example, let's assume that a decedent dies on December 31, 1986. Now if the heirs sell appreciated assets, they have to go back ten years to December 31, 1976 to determine their cost basis. This is an extremely important part of estate planning for a property owner. Because of the carryover provision, accurate records of the cost basis of real estate must be retained by the testator for the benefit of his or her legal representative and the heirs.

The carryover cost basis provision applies to all assets that, if sold during life, would have produced a capital gain or loss. It specifically does not apply to life insurance proceeds (regardless of how few premiums might have been paid), nor to a joint and survivor agreement or to a deferred compensation agreement. Ordinarily most personal and household effects would be included, but there is a special provision of the law that allows a legal representative to exclude up to $10,000 of this tangible personal property from the carryover provision. Instead these assets take on a stepped-up cost basis equal to their appraised value in the estate for estate tax purposes, just as all assets did prior to the Tax Reform Act of 1976.

The "fresh start" basis for determining cost (December 31, 1976) does not apply to a loss.

Example. The decedent bought a stock for $40 per share. On December 31, 1976 it was worth $80 per share, and subsequently the recipient of the stock sold it for $70 per share. The heir cannot take a $10 loss per share ($80 − $70). The only time a loss can be taken is when the heir sells at a price that is below the decedent's original cost basis. If the recipient should sell the above stock for $30, he or she may take a $10 loss per share ($40 − $30).

There are also several special rules that apply to the carryover provision.

1. The cost basis of carryover assets may be increased by the amount of the federal and state death taxes paid by the estate that is attributable to the appreciation in such property after December 31, 1976. However, this rule applies only to assets that were subject to the estate tax. It does not apply to property that qualified for the marital deduction, the charitable deduction (explained later), or the survivor's one-half of community property in community property states.

2. In small estates, if the cost basis of all appreciated carryover property does not amount to $60,000, then the difference between the actual cost basis and $60,000 may be prorated among all of the carryover assets, but no one asset may have its value increased beyond what it was appraised for in the estate.

Phylis Freeman's estate had a total cost basis of $40,000 in four carryover assets ($10,000 per asset). The difference between $40,000 and $60,000 is $20,000. Her legal representative was allowed to divide this $20,000 among the four assets, thereby increasing the cost basis of each asset to $15,000 ($20,000 divided by 4), plus the cost basis of each asset.

3. The cost basis of appreciated carryover property may be increased (but not above the estate tax value) by the amount of the state death taxes *that the recipient is required to pay* and which the estate has no obligation to pay.

The law states that these adjustments must be made in the order listed above, and applied on an asset by asset basis. Also the recipient stands in the shoes of the decedent so far as any provisions that require that a long-term capital gain be taxed as ordinary income, such as the recapture of depreciation on real estate. Furthermore, any property that is acquired *after* December 31, 1976 is not granted a "fresh start" basis.

The law requires the executor of an estate to provide each heir, and the Internal Revenue Service, with the adjusted cost basis of all carryover appreciated assets, and imposes severe penalties for failure to comply.

Other Rules Involving Estate Settlement

Lump-sum death benefits and installment payments from qualified corporate pension plans, Keogh Plans, and individual retirement accounts

Lump-sum death benefits from these plans are included in the appraisal of an estate for estate tax purposes. Installment payments from qualified corporate plans are not included in the estate appraisal, but installment payments from a Keogh Plan or an IRA *are* included.[9]

9. Except payments from the voluntary portion of a Keogh Plan.

The orphans' exclusion

This exclusion from estate taxes is important to parents who
have children who are under twenty-one years of age. Where
the only surviving parent dies (whether the child is natural or
adopted) and the child is not yet twenty-one, a special orphans'
exclusion is granted. The exemption from the estate tax
amounts to $5,000, multiplied by the number of years by which
the child is under twenty-one years of age. For example, the
only surviving parent dies when a child is fourteen years old. In
this event $35,000 is the amount of the orphans' exclusion (7
× $5,000).

Appraising real estate used for farming or ranching, or owned by a closely held business

An executor may elect to appraise this real estate based on its
current "use" value. Prior to 1977 the property had to be
valued at its *highest and best* "use." This prior classification
resulted in too high an estate tax being imposed and forced
many farms and small businesses out of existence when the
heirs inherited the property.

Granting deferral of estate taxes

Deferral of estate taxes may be granted to an executor by
permitting installment payment of these taxes over a period of
10 years, providing an executor can show "reasonable cause"
for the deferral.[10] However, no "reasonable cause" has to be
shown if the value of a decedent's closely held business is 35
percent of the gross estate or 50 percent of the taxable estate.
The ten-year deferral will be automatically granted. In addition
to a ten-year deferral, a fifteen-year deferral will be automatically granted if the value of a farm, ranch, or closely held busi-

10. Formerly deferral of payment of estate taxes was granted if payment
would cause "undue hardship."

ness is 65 percent or more of the decedent's adjusted gross estate. In this event interest only has to be paid for five years (at the rate of 4 percent on the first $1 million). Thereafter the tax is payable in equal installments over a ten-year period.

Redemption of stock by the executor in a closely held business in order to pay estate taxes and administration and funeral expenses

If the value of the decedent's business interest is at least 50 percent of the adjusted gross estate, the executor may redeem enough stock to pay these expenses without having the redemption treated as a taxable dividend, but the value of the redeemed stock would still be subject to the capital gains tax under the carryover provision.

State Inheritance Taxes

Not only is a federal estate tax imposed when a property owner dies, but in most states a state inheritance tax is assessed as well.[11] The estate tax, as we have seen, is a tax imposed upon the estate on the right of a decedent to transfer his or her property to heirs. The state death tax is a true *inheritance tax* imposed upon each individual heir. State inheritance taxes vary widely, so it is hard to generalize. Broadly speaking this tax rate is between 2 and 6 percent. The exemption amount that each individual heir receives, and the tax rate, depend upon the heir's relationship to the deceased. A widow normally obtains a generous exemption and a low rate, with minor children obtaining the next most beneficial tax treatment. Strangers who inherit get the worst treatment, as high as a 10 percent rate and virtually no exemption. An example of a state inheritance tax schedule is the one in California, which is reproduced here.

Geoffrey Fulton, a widower, died in California possessed of

---

11. The only exceptions are Georgia, Florida, and Nevada.

CALIFORNIA INHERITANCE AND GIFT TAX[1]—RATES AND EXEMPTIONS

Effective as to { decedents dying / gifts made } on or after January 1, 1976

CLASSIFICATION	EXEMPTION	up to $25,000.00	$25,000 to $50,000	$50,000 to $100,000	$100,000 to $200,000	$200,000 to $300,000	$300,000 to $400,000	Over $400,000
Husband or Wife — One-half of community property, quasi-community property or decedent's separate property[2]	60,000	—	—	Rate of tax on amount left after deducting exemption from $100,000 **6%**	8%	10%	12%	14%
Minor Child (Includes Adopted)	12,000	Rate of tax on amount left after deducting exemption from $25,000 **3%**	4%	6%	8%	10%	12%	14%
Adult Child, Grandchild, Parent, Grandparent (Relationship may be by Blood or Adoption) / **Mutually Acknowledged Child** / **Descendant of Mutually Acknowledged Child**	5,000	Rate of tax on amount left after deducting exemption from $25,000 **3%**	4%	6%	8%	10%	12%	14%
Brother, Sister (Excludes Brothers- and Sisters-in-law) / **Descendant of Brother or Sister** (Includes Descendant by Adoption) / **Wife or Widow of Son, Husband or Widower of Daughter**	2,000	Rate of tax on amount left after deducting exemption from $25,000 **6%**	10%	12%	14%	16%	18%	20%
Strangers in Blood and Relationships not Specified Above	300	Rate of tax on amount left after deducting exemption from $25,000 **10%**	14%	16%	18%	20%	22%	24%

[1] GIFT TAX ANNUAL EXEMPTION. Value of $3,000.00 transferred to each donee in any calendar year is excluded from tax unless transfer is of a future interest.

[2] The one-half exclusion of decedent's separate property does not apply if it is the result of a division of community or quasi-community property between spouses.

CONTROLLER OF STATE OF CALIFORNIA

IT-72 (REV. 11-75)

OSP

$80,000 which he left to his only son. His executor had to compute the amount of the state inheritance tax according to the California State Inheritance Tax Schedule.

Since an adult child has a low exemption of just $5,000, this was subtracted from the first $25,000, leaving $20,000 to be taxed at the rate of 3 percent. The next $25,000 was taxed at 4 percent, and the remaining $30,000 was taxed at 6 percent. This resulted in a state inheritance tax assessed against Geoffrey Fulton's son of $3,400. The computation looked like this:

$25,000–$5,000 = $20,000 at 3%	$ 600
$25,000 taxed at 4%	1,000
$30,000 taxed at 6%	1,800
State inheritance tax	$3,400

This is a sizable sum against an estate worth only $80,000, the major portion of which was Geoffrey Fulton's free and clear home.

Dale Douglas died in California and his only son fared much worse, for his estate was worth $150,000. His assets consisted of a $70,000 home, $20,000 in death benefit life insurance, $40,000 in a corporate pension plan payable in a lump-sum to his beneficiary, and $20,000 in a savings and loan account.

Dale Douglas, when he was alive, did not think of himself as a well-to-do man. He received no income from his home or his life insurance, and the income from his pension and his savings, when added to his Social Security check, did not amount to a great deal. Actually he was just getting by.

The inheritance tax assessed against his son, however, was $8,600. The computation looked like this:

$25,000–$5,000 exemption = $20,000 at 3%	$ 600
$25,000 taxed at 4%	1,000
$50,000 taxed at 6%	3,000
$50,000 taxed at 8%	4,000
State inheritance tax	$8,600

When trusts are created to save estate taxes, the grantor should realize that state inheritance taxes are imposed against the eventual remaindermen of the trust at the time of the grantor's death, even though the heirs will not inherit the corpus of the trust for many years. Therefore the grantor should direct his or her executor to pay these taxes out of the estate.

Flexibility by Granting Powers of Appointment

Considerable flexibility can be provided by a testator by granting powers of appointment to heirs, or to a trustee, at the time the will or trust agreement is drawn. Most people, and some attorneys, don't understand what is meant by a power of appointment. As a consequence this testamentary device is not used as often as it should be.

A power of appointment is the right given by one person to another to control the use or enjoyment of property. A power of appointment can be broad or limited. If, when creating a marital deduction trust, a spouse gives the surviving consort as trustee the right to leave the trust property to whom he or she pleases, the creator of the trust has granted a general power of appointment. On the other hand, if a provision is inserted in the trust agreement that the survivor, as trustee, may leave the trust property only by distribution in his or her will, the grantor has given a limited power of appointment.

The terms of a power of appointment determine its tax status. Generally speaking, a general power is taxed, a limited power is not taxed.

If a husband fears that his wife will succumb to the pleas of children and/or other relations for substantial withdrawals from her one-half of the estate, he can limit her right of withdrawal to distribution according to her will. This limited power of appointment will not violate the five conditions of the marital deduction rule; therefore the power is nontaxable.

Sometimes a limited power of appointment is given to the survivor, as trustee, concerning the use and enjoyment of the residuary trust. The survivor is given the power to change the disposition of the income and principal of the trust "on down the line" as he or she continues to live and the fortunes of the children and grandchildren change, sometimes in a completely unforeseen manner.

Mr. and Mrs. Samuel Homer had two children and a sizable estate. They had a simple will that stated the children inherited their estate outright, share and share alike. When they became aware of their death tax problem they created a marital deduction trust. They also arranged for the trust to continue after the death of both of them, providing that income only was to paid to their children, with the grandchildren inheriting the corpus outright.

This disposition of the trust property was what Mr. and Mrs. Homer both wanted at the time the trust agreement was drawn. But they fully realized that if one of them died, and the survivor continued to live for many years thereafter, that this distribution could well be all wrong. Therefore the trust agreement provided the survivor with a limited power of appointment that gave the trustee the right to alter the disposition of the trust assets to their children and/or other descendents in any way that he or she might later decide. Since this was a limited power of appointment the granting of this power did not change the tax-free status of the trust. The corpus of the trust that was left to the grandchildren would still go tax-free to them.

Mr. and Mrs. Homer inserted this limited power of appointment in their trust agreement because they were concerned about the status of their son's second marriage, and the fact that he had two stepchildren by his second wife whom they hadn't met. The possibility, after they were both gone, that their son might die bothered them. They did not want his second wife's children to inherit any part of their estate. Thus the trust agreement specifically stated that at the termination of the trust, the remaindermen were the *daughter's children* only, and no one else. On the other hand, they realized that their son's recent second marriage could be successful, and that the survivor of the two of them (either Mr. or Mrs. Homer) could come to know and like the second wife and her children; therefore they might want to alter the distribution of the trust assets by using the limited power of appointment to include their son's stepchildren. As one attorney is fond of saying: "It's better to grant a power of appointment that is never used, than to omit one and wish that you had it."

When a trust agreement provides only for the grandchildren after a son or daughter dies, the son-in-law or the daughter-in-law becomes the forgotten person. This also bothered Mr. and Mrs. Homer. Their daughter had a successful marriage and two children. But what about her husband if she should die? Their daughter's marriage was a good one, and the Homers liked their son-in-law. If their daughter should die while either Mr. or Mrs. Homer were still living, it would be advisable in that event to provide for the son-in-law in some manner. By using the same special power of appointment, this also could be arranged by the survivor.

Generation-Skipping Trusts

For many years the creation of generation-skipping trusts has been a favorite device used by the super-rich to avoid payment of estate taxes. A generation-skipping trust is one in which beneficiaries of at least two generations, each of which is younger than the generation of the person creating the trust, have a present or future interest or power in the trust.

Under the law that was in existence before the Tax Reform Act of 1976, a super-rich testator could leave property in trust for the benefit of a child, and then for the benefit of grandchildren, with the ultimate distribution of the trust assets to great-grandchildren; and if income only was paid to the child, and then the grandchildren, the trust property would escape estate taxes for two generations. The estate would not be subject to transfer taxes until the deaths of the great-grandchildren. The current law changes this.

Mrs. Vernon Lake, a well-to-do widow, with one son and three grandchildren, created a generation-skipping trust under current law. Her will provided that her son was to receive all of the income, and that her grandchildren would inherit the corpus of the trust upon the death of her son. This was a generation-skipping trust, with her son as the skipped generation. She also gave her son the right to distribute principal from the trust to his children, if he so desired. This was a limited power of appointment; therefore it did not change the tax status of the trust.

The imposition of the federal estate tax would be triggered either by the son's death, or by his use of his special power of appointment, subject however to a special exclusion of $250,000, which will be explained later.

If the son distributed part of the principal during his lifetime, this would cause the imposition of the estate tax. The trustee would enter the combined rate schedule with the value of the transferred property, *after* all previous generation-skipping transfers had been added to it, plus the addition of any taxable gifts made by the son since December 31, 1976. The tax would be paid by the trust, which would be a tax advantage to the son, for he would not have to pay it.

The son's death would also trigger the imposition of the estate tax. The tax would be computed from the combined rate schedule, as if the value of the trust property were included in the son's estate on top of all the property the son owned. Once again the generation-skipping estate tax is paid from the trust property, not from the son's assets.

As we stated earlier, the assessment of the estate tax upon the son's death is subject to a $250,000 exclusion. The law provides for an exclusion of the first $250,000 that is transferred to the grandchildren of the grantor upon a termination of an interest of a child. This is a very precise definition of when the exclusion comes into play, and it is the only time that it can be used. This grandchild exclusion, which became effective for the first time in 1977, really affects only the super-rich. Certainly one has to be wealthy indeed to leave $250,000 to grandchildren in such a manner as to avoid payment of estate taxes in the first generation that follows behind you.

Another rule that for all practical purposes helps only the super-rich is that any other relatives besides direct lineal descendants may be included when creating a generation-skipping trust. Also the first younger generation following the donor can be bypassed entirely, with the donor's grandchild as the first beneficiary, and with the donor's great-grandchildren as the ultimate beneficiaries. The only rule that has to be followed in this event is the one governing the perpetuity of a trust. It cannot last forever. A trust cannot extend beyond lives in being, plus twenty-one years. Thus a great-grandchild must be alive at the time the trust is created, and the trust must terminate twenty-one years after he or she is dead. Conceivably this event might not take place for a hundred years.

There are rules set up for determining who belongs to a younger generation when creating a generation-skipping trust. A husband and wife, regardless of their respective ages, are considered to be of the same generation. Other persons (besides direct lineal descendents) have their generation determined by the difference between their age and the age of the person creating the trust. A person who is not more than 12½ years younger or older than the creator of the trust is deemed to be of the same generation. If a person is more than 12½ years younger but not more than 37½ years younger, that individual is classified as being in the first generation younger than the person who created the trust. If a person is more than 37½ years younger but not more than 62½ years younger than the person who created the trust, that individual is classified as being in the second generation younger than the grantor.

There must be three generations involved in a generation-skipping. A marital deduction trust that provides income only to a surviving spouse, with distribution to children upon the survivor's death, is not a generation-skipping trust. Only two generations are involved. The spouses are one generation and the children are the second generation.

For generation-skipping trusts that were in existence prior to the Tax Reform Act of 1976, there are two dates that are important. The new tax rules don't apply to a generation-skipping trust created under the will of a testator who died on or before April 30, 1976, nor does it apply to trusts created during a property owner's lifetime that were irrevocable on April 30, 1976. The second date that is important is January 1, 1982. The new rules don't apply to a generation-skipping trust that was created under a will on or before April 30, 1976, *by a grantor who is still alive,* provided the trustor (1) dies before January 1, 1982, and (2) does not change his or her will in any way that increases any generation-skipping transfer. As January 1, 1982 approaches, however, generation-skipping trusts of living grantors will have to be revised to comply with the new rules. These same rules also apply to a *revocable* living trust that was in existence on or before April 30, 1976, and that has not been changed since then.

Besides the tax advantage offered by generation-skipping trusts, it should be understood by property owners that testamentary dispositions made at any time that leave assets outright to charity remain, as before, free of the federal estate tax.

General Estate Rules to Follow

In addition to saving death taxes through properly drawn wills and trust agreements, and by lifetime gifts, there are other rules to follow that will help conserve an estate for the heirs and make the job of the executor an easier one. These rules apply to all estates, large and small.

1. *Don't leave your heirs too much cash.*

"Easy come, easy go" is an old expression, but still a true one; as a consequence, cash will too often be spent. Your heirs are normally much younger and less experienced than you, and therefore you should exercise your mature judgment and invest the money. If heirs are left a sound investment with a good income, they are more inclined to leave it alone. If they don't spend the cash, but through lack of experience make a bad investment instead, the money will again be gone and this way more tragically dissipated because no one will have actually enjoyed it. It's true that decisions are always difficult, and when you are older and getting along on what you have, it's easier to do nothing. But in the best interests of conserving your estate for your heirs, you should make a decision and invest your excess cash.

Mr. and Mrs. Mark Hoving had accomplished the difficult task of accumulating an estate of $200,000, made particularly noteworthy because neither one of them had gone beyond the sixth grade in school, and Mr. Hoving had never made much money. They had one son, who unfortunately had not inherited his parents' acquisitive instincts, and in addition was a ne'er-do-well who couldn't seem to hold a job much longer than six months. Mr. and Mrs. Hoving's estate was entirely in cash. Repeated efforts by both their bank's trust department and an investment representative to have them either invest the money, or create a trust for their son's protection, were to no avail. When the son eventually inherited the estate, it was all gone within two years. This seems almost impossible today with the fine laws that have been passed, both federal and state, that protect the investor. Since the son knew nothing about money, he was easy prey for an unscrupulous promoter. The scheme was underfinanced, and eventually declared bankrupt, with the result that the boy lost in a very short time an estate that took a lifetime to build.

2. *If income real estate is presenting such a management problem that you cannot retire and enjoy your golden years, you should sell it and invest the money elsewhere.*

Real estate has been an excellent estate-building vehicle for a great many people; however, in too many cases it is not a good retirement investment, and the reason for it stems from the times. Retired people who no longer want the management headache, or who are physically incapable of taking care of real estate themselves, cannot call in a painter or a plumber every time an apartment has to be redecorated or a leaky faucet repaired, for the high cost of these services will reduce their net income to a very low figure indeed. It might be advisable under these circumstances to sell the real estate and invest the money where it doesn't require your personal daily attention. It should be realized that no one is truly retired who is still managing property.

3. *If you own securities, and you have inexperienced heirs, either create a bank trust or start training them immediately in how to manage your investments.*

It is surprising how different your stocks and bonds look to you when viewed as being in the hands of your heirs. Many a testator will have to admit that the future expert management of his or her investment portfolio is a dim prospect indeed. If this is true in your case, you had better create a testamentary bank trust; or better yet, transfer some of your securities to your heirs and observe how well they manage them. They may surprise you, and if they do, or if they learn under your direction, then a trust will not be necessary and they can inherit the investments outright, which is the best possible solution.

4. *Don't own too many assets.*

They present a management problem to you in your living estate, and create extra work for your executor in your death estate. An investor simply cannot effectively supervise, say, thirty different securities. If you will review them with your stockbroker, you should be able to reduce your portfolio to a manageable six or seven stocks and bonds that meet your over-all objective and, for that matter, it might even improve your investment results.

5. *Don't keep assets that have a small monetary value.*

Assets that have a small monetary value simply clutter up your living estate and your death estate. Five shares of a $5 stock are worth $25.00, and one matured E bond for which you paid $75 is now worth $100. Such small assets are hardly worth keeping in your estate, yet people do retain them. They should be sold and the money put into a bank, for at the very least they will prove to be a nuisance factor to your executor. Small assets that are acquired over a lifetime are often retained through sheer inertia on the part of the property owner; frequently he or she has forgotten how they were acquired in the first place.

6. *Don't make yourself financially responsible for your grandchildren.*

You don't have to put yourself in this position if your son or son-in-law is insurable and can pass a physical examination. If your son-in-law, for instance, does not believe in life insurance and refuses as the breadwinner to protect his young family through an adequate life insurance program, you should take out insurance on his life and pay the premiums. Life insurance is the only way that a sizable estate can be created for a widow and dependent children where the head of the family hasn't had the time, or the inclination, to save enough for their protection. You may not object to acting as a baby-sitter if your son-in-law should die, but you shouldn't put yourself in the position of reducing your living estate in order to help your daughter financially, or to send your grandchildren through college. A $100,000 reducing term policy for twenty years at a premium of around $30 per month (depending upon the age of the insured) is a lot easier to pay than $100,000 in cash.

Conclusion

No one should pay more in death taxes than the law demands.

The combined estate and gift tax is a progressive tax, and like the income tax, the burden falls most heavily upon the middle class. This is because they are often not aware of the problem, or if aware of it, they don't know what to do about it. The well-to-do and the super-rich, as usual, hire tax experts to effectively make use of the deductions that are allowed.

Estate tax savings are mainly achieved by testators themselves by a properly drawn will and/or trust agreement. A marital deduction trust should seriously be considered by all spouses who have a joint estate of such a size that the exemption "equivalents" will not solve their death tax problem. In these situations pyramiding assets in the estate of the survivor should be avoided by the creation of a trust rather than by leaving the entire combined estate to the surviving spouse.

Gifts made during life can also considerably reduce estate taxes. If these gifts are made with full understanding of the annual exclusion, and the three-year rule, they can be donated without incurring a tax of any kind.

Every property owner should understand the carryover provision of appreciated assets, particularly as applied to real estate. It is today more important than ever that a testator keep complete and careful records of the cost basis of all of his or her property. State inheritance taxes also cannot be ignored, for they have seriously escalated in recent years.

In larger estates, the use of powers of appointment is often advisable, and if you are very well-to-do or super-rich, a generation-skipping trust is still advantageous despite the fact that such trusts are now confined to just two younger generations with, of course, the generous grandchild exclusion.

14

Conclusions

The financial problems confronting retired people, and those planning for retirement, seem to be insurmountable. But they are not. Careful planning, and willingness to make difficult decisions, even though they are in many instances contrary to life-long convictions, can still improve almost anyone's financial position.

If you are 65 and still counting, don't hang on for dear life to all of your assets, refusing to spend anything but the income from them. Inflation the last few years has reduced the standard of living of most of us. For the vast majority of retired people this requires a basic change in their thinking. They must decide to spend a small percentage of their capital each year in order to increase their cash flow. This isn't such a bad thing to do when you think about it, for why not leave your heirs a little less, so you can enjoy yourself more? At the very least, you should be sure that you are getting an income from all of your assets. Many retired people are not. They are still saving for their heirs, without being fully aware of it.

Practically all retired people would like to avoid probate.

There are three ways to do this, all involving correct owner-ship. Married couples should hold all of their assets in joint tenancy with right of survivorship. Individuals can name a beneficiary. But if an estate is of such a size that death taxes are a problem, a living trust should be created.

One of the major objectives for retired people in the management of their finances should be to minimize their income taxes. Despite this, one-half of all people who are 65 overpay their income taxes. New rules and new problems face the retired person in dealing with the Internal Revenue Service. This is because property at work has replaced a person at work as the primary source of income. A retired person should realize that the income tax return is not that complicated and can be understood even by someone who has never before had to file Form 1040.

As Judge Learned Hand said: "There is nothing sinister in so arranging one's affairs to keep taxes as low as possible. To demand more in the name of morals is mere cant."

Despite the fact that the process can be avoided, too many times a widow is confronted with the probate of her husband's estate. A complete understanding of the probate process, in advance of having to deal with it, can be of tremendous help to the potential widow.

Annuities are too often ignored by retired people. When more income is badly needed, annuities offer an excellent method of providing a higher monthly cash benefit, particularly if the annuitant is 75 years of age or older. Fourteen percent can be obtained on money at this age, which is about double the guarantee that can be obtained elsewhere. What's more, the benefit is guaranteed for life.

Oddly enough, those who are well-off financially can also use annuities to their advantage. By buying non-refund annuities they can reduce death taxes and increase family income to a greater extent than would otherwise be possible.

Holding correct title to all of the assets in an estate is of the utmost importance. It will determine which assets will be subject to probate administration and which will not. It will determine who will be in immediate possession of part of the estate, and who of the heirs will have to wait for months, and maybe years, to inherit what has been left to them.

Carelessness in how you hold your assets can completely disrupt your estate plan. It can seriously escalate death taxes, and it can result in disinheriting your wife of two-thirds of your estate, even though it is your intention that she should inherit the whole of it. It could result in such bad management of your assets that your widow will be broke in just four years. Improper ownership can allow relatives, friends, and even absolute strangers to participate in the fruits of your labor, although this is the last thing in the world that you wanted to have happen.

In many estates, title is left to chance. Titles that were correct, or that seemed to be correct at the time the property was acquired, no longer apply. Ownership can become obsolete for many reasons, the most obvious being death, births, marriage, or divorce. If any of these events take place, the testator should be alert that all titles to his or her estate should be reviewed.

It should be realized that non-probate assets, while avoiding court administration, are quite often assets without a plan. Such property should not be looked at individually but as part of an economic whole so that the assets will accomplish the testator's overall objectives. When there are such assets in an estate the property owner should do the following:

1. Recognize them as such.
2. Determine the tax consequences.
3. Provide for the payment of death taxes.
4. Coordinate the disposition of these non-probate assets with the assets that will pass under the will.

Retired people should not pay premiums on individual permanent life insurance policies. These premiums cut into retirement income, and the cash surrender value can be put to better use. Too often policyholders have been brainwashed by the insurance industry into believing that they must pay on permanent insurance for the whole of life. This just isn't so. It should be remembered that we don't live to save, we save to live.

The permanent insurance policyholder should make use of the cash surrender value by choosing one of three options:

1. The policyholder should surrender the contract and take the cash.
2. The policyholder should convert to a paid-up policy.
3. The policyholder should take out extended term insurance for the face amount.

Under any one of these three options the insured stops paying insurance premiums for the rest of his or her life. And under option one, he or she receives the cash surrender value as well.

Quite often a married couple would like to enjoy together the increased income, or the cash, rather than to have the widow spend it later alone.

Everyone should have a will drawn by a competent attorney. It is often the most important document a person ever signs, for it disposes of a lifetime accumulation of property, and determines who inherits it and in what amounts.

Before you have your final will and testament drawn, add up your assets first. You might be surprised to find out that you are worth more than you think! If you are, you must consider the very serious problem of death taxes. The federal estate tax on an estate of $250,000 is $36,800 in 1978. By 1981 (because a tax credit of $47,000 will be in effect) the estate tax on $250,000 will be reduced to $23,800, but this is still a sizable sum. To this must be added inheritance taxes in most states and, in all of them, probate costs.

Reduction of these expenses is mainly achieved by testators themselves through properly drawn wills and/or trust agreements that give full recognition to the taxes involved. And in sizable estates, expenses can be further reduced by a program of gifts that are completely tax-free.

In general, a man may will everything away from his relatives (except his wife), including his children. It doesn't seem right somehow that, no matter how harshly a testator may treat his relatives, his or her wishes in a properly drawn document will be upheld by the courts. But they will.

Probate is bad enough. But ancillary probate proceedings, which means court administration in another state besides the state of domicile, should be avoided whenever possible. With personal property, the simplest way to accomplish this is to physically transfer the property into the state where the testator lives. When real estate is involved, five different methods may be used to avoid ancillary probate of the property, once the decision has been made to retain it rather than to sell.

The effect of dying intestate can be disastrous, particularly for a spouse when it is the couple's intention that the survivor should inherit everything; yet every year great numbers of people die without a will. Therefore many people should know how to draw their own wills, for if they are drawn right, they can be legal. Holographic wills are not recommended, but they are better than dying intestate, and they can be very useful when a property owner is taken suddenly and seriously ill.

The ownership of real estate presents many perplexing problems for retired people. One of the most difficult is the computation of the capital gains tax when property (usually a home) is sold. If improper records have been kept, which makes the cost basis difficult or impossible to determine, the property owner may be faced with paying more in taxes than he or she actually owes. Even when this isn't a problem, too many people who are 65 fail to take the exclusion that is available to them. And everyone should understand that if you buy or build another home within the prescribed time limit, no capital gains tax is owed at all.

Income property is a good investment when it is owned by knowledgeable retired people. If they live on the property and have a small number of reliable tenants, and the husband is good at do-it-yourself work, it can provide an excellent retirement income. It's a bad investment vehicle, however, for a widow who is not in this position.

It's difficult to determine sometimes how real property should be divided among several heirs. Quite often the best way is for the testator to turn the problem over to his or her executor, giving the legal representative the right to sell the property and divide the proceeds.

When a widow inherits a home, it presents a different problem. Quite often she should dispose of it, but not right away. If selling it proves to have been a mistake, it too often can't be rectified. It's better to wait a year or two before making such an important and irrevocable decision.

Where money is an important consideration, many retired people don't know how to compute the comparative costs of continuing to live in their home against renting an apartment instead. The two costs are easily determined if the home-owner realizes that added to the costs of property taxes, insurance, utilities, and maintenance must be added the loss of interest on the equity in the house. Now the two costs, of owning or renting, can be accurately determined.

Every Social Security beneficiary should have his or her monthly check deposited directly to a savings or checking account. This direct deposit option was first offered in 1975 and has several advantages. You don't have to stand in line each month to cash your check, and if you are out of town it's not in your mailbox. Nor do you have to worry each month about your check being lost or stolen. You can arrange for a direct deposit of your check by filling out a simple form at your bank or savings and loan institution.

The wonderful benefits provided by Medicare, which is the health insurance portion of Social Security, are not understood by many people. Because of Medicare the former nightmare of hospital and doctors costs utterly depleting a person's life savings has been eliminated. No Social Security recipient, who is about to retire, should refuse to participate in Part B of Medicare (which takes care of the majority of a patient's doctor bills). It's true it costs a few premium dollars per month, but it's worth it.

As people approach retirement their main concern is how they are going to solve the problem of living on a reduced income after they stop working. Very simply stated, property at work has to take the place of a person at work. This can be better accomplished if the prospective retiree can free himself or herself of all debt, including the mortgage on a home, and particularly of installment loans. Monthly payments are murderous when one is retired.

For those who have enough time left before retirement, there are nine basic rules to follow that will make them more financially independent. These were discussed in Chapter 11.

In addition, prospective retirees should realize the importance of receiving a pension to supplement their Social Security check. This was impossible to arrange in the past if an employer did not provide a qualified plan. But no more. With the passage of pension reform legislation in 1974 everyone (an employee or the self-employed) can provide for himself or herself a continuing income after retirement, *if he or she doesn't have a qualified pension plan at work.* This is accomplished by establishing a Keogh Plan for the self-employed, or setting up an IRA account for those who are not.

The benefits from a Keogh Plan or an IRA account are substantial.

An individual retirement account, with a maximum contribution of $1,500 per year for twenty-five years, compounded at 6 percent, will amount to $87,234! A Keogh Plan, with a maximum contribution of $7,500 per year for twenty years, compounded at 6 percent, will amount to $282,447.50! With such plans available, no one should retire broke.

APPENDIXES

Simple Form for a Temporary Will
LAST WILL AND TESTAMENT OF
. . . .

I, ... of . . . . ,
City of . . . . , State of . . . . , do hereby make,
publish and declare this to be my last will and testament and I do
hereby revoke all former wills and codicils thereto by me at any time
made.

First: I desire that my just debts, including the expenses of my last
illness and funeral, be paid as soon as may be practicable after my
death.

Second: All of the residue of my estate, whether real, personal or
mixed, wheresoever situate, and whether now owned or hereafter
acquired, I give, devise and bequeath unto my beloved wife (husband)
. . . . , for her (his) own use and benefit forever.

*Note: If there are children, they should be specifically mentioned, or
the will may be set aside.*

Third: I appoint as executrix (executor) of my will my wife (husband);
I request that she (he) be permitted to serve without sureties on her
(his) bond and that, without application to or order of courts, she (he)
have full power and authority to sell, transfer, grant, convey, exchange,
lease, mortgage, pledge, or otherwise encumber or dispose of, any or
all of the real and personal property of my estate.

In Witness Whereof, I have hereunto subscribed my name this
. . . . day of . . . . , 19 . . . .

The foregoing instrument, consisting of _____ pages, handwritten
(typewritten), including this one, each page being identified by the
signature or initials of the testator (testatrix), was subscribed, published
and declared by the above named testator (testatrix) to be his (her) last

will and testament, in the presence of us, who, in his (her) presence, at his (her) request, and in the presence of each other, have hereunto subscribed our names as witnesses; and we declare that at the time of the execution of this instrument said testator (testatrix), according to our best knowledge and belief, was of sound mind and memory and under no constraint.

Dated at . . . . , ... , this . . . . day of . . . . , 19 . . . . . .

. . . .   Address . . . .

. . . .   Address . . . .

. . . .   Address . . . .

Where to Send Your
Medical Insurance Claims

The list below gives the names and addresses of the organizations selected by the Social Security Administration to handle medical insurance claims. These organizations are called carriers. In most cases, one carrier handles claims for an entire state. But some carriers handle claims for only part of a state. To find out which carrier to use, look in the list for the state **where you received the services.** Under the name of the state, you will find the name of the carrier. If there is more than one carrier in the state, look for the **county** where you received services. If you are not sure where to send your first claim and happen to send it to the wrong office, your claim will be forwarded to the right place. Whenever you send in a claim, be sure to include the word Medicare in the address on the envelope.

After you make a claim, the carrier will usually send you another *Request for Medicare Payment* form for later use. This form will show the carrier's name and address in the top left-hand corner. If you ever need to file a medical insurance claim and don't have a claim form, you can get one by phoning a Social Security office.

NOTE: If you are entitled to Medicare under the railroad retirement system, send your medical insurance claims to The Travelers Insurance Company office which is nearest to your home—no matter where you received services.

Alabama
Medicare
Blue Cross-Blue Shield of
Alabama
930 South 20th Street
Birmingham, Alabama 35205

Alaska
Medicare
Aetna Life & Casualty

Crown Plaza
1500 S.W. First Avenue
Portland, Oregon
97201

Arizona
Medicare
Aetna Life & Casualty
Medicare Claim Administration
3010 West Fairmount Avenue

Phoenix, Arizona
85017

Arkansas
Medicare
Arkansas Blue Cross and Blue
Shield
P.O. Box 2181
Little Rock, Arkansas 72203

California
Counties of: Los Angeles,
Orange, San Diego, Ventura,
San Bernadino, Imperial, San
Luis Obispo, Riverside, Santa
Barbara
Medicare
Occidental Life Insurance Co.
of California
Box 54905
Terminal Annex
Los Angeles, California 90054

Rest of State:
Medicare
Blue Shield of California
P.O. Box 7968, Rincon Annex
San Francisco, California 94120

Colorado
Medicare
Colorado Medical Service, Inc.
700 Broadway
Denver, Colorado 80203

Connecticut
Medicare
Connecticut General Life
Insurance Co.
200 Pratt Street
Meriden, Connecticut 06450

Delaware
Medicare

Blue Cross and Blue Shield of
Delaware
201 West 14th Street
Wilmington, Delaware 19899

District of Columbia
Medicare
Medical Service of D.C.
550–12th St., S.W.
Washington, D.C. 20024

Florida
Counties of: Dade, Monroe
Medicare
Group Health, Inc.
P.O. Box 341370
Miami, Florida 33134

Rest of State:
Medicare
Blue Shield of Florida, Inc.
P.O. Box 2525
Jacksonville, Florida 32203

Georgia
The Prudential Insurance Co. of
America
Medicare Part B
P.O. Box 95466 Executive Park
Station
Atlanta, Georgia 30347

Hawaii
Medicare
Aetna Life & Casualty
P.O. Box 3947
Honolulu, Hawaii 96812

Idaho
Medicare
The Equitable Life Assurance
Society
P.O. Box 8048
Boise, Idaho 83707

Illinois
Cook County
Medicare Part B
Illinois Medical Service
P.O. Box 210
Chicago, Illinois 60690

Rest of State:
Medicare
CNA Insurance
Medicare Benefits Division
P.O. Box 910
Chicago, Illinois 60690

Indiana
Medicare Part B
120 West Market Street
Indianapolis, Indiana 46204

Iowa
Medicare
Blue Shield of Iowa
636 Grand Avenue
Des Moines, Iowa 50307

Kansas
Counties of: Johnson,
Wyandotte
Medicare
Blue Shield of Kansas City
P.O. Box 169
Kansas City, Missouri 64141

Rest of State:
Medicare
Kansas Blue Shield
P.O. Box 239
Topeka, Kansas 66601

Kentucky
Medicare
Metropolitan Life Insurance
Co.

1218 Harrodsburg Road
Lexington, Kentucky 40504

Louisiana
Medicare
Pan-American Life Insurance
Co.
P.O. Box 60450
New Orleans, Louisiana 70160

Maine
Medicare
Union Mutual Life Insurance
Co.
Box 4629
Portland, Maine 04112

Maryland
Counties of: Montgomery,
Prince Georges
Medicare
Medical Service of D.C.
550–12th St., S.W.
Washington, D.C. 20024

Rest of State:
Maryland Blue Shield,
Inc.
700 East Joppa Road
Towson, Maryland 21204

Massachusetts
Medicare
Blue Shield of Massachusetts,
Inc.
P.O. Box 2137
Boston, Massachusetts 02106

Michigan
Medicare
Blue Shield of Michigan
P.O. Box 2201
Detroit, Michigan 48231

Minnesota
Counties of: Anoka, Dakota,
Filmore, Goodhue, Hennepin,
Houston, Olmstead, Ramsey,
Wabasha, Washington, Winona
Medicare
The Travelers Insurance
Company
8120 Penn Avenue, South
Bloomington, Minnesota 55431

Rest of State:
Medicare
Blue Shield of Minnesota
P.O. Box 8899
Minneapolis, Minnesota 55408

Mississippi
Medicare
The Travelers Insurance Co.
P.O. Box 22545
Jackson, Mississippi 39205

Missouri
Counties of: Andrew, Atchison,
Bates, Benton, Buchanan,
Caldwell, Carroll, Cass, Clay,
Clinton, Daviess, DeKalb,
Gentry, Grundy, Harrison,
Henry, Holt, Jackson, Johnson,
Lafayette, Livingston, Mercer,
Nodaway, Pettis, Platte, Ray, St.
Clair, Saline, Vernon, Worth
Medicare
Blue Shield of Kansas City
P.O. Box 169
Kansas City, Missouri 64141

Rest of State:
Medicare
General American Life

Insurance Co.
P.O. Box 505
St. Louis, Missouri
63166

Montana
Medicare
Montana Physicians' Service
P.O. Box 2510
Helena, Montana 59601

Nebraska
Medicare
Mutual of Omaha Insurance
Co.
P.O. Box 456, Downtown
Station
Omaha, Nebraska 68101

Nevada
Medicare
Aetna Life & Casualty
1535 Vassar Street
P.O. Box 3077
Reno, Nevada 89505

New Hampshire
Medicare
New Hampshire-Vermont
Physician Service
Two Pillsbury Street
Concord, New Hampshire
03301

New Jersey
Medicare
The Prudential Insurance Co.
of America
P.O. Box 3000
Linwood, New Jersey 08221

New Mexico
Medicare
The Equitable Life Assurance
Society
P.O. Box 3070, Station D
Albuquerque, New Mexico
87110

New York
*Counties of: Bronx, Columbia,
Delaware, Dutchess, Greene,
Kings, Nassau, New York,
Orange, Putnam, Richmond,
Rockland, Suffolk, Sullivan,
Ulster, Westchester*
Medicare
Blue Cross-Blue Shield of
Greater New York
Two Park Avenue
New York, New York 10016

County of: Queens
Medicare
Group Health, Inc.
P.O. Box 233—Midtown
Station
New York, New York 10018

*Counties of: Livingston,
Monroe, Ontario, Seneca,
Wayne, Yates*
Medicare
Genessee Valley Medical Care,
Inc.
41 Chestnut Street
Rochester, New York 14647

*Counties of: Allegany,
Cattaraugus, Erie, Genesee,
Niagara, Orleans, Wyoming*
Medicare
Blue Shield of Western New

York, Inc.
298 Main Street
Buffalo, New York
14202

*Counties of: Albany, Broome,
Cayuga, Chautauqua, Chemung,
Chenango, Clinton, Cortland,
Essex, Franklin, Fulton,
Hamilton, Herkimer, Jefferson,
Lewis, Madison, Montgomery,
Oneida, Onondaga, Oswego,
Otsego, Rensselaer, Saratoga,
Schenectady, Schoharie,
Schuyler, Steuben, St. Lawrence,
Tioga, Tompkins, Warren,
Washington*
Medicare
Metropolitan Life Insurance
Co.
276 Genesee Street
P.O. Box 393
Utica, New York 13503

North Carolina
The Prudential Insurance Co.
of America
Medicare B Division
P.O. Box 2126
High Point, North Carolina
27261

North Dakota
Medicare
Blue Shield of North Dakota
301 Eighth Street, South
Fargo, North Dakota
58102

Ohio
Medicare

Nationwide Mutual Insurance
Co.
P.O. Box 57
Columbus, Ohio 43216

Oklahoma
Medicare
Aetna Life & Casualty
1140 N.W. 63rd Street
Oklahoma City, Oklahoma
73116

Oregon
Medicare
Aetna Life & Casualty
Crown Plaza
1500 S.W. First Avenue
Portland, Oregon 97201

Pennsylvania
Medicare
Pennsylvania Blue Shield
Box 65 Blue Shield Bldg.
Camp Hill, Pennsylvania
17011

Rhode Island
Medicare
Blue Shield of Rhode Island
444 Westminster Mall
Providence, Rhode Island 02901

South Carolina
Medicare
Blue Shield of South Carolina
Drawer F, Forest Acres Branch
Columbia, South Carolina 29260

South Dakota
Medicare
South Dakota Medical Service,
Inc.
711 North Lake Avenue
Sioux Falls, South Dakota 57104

Tennessee
Medicare
The Equitable Life Assurance
Society
P.O. Box 1465
Nashville, Tennessee 37202

Texas
Medicare
Group Medical and Surgical
Service
P.O. Box 22147
Dallas, Texas 75222

Utah
Medicare
Blue Shield of Utah
P.O. Box 270
2455 Parley's Way
Salt Lake City, Utah 84110

Vermont
Medicare
New Hampshire-Vermont
Physician Service
Two Pillsbury Street
Concord, New Hampshire
03301

Virginia
Counties of: Arlington, Fairfax
Cities of: Alexandria, Falls
Church, Fairfax
Medicare
Medical Service of D.C.
550–12th St., S.W.
Washington, D.C. 20024

Rest of State:
Medicare
The Travelers Insurance Co.
P.O. Box 26463
Richmond, Virginia 23261

Washington
Medicare
Washington Physicians' Service
Mail to your local Medical
Service Bureau
*If you do not know which
bureau handles your claim,
mail to:*
Medicare
Washington Physicians'
Service
220 West Harrison
Seattle, Washington 98119

West Virginia
Medicare
Nationwide Mutual Insurance
Co.
P.O. Box 57
Columbus, Ohio 43216

Wisconsin
County of Milwaukee
Medicare
Surgical Care—Blue Shield
P.O. Box 2049
Milwaukee, Wisconsin 53201

Rest of State:
Medicare
Wisconsin Physicians
Service
Box 1787
Madison, Wisconsin 53701

Wyoming
Medicare
The Equitable Life Assurance
Society
P.O. Box 628
Cheyenne, Wyoming 82001

Puerto Rico
Medicare
Seguros De Servicio De Salud
De Puerto Rico
P.O. Box 3628
104 Ponce de Leon Avenue
Hato Rey, Puerto Rico 00936

Virgin Islands
Medicare
Seguros De Servicio De Salud
De Puerto Rico
P.O. Box 3628
104 Ponce de Leon Avenue
Hato Rey, Puerto Rico 00936

American Samoa
Medicare
Hawaii Medical Service Assn.
P.O. Box 860
Honolulu, Hawaii 96808

Guam
Medicare
Aetna Life & Casualty
P.O. Box 3947
Honolulu, Hawaii 96812

To Call IRS Toll Free For Answers to Your Federal Tax Questions, Use Only the Number Listed Below for Your Area

Caution: *"Toll-free" is a telephone call for which you pay only local charges and no long-distance charge is involved. Therefore, please use a local city number only if it is not a long-distance call for you. Otherwise, use the general toll-free number provided.*

To help us provide courteous responses and accurate information, IRS occasionally monitors telephone calls. No record is maintained of the taxpayer's name, address or social security number.

If you find it necessary to write rather than call us, please address your letter to your IRS District Director for a prompt reply.

Tax Advice to Taxpayers.—We are happy to answer questions to help you prepare your return. But you should know that you are responsible for the accuracy of your return and for the payment of the correct tax. If we do make an error, you are still responsible for the payment of the correct tax, and we are generally required by law to charge interest.

Telephone Assistance Services for Deaf/Hearing Impaired Taxpayers Who have Access to TV-phone/ teletypewriter Equipment.
Hours of Operation
8:30 A.M. to 6:45 P.M. EST
Indiana residents, 800–382–4059
Elsewhere in contiguous U.S., 800–428–4732

ALABAMA
Birmingham, 252–1155
Decatur, 355–1855
Huntsville, 539–2751
Mobile, 433–5532
Montgomery, 264–8441
Muscle Shoals Area, 767–0301
Tuscaloosa, 758–4434
Elsewhere in Alabama, 800–292–6300

ALASKA
Anchorage, 276–1040
Elsewhere in Alaska, call operator and ask for Zenith 3700

ARIZONA
Phoenix, 257–1233
Tucson, 882–4181
Elsewhere in Arizona, 800–352–6911

ARKANSAS
Little Rock, 376–4401
Elsewhere in Arkansas, 800–482–9350

CALIFORNIA
Please call the telephone number shown in the white pages of your local telephone directory under U.S. Government, Internal Revenue Service, Federal Tax Assistance

COLORADO
Colorado Springs, 634–6684
Denver, 825–7041
Elsewhere in Colorado, 800–332–2060

CONNECTICUT
Bridgeport, 576–1433
Hartford, 249–8251
Stamford, 348–6235
Elsewhere in Connecticut, 1–800–842–1120

DELAWARE
Wilmington, 571–6400
Elsewhere in Delaware, 800–292–9575
DISTRICT OF COLUMBIA
Call 488–3100

FLORIDA
Fort Lauderdale, 491–3311
Jacksonville, 354–1760
Miami, 358–5072
Orlando, 422–2550
Pensacola, 434–5215
St. Petersburg, 823–7459
Tampa, 223–9741
West Palm Beach, 655–7250
Elsewhere in Florida, 1–800–342–8300

GEORGIA
Atlanta, 522–0050

Augusta, 724–9946
Columbus, 327–7491
Macon, 746–4993
Savannah, 355–1045
Elsewhere in Georgia, 1–800–222–1040

HAWAII
Hawaii, 935–4895
Oahu, 546–8660
Kauai, 245–2731
Lanai, call operator and ask for Enterprise 8036
Maui, 244–7654
Molokai, call operator and ask for Enterprise 8034

IDAHO
Boise, 336–1040
Elsewhere in Idaho, 800–632–5990

ILLINOIS
Chicago, 435–1040
Elsewhere in area code 312 (except city of Chicago) and residents in Joliet Region Telephone Directory, 800–972–5400
Springfield, 789–4220
Elsewhere in all other locations in Illinois, 800–252–2921

INDIANA
Evansville, 424–6481
Fort Wayne, 423–2331
Gary, 938–0560
Hammond, 938–0560
Indianapolis, 269–5477
Muncie, 288–4594
South Bend, 232–3981
Terre Haute, 232–9421
Elsewhere in Indiana, 800–382–9740

IOWA
Cedar Rapids, 366–8771
Des Moines, 284–4850
Elsewhere in Iowa, 800–362–2600

KANSAS
Kansas City, 722–2910
Topeka, 357–5311
Wichita, 263–2161
Elsewhere in Kansas, 800–362–2190

KENTUCKY
Lexington, 255–2333
Louisville, 584–1361
Northern Kentucky (Cincinnati local dialing area), 621–6281
Elsewhere in Kentucky, 800–292–6570

LOUISIANA
Baton Rouge, 387–2206
New Orleans, 581–2440
Shreveport, 424–6301
Elsewhere in Louisiana, 800–362–6900

MAINE
Augusta, 622–7101
Portland, 775–7401
Elsewhere in Maine, 1–800–452–8750

MARYLAND
Baltimore, 962–2590
Prince Georges County, 488–3100
Montgomery County, 488–3100
Elsewhere in Maryland, 800–492–0460
MASSACHUSETTS
Boston, 523–1040
Brockton, 580–1770
Fitchburg, 345–1031
Lawrence, 682–4344
Lowell, 957–4470
New Bedford, 996–3111
Springfield, 785–1201
Worcester, 757–2712
Elsewhere in Massachusetts, 1–800–392–6288

MICHIGAN
Ann Arbor, 769–9850
Bay City, 771–2153
Detroit, 237–0800
Flint, 767–8830
Jackson, 750–4677
Kalamazoo, 385–4410
Grand Rapids, 774–8300
Lansing, 394–1550
Mount Clemens, 469–4200
Muskegon, 726–4971
Pontiac, 858–2530
Saginaw, 771–2153
Elsewhere in area code 313, call 800–462–0830
Elsewhere in area codes 517, 616, and 906, call 800–482–0670

MINNESOTA
Minneapolis, 291–1422
St. Paul, 291–1422
Elsewhere in Minnesota, 800–652–9062

MISSISSIPPI
Biloxi, 868–2122
Gulfport, 868–2122
Jackson, 948–4500
Elsewhere in Mississippi, 1–800–222–8070

MISSOURI
Columbia, 443–2491
Jefferson City, 635–9141
Joplin, 781–8500
Kansas City, 474–0350
St. Joseph, 364–3111
St. Louis, 342–1040
Springfield, 887–5000
Elsewhere in Missouri, 800–392–4200

MONTANA
Helena, 443–2320
Elsewhere in Montana, 1–800–332–2275

NEBRASKA
Lincoln, 475–3611
Omaha, 422–1500
Elsewhere in Nebraska, 800–642–9960

NEVADA
Las Vegas, 385–6291
Reno, 784–5521
Elsewhere in Nevada, 800–492–6552

NEW HAMPSHIRE
Manchester, 668–2100
Portsmouth, 436–8810
Elsewhere in New Hampshire, 1–800–582–7200

NEW JERSEY
Camden, 966–7333
Hackensack, 487–8981
Jersey City, 622–0600
Newark, 622–0600
Paterson, 279–9400
Trenton, 394–7113
Elsewhere in New Jersey, 800–242–6750

NEW MEXICO
Albuquerque, 243–8641
Elsewhere in New Mexico, 800–527–3880

NEW YORK
Albany District *(Eastern Upstate New York)*
Albany, 449–3120
Poughkeepsie, 452–7800
Elsewhere in Eastern Upstate New York, 1–800–342–3700
Brooklyn District
Brooklyn, 596–3770
Nassau, 294–3600
Queens, 596–3770
Suffolk, 724–5000
Buffalo District *(Western Upstate New York)*
Binghamton, 772–1540
Buffalo, 855–3955
Niagara Falls, 285–9361
Rochester, 263–6770
Syracuse, 425–8111
Utica, 797–2550
Elsewhere in Western Upstate New York, 1–800–462–1560
Manhattan District
Bronx, 732–0100
Manhattan, 732–0100
Rockland County, 352–8900
Staten Island, 732–0100
Westchester County:
North (Peekskill Area), 739–9191
South (Mt. Vernon, New Rochelle, White Plains—Yonkers Area), 212–732–0100

NORTH CAROLINA
Charlotte, 372–7750
Greensboro, 274–3711
Raleigh, 020–6278
Elsewhere in North Carolina, 800–822–8800

NORTH DAKOTA
Fargo, 293–0650
Elsewhere in North Dakota, 800–342–4710

OHIO
Akron, 253–1141
Canton, 455–6781
Cincinnati, 621–6281
Cleveland, 522–3000
Columbus, 228–0520
Dayton, 228–0557
Toledo, 255–3730
Youngstown, 746–1811
Elsewhere in Northern Ohio, 800–362–9050
Elsewhere in Southern Ohio, 800–582–1700

OKLAHOMA
Oklahoma City, 272–9531
Tulsa, 583–5121
Elsewhere in Oklahoma, 800–962–3456

OREGON
Eugene, 485–8285
Medford, 779–3375
Portland, 221–3960
Salem, 581–8720
Elsewhere in Oregon, 800–452–1980

PENNSYLVANIA
Allentown, 437–6966
Bethlehem, 437–6966
Erie 453–5671
Harrisburg, 783–8700
Philadelphia, 574–9900
Pittsburgh, 281–0112
Elsewhere in area codes 215 and 717, call 800–462–4000
Elsewhere in area codes 412 and 814, call 800–242–0250

RHODE ISLAND
Block Island, call operator and ask for Enterprise 1040
Burrillville—Glocester, 568–3100
Hope Valley—South County, 539–2361
Newport, 847–2463
Providence, 274–1040
Tiverton—Little Compton, 624–6647
Woonsocket, 722–9245

SOUTH CAROLINA
Charleston, 722–1601
Columbia, 799–1000
Greenville, 242–5434
Elsewhere in South Carolina, 1–800–922–8810

SOUTH DAKOTA
Aberdeen, 225–9112
Rapid City, 348–9400
Sioux Falls, 334–6600
Elsewhere in South Dakota, 800–592–1870

TENNESSEE
Chattanooga, 892–3010
Johnson City, 929–0181
Knoxville, 637–0190
Memphis, 522–1250
Nashville, 259–4601
Elsewhere in Tennessee, 800–342–8420

TEXAS
Amarillo, 376–2184
Austin, 472–1974
Beaumont, 835–5076
Corpus Christi, 888–9431
Dallas, 742–2440
El Paso, 532–6116
Ft. Worth, 335–1370
Houston, 965–0440
Lubbock, 747–4365
San Antonio, 229–1700
Waco, 752–6535
Wichita Falls, 723–6702
Elsewhere in Texas, 800–492–4830

UTAH
Salt Lake City, 524–4060
Elsewhere in Utah, 1–800–662–5370

VERMONT
Burlington, 658–1870
Elsewhere in Vermont, 1–800–642–3110

VIRGINIA
Baileys Crossroads (Northern Virginia), 557–9230
Chesapeake, 461–3770
Norfolk, 461–3770
Portsmouth, 461–3770
Richmond, 649–2361
Virginia Beach, 461–3770
Elsewhere in Virginia, 800–552–9500

WASHINGTON
Everett, 259–0861
Seattle, 441–1040
Spokane, 456–8350
Tacoma, 383–2021
Vancouver, 695–9252
Yakima, 248–6891
Elsewhere in Washington, 800–732–1040

WEST VIRGINIA
Charleston, 345–2210
Huntington, 523–0213
Parkersburg, 485–1601
Wheeling, 845–8290
Elsewhere in West Virginia, 800–642–1931

WISCONSIN
Milwaukee, 271–3780
Elsewhere in Wisconsin, 800–452–9100

WYOMING
Cheyenne, 635–4124
Elsewhere in Wyoming, 800–525–6060

Department of the Treasury
Internal Revenue Service

Instructions for Form 709

(Revised June 1977)

United States Quarterly Gift Tax Return

(For gifts made after December 31, 1976)

For "Privacy Act" Notification, see the Instructions for Form 1040

The Federal gift tax applies to any gift by an individual of real or personal property, whether tangible or intangible, and whether given directly to a donee, in trust, or by any other means. The tax is applicable to the gratuitous transfer of all types of property or interests in property, including, for example, real estate, securities, life insurance policies, annuities, contract rights, jewelry, art objects, and personal belongings. The gift tax is applicable regardless of whether any other tax, such as Federal income tax, has been paid or is payable with respect to the transferred property.

(References are to the Internal Revenue Code, unless otherwise noted.)

1. Who must file.—Any individual citizen or resident of the U.S. who within a calendar quarter(s) gives (or as explained in instructions 8 and 10 is considered as giving) a present interest or a future interest in property to any one donee must file a gift tax return on Form 709 with respect to such quarter(s), subject to the following exceptions: (1) no return with respect to a calendar quarter is required for a gift of a present interest to any one donee unless in such quarter, and any preceding quarter or quarters of the calendar year involved, all such gifts to such donee aggregate more than $3,000, and (2) certain qualified charitable transfers (see the fifth paragraph). Gifts of present interests to any one donee of $3,000

or less made in previous quarters of a calendar year must be reported on a return with respect to the calendar quarter at the close of which the total of such gifts made to such donee is more than $3,000.

Joint gift tax returns are not permitted. The return is required even though, because of authorized deductions, a tax may not be due. The term "citizen of the U.S." includes a person who, at the time of making the gift, was domiciled in a possession of the U.S. and was a U.S. citizen, and who did not acquire U.S. citizenship solely by reason of being a citizen of a possession or by reason of birth or residence within a possession.

A nonresident alien is similarly required to file a gift tax return for gifts of tangible property situated in the U.S. A nonresident alien who has lost U.S. citizenship may also be required to file a gift tax return for gifts of intangible property, shares of stock issued by a domestic corporation, and debt obligations of a domestic person or domestic governmental organization. (Sections 2501(a)(3) and 2511 (b)). As used above, the term nonresident alien includes a person who at the time of making the gift was domiciled in a possession of the U.S. and was a U.S. citizen, and who acquired U.S. citizenship solely by reason of being a citizen of a possession or by reason of birth or residence within a possession.

Only individuals are required to file returns. If gifts are made by trusts, estates, partnerships, or corporations, the individual beneficiaries, partners, or stockholders become donors and may incur liability under the Federal gift tax law. If the donor dies before filing the return, the deceased's personal representative must file the return.

A return for qualified charitable transfers is not required on a quarterly basis, but donors must report such transfers on a return for the fourth quarter of the calendar year, or for an earlier quarter for which the donor is required to file a return for other than a qualified charitable transfer. A qualified charitable transfer is one for which a deduction is allowable under section 2522 for the full amount of the gift to the extent not excludable under section 2503(b) and the regulations thereunder. For any transfer reported as a qualified charitable transfer, the return shall be deemed to be a return for the calendar quarter in which such transfer was made.

If the gift is community property, the gift tax provisions, including the requirement of a return, apply separately to the one-half interest of each spouse. For example, a gift of $100,-000 of community property is considered a gift of $50,000 by each spouse, and a return is due from each spouse for the one-half interest.

The donor must sign the return. The person, firm, or corporation preparing the return for compensation must also sign the return. This verification is not required if the return is prepared by a regular full-time employee of the donor.

2. When to file.—If the total amount of taxable gifts during a calendar quarter exceeds $25,000 ($12,500 for a nonresident not a U.S. citizen donor), the return must be filed on or before the 15th day of the second month following the close of the calendar quarter in which the gifts were made, unless an extension of time for filing has been granted.

If the total amount of taxable gifts during a calendar quarter is $25,000 or less ($12,500 for a nonresident not a U.S. citizen donor), the return must be filed on or before the 15th day of the second month after the close of the first subsequent calendar quarter in the calendar year in which the sum of the taxable gifts made during such subsequent quarter plus other taxable gifts made during the calendar year and for which no return has been filed exceed $25,000 ($12,500 for a nonresident not a

U.S. citizen donor); this rule never extends the filing date for a return beyond February 15 of the following calendar year.

If a return is due for taxable gifts during the calendar year which do not exceed $25,000 ($12,500 for a nonresident not a U.S. citizen donor), the return must be filed on or before February 15 of the following calendar year.

3. Where to file.—Unless the return is hand carried to the office of the district director, it must be filed at the service center listed below for the State in which the donor has legal residence or principal place of business or, if the donor has neither in the U.S., with the Internal Revenue Service Center, 11601 Roosevelt Boulevard, Philadelphia, Pennsylvania 19155, U.S.A.

New Jersey, New York City and counties of Nassau, Rockland, Suffolk, and Westchester	Internal Revenue Service Center 1040 Waverly Avenue Holtsville, New York 11799
New York (all other counties), Connecticut, Maine, Massachusetts, New Hampshire, Rhode Island, Vermont	Internal Revenue Service Center 310 Lowell Street Andover, Mass. 01812
Alabama, Florida, Georgia, Mississippi, South Carolina	Internal Revenue Service Center 4800 Buford Highway Chamblee, Georgia 30006
Michigan, Ohio	Internal Revenue Service Center Cincinnati, Ohio 45298
Arkansas, Kansas, Louisiana, New Mexico, Oklahoma, Texas	Internal Revenue Service Center 3651 S. Interregional Highway Austin, Texas 78740
Alaska, Arizona, Colorado, Idaho, Minnesota, Montana, Nebraska, Nevada, North Dakota, Oregon, South Dakota, Utah, Washington, Wyoming	Internal Revenue Service Center 1160 West 1200 South St. Ogden, Utah 84201
Illinois, Iowa, Missouri, Wisconsin	Internal Revenue Service Center 2306 East Bannister Road Kansas City, Missouri 64170
California, Hawaii	Internal Revenue Service Center 5045 East Butler Avenue Fresno, California 93888
Indiana, Kentucky, North Carolina, Tennessee, Virginia, West Virginia	Internal Revenue Service Center 3131 Democrat Road Memphis, Tenn. 38110
Delaware, District of Columbia, Maryland, Pennsylvania	Internal Revenue Service Center 11601 Roosevelt Boulevard Philadelphia, Pa. 19155

4. Tax.—The tax must be paid by the donor on or before the 15th day of the second month following the close of the calendar quarter in which the gifts were made and a return with respect thereto became due, unless an extension of time for payment has been granted.

Please make the check or money order payable to Internal Revenue Service and write the donor's social security number on it.

5. Penalties.—Section 6651 provides for additions to the tax for both delinquent returns and for delinquent payments of tax unless due to reasonable cause. The law also provides penalties for willful failure to file a return on time and ·for willful attempt to evade or defeat payment of tax.

6. Transfers for a consideration in money or money's worth.—Gifts include not only transfers without consideration, but also sales and exchanges for less than an adequate and full consideration in money or money's worth not made in the ordinary course of business to the extent the value of the sale or exchange exceeds the value of the consideration received.

For the rules governing certain property settlements in divorce cases, see section 2516 and the regulations thereunder. Also see section 25.6019–3(b) of the regulations for the information to be disclosed on the gift tax return in such cases.

For the rules governing certain survivorship annuities, see section 2517 and the regulations thereunder. In the case of a taxable gift (certain employee contributions, for example), the gift is considered a future interest and, therefore, not subject to the $3,000 annual exclusion.

7. Powers of appointment and disclaimers.—The exercise or release of a power of appointment may constitute a gift by the individual possessing the power. For additional information, see section 2514 and the regulations thereunder.

For the rules governing a qualified disclaimer with respect to an interest in property, see section 2518.

8. Gifts by husband or wife to third parties.—Section 2513 provides that if husband and wife consent, all gifts made by either to third parties during the calendar quarter may be considered as made one-half by each. If the consent is effective for the entire calendar quarter, all gifts by husband or wife to third parties during the calendar quarter must be treated in the same way. An individual is considered the spouse of another individual only if the individual is married to the other individual at the time of the gift and does not remarry during the remainder of the calendar quarter. This provision applies only for a calendar quarter for which both spouses signify their consent as explained below, and does not apply (a) if the consenting spouses were not married to each other on the date of gift, (b) if either spouse was a nonresident alien on the date of gift, (c) to a gift by one spouse if the donor spouse created in the other spouse a general power of appointment over the property interest transferred. If the donor spouse transferred property in part to the donee spouse and in part to third parties, the consent is effective only to the extent the interest transferred to third parties is ascertainable at the time of the gift. If the consent is effective the liability for the entire gift tax of each spouse is joint and several.

The consent may be signified, by the spouse filing the return, by answering "Yes" to question A on the face of the return and, by the other spouse, by executing the "Consent of Spouse" appearing on the face of the same return. The consent may be signified at any time after the close of the calendar quarter, subject to the following limitations: (a) the consent may not be signified after the 15th day of the second month following the close of the quarter, except if neither spouse has filed a return for the quarter on or before that date, the consent may be signified on the first return for the quarter filed by either spouse, but not thereafter; and (b) the consent may not be signified after a notice of deficiency with respect to the tax for the quarter has been sent to either spouse. The personal representative for a deceased spouse or the guardian of a legally incompetent spouse may signify the consent. If the consent is effective for gifts made in a previous quarter(s) of the calendar year and no return was filed for such previous quarter(s) (see instruction 1) and such gifts are being reported on the current return (see instruction 10), write the previous quarter(s) in addition to the current quarter in item 2 of question A.

9. Joint tenancy.—If the donor with the donor's own funds purchases property and has the title conveyed to the donor and the donee as joint tenants with right of survivorship or converts the donor's separate property into a joint tenancy with right of survivorship with the donee (other than a joint bank account or a United States savings bond registered in coownership as described below) but which rights may be defeated by either party severing that party's interests, there is a gift to the donee in the amount of half the value of the property. However, for the rules relative to the creation of a joint tenancy (or tenancy by the entirety) between husband and wife in real property with right of survivorship, see the next paragraph. If the donor creates a joint bank account for the donor and the donee (or a similar type of ownership by which the donor can regain the entire fund without the donee's consent), there is a gift to the donee when the donee draws upon the account for the donee's own benefit, to the extent of the amount drawn without any obligation to account for a part of the proceeds to the donor. If the donor purchases a United States savings bond registered as payable to the donor or the donee, there is a gift to the donee when the donee surrenders the bond for cash without any obligation to account for a part of the proceeds to the donor.

The creation between husband and wife of a tenancy by the entirety or joint tenancy with right of survivorship in real property is not treated as a gift unless the donor spouse so elects in a timely filed gift tax return. If the donor spouse does so elect by a full disclosure of the gift on Form 709, page 2, Schedule A, the election applies to all subsequent additions in value (including debt reduction and improvements but excluding appreciation), additional returns will be due with respect to additions which exceed the $3,000 annual exclusion, and the retained interest of each spouse is treated as one-half of the value of the joint interest; also, for estate tax purposes, one-half of the value of the joint property will be includible in the gross estate of the decedent regardless of which spouse furnished the consideration. If the donor does not elect in a timely filed return to have such tenancy, or addition, treated as a gift during the calendar quarter within which the tenancy was created, or addition made, the termination of the tenancy, other than by reason of the death of a spouse, is considered a gift to the extent the proportion of the proceeds received by either spouse is not equal to the proportion of the consideration furnished by the spouse in acquiring or improving the property; if the tenancy is terminated by the death of a spouse, the joint property is subject to inclusion in the gross estate of the decedent at the full value less the value attributable to any contribution that can be traced to the surviving spouse.

10. The $3,000 annual exclusion.—The first $3,000 of gifts (other than gifts of future interests in property) to any one donee during the calendar year is deducted in computing the amount of taxable gifts for the calendar quarter(s). Gifts of present interests to any one donee of $3,000 or less made in previous quarters of a calendar year must be reported on a return with respect to the calendar quarter at the close of which the total of such gifts made to such donee is more than $3,000. If section 2513 is applicable, all gifts of a present interest to any third party donee during the year totaling more than $3,000 must be reported although by reason of such consent neither spouse is considered to have made gifts of a present interest in excess of $3,000. If section 2513 is applicable and if the total gifts of a present interest of the husband and wife for the taxable year to one donee exceeded $6,000, the other spouse must file a return also and report the gifts to the same donee regardless of the amount. The entire value of any gift of a future interest in property must be included in the return with respect to the calendar quarter in which the gift is made and no amount may be deducted for the annual exclusion. If section 2513 is applicable, a return must be filed by each spouse for a gift of a future interest of any value. For the definition of future interests, see section 25.2503–3 of the regulations. Also, see section 25.2503–4 of the regulations for gifts of future interests to minors.

11. Schedule A.—All gifts (including charitable, public, and similar gifts) by the donor during the calendar quarter(s) with respect to which the return is filed must, to the extent indicated in instruction 10, be reported in Schedule A. In addition, gifts made during previous quarters of the calendar year may also be required to be reported to the extent indicated in the second sentence of instruction 10; if prior returns were filed for such previous quarters with a "Yes" answer to question A on page 1 of Form 709 (question B on prior revi-

sions), this fact must also be noted in Schedule A. If a transfer results in gifts to two individuals (such as a life estate to one with remainder to the other) the gift to each must be listed separately. If section 2513 is applicable but only one spouse in fact makes gifts for which a return is required, the full value of all gifts made by the spouse filing the return must be included, one-half of the full value of all gifts to all third party donees entered on line (b), and no entry made on line (d). If section 2513 is applicable and only one spouse in fact makes gifts for which a return is required but the second spouse is considered to have made gifts for which a return is required because of the provisions of section 2513, the full value of all gifts made by the donor spouse must be included on the return for the donor spouse, one-half of the full value of all gifts to all third party donees entered on line (b), and no entry made on line (d); the preceding amount from line (b) must also be entered on line (d) of the return filed for the second spouse, but this amount is excluded from lines (a), (b), and (c) on the return filed for the second spouse. If section 2513 is applicable and each spouse in fact makes gifts for which a return is required, the full value of all gifts in fact made by each spouse must be included on the separate return filed for each spouse, one-half of the full value of all gifts to all third party donees in fact made by each spouse entered on line (b) of the separate return filed for each spouse, and then the respective amounts entered on line (b) of one return must also be entered on line (d) of the other return. To facilitate the computations for lines (b) and (h), the items should be segregated into the following categories: (1) gifts to spouse, (2) gifts for charitable, public, and similar uses, and (3) all other gifts. In all cases in which it is not apparent how the amounts entered on lines (b) and (h) were computed, report the computations in detail on an attached sheet. The amount entered on line (j) must be carried forward to line 1 in "Computation of Tax" on page 1 of the return.

12. Description of property.—The description of the gifts must be complete enough to readily identify the property. Thus a legal description must be given for each parcel of real estate, and, if located in a city, the street number and name, its area, and, if improved, a short statement of the character of the improvements. Description of bonds must include the number transferred, principal amount, name of obligor, date of maturity, rate of interest, date or dates on which interest is payable, series number where there is more than one issue, the exchange where listed, or the principal business office of the corporation, if unlisted. Description of stocks must include number of shares, whether common or preferred, and, if preferred, what issue, par value, quotation at which returned, exact name of corporation, and, if the stock is unlisted, the location of the principal business office and State in which incorporated and the date of incorporation. If a listed security, state principal exchange where sold. In describing an interest in property based on the duration of a person's life, the date of birth and sex of that person must be stated. Description of life insurance policies must include the name of the insurer and the policy number.

13. Donor's adjusted basis of gift.—Enter the donor's basis that would be used for income tax purposes if the gift were sold or exchanged. For additional information see the Instructions for Schedule D (Form 1040) and section 1011 and the regulations thereunder.

14. Date and valuation of property.—If the gift is made in property other than money, determine the value on the date of the gift. For the rules to determine fair market value

for various types of property see the regulations under section 2512.

15. Supplemental documents.— For every policy of life insurance listed on the return, the donor must attach Form 712 to the return. If the gift was made by means of a trust, a certified or verified copy of the trust instrument must be attached. In the case of stock of close corporations or inactive stock (which must be valued on the basis of net worth, earning and dividend paying capacity, and other relevant factors), there must be attached balance sheets, particularly the one nearest the date of the gift, and statements of the net earnings or operating results and dividends paid for each of the 5 preceding years. Any other documents, such as appraisal lists, required for an adequate explanation, must be attached to the return. For example, attach a copy of any appraisal used to determine the value of real estate; otherwise full information to explain how the value was determined must be included in Schedule A.

16. Marital deduction.—If the donor was a citizen or resident of the United States at the time the gift was made, compute the marital deduction on Schedule A, lines (h)(1) through (h)(6), for the value of any property interest (except as otherwise indicated below) given to a donee who at the time of the gift was the donor's spouse.

For the purpose of the marital deduction, a property interest, whether or not in trust, is considered as given to the donee spouse (and to no other person), if (a) the donee spouse is entitled for life to all of the income from the entire interest; (b) the income is payable annually or at more frequent intervals; (c) the donee spouse has the power, exercisable in favor of the donee spouse or the estate of the donee spouse, to appoint the entire interest; (d) the power is exercisable by the donee spouse alone and (whether exercisable by will or during life) is exercisable by the donee spouse in all events; and (e) no part of the entire interest is subject to a power in any other person to appoint any part to any person other than the donee spouse. If these five conditions are satisfied only for a specific portion of the entire interest, see section 25.2523(e)–1 of the regulations for the portion which qualifies for the marital deduction.

If income from property is payable to the donor or a third party for life, or for a term of years, with remainder absolutely to the donor's spouse or the estate of the donor's spouse, use the present value of the remainder in computing the marital deduction.

The marital deduction is generally not allowable if the gift to the donee spouse is a terminable interest. Terminable interest includes a life estate, an estate for years, or any other property interest which, after the lapse of time, occurrence of an event or contingency, or failure of an event or contingency to occur, will terminate or fail. If the interest is transferred to the donee spouse as sole joint tenant with the donor or as tenant by the entirety, the interest is not considered a terminable interest solely because of the possibility that the donor may survive the donee spouse, or that there may occur a severance of the tenancy. A retiring Federal employee who receives a reduced annuity in order that the donee spouse can receive a survivor annuity after the retiring Federal employee's death is considered to give a terminable interest to the spouse when the Federal employee retires, and, therefore, no marital deduction is allowable; also, no amount may be deducted for the annual exclusion because the gift of the survivor annuity is a future interest. The marital deduction is not allowable if the property was held as community property. Community property is defined in section 25.2523(f)–1(b) of the regulations.

17. Deductions for charitable, public, and similar gifts.—Add all the charitable, public, and similar gifts reported in Schedule A for which a deduction is claimed under section 2522, subtract the total exclusions claimed in Schedule A for such gifts, and enter the balance on line (h)(7). See section 2522 and the regulations thereunder for the rules governing the charitable deduction.

18. Unified credit against gift tax.—If the donor is a citizen or resident of the United States, a credit against gift tax is allowable for gifts made after December 31, 1976. The credit is computed on Form 709, page 1, lines 7 through 12. The amount of credit allowable for prior periods must be reported on Form 709, page 2, Schedule B, third column.

19. Schedule B.—Gift tax returns, Form 709, filed for prior calendar years preceding 1971 and for prior calendar quarters in 1971 and subsequent years must be indicated in Schedule B. The donor's name used in each return filed for prior periods must be shown in Schedule B if there has been a change in name in this or any prior return. Any variation such as the use of full given names instead of initials must also be indicated. The correct amount of the taxable gifts for each prior period during which gifts were made (the amount finally determined), and not necessarily the amount previously reported, must be entered in the last column. The amount of the specific exemption claimed and allowed for each prior period ending before January 1, 1977, must be entered in the fourth column. Enter on line (b) any amount by which the total specific exemption claimed and allowed for prior periods ending before January 1, 1977, (line (a)) exceeds $30,000. Any amount entered on line (b) must be added to the amount entered in the last column on line (a), and the sum thus obtained must be entered on line (c). The amount entered on line (c) must be carried forward to line 2 in "Computation of Tax" on the first page of the return.

20. Gift tax conventions.—Gift tax conventions are in effect with Australia and Japan. If credit is claimed for payment of foreign gift taxes, compute the credit on an attached sheet and submit evidence of payment of the foreign gift taxes.

Table A
Table for Computing Gift Tax

Column A	Column B	Column C	Column D
Taxable Amount Over—	Taxable Amount Not Over—	Tax on Amount in Column A	Rate of Tax on Excess Over Amount in Column A
. . . .	$10,000	. . . .	18%
$10,000	20,000	$1,800	20%
20,000	40,000	3,800	22%
40,000	60,000	8,200	24%
60,000	80,000	13,000	26%
80,000	100,000	18,200	28%
100,000	150,000	23,800	30%
150,000	250,000	38,800	32%
250,000	500,000	70,800	34%
500,000	750,000	155,800	37%
750,000	1,000,000	248,300	39%
1,000,000	1,250,000	345,800	41%
1,250,000	1,500,000	448,300	43%
1,500,000	2,000,000	555,800	45%
2,000,000	2,500,000	780,800	49%
2,500,000	3,000,000	1,025,800	53%
3,000,000	3,500,000	1,290,800	57%
3,500,000	4,000,000	1,575,800	61%
4,000,000	4,500,000	1,880,800	65%
4,500,000	5,000,000	2,205,800	69%
5,000,000	. . . .	2,550,800	70%

Table B
Table for Unified Credit Against Gift Tax
United States Citizen or Resident Donor

For gifts made—	The credit is—
After December 31, 1976, and before July 1, 1977	$6,000
After June 30, 1977, and before January 1, 1978	30,000
After December 31, 1977, and before January 1, 1979	34,000
After December 31, 1978, and before January 1, 1980	38,000
After December 31, 1979, and before January 1, 1981	42,500
After December 31, 1980	47,000

INDEX